D1572414

A Companion to Schubert's *Schwanengesang*

A Companion to
Schubert's
Schwanengesang

History, Poets, Analysis, Performance

Edited by

MARTIN CHUSID

Yale University Press   New Haven & London

WITHDRAWN
LIBRARY MSU-BILLINGS

Copyright © 2000 by Yale University.
All rights reserved.
This book may not be reproduced, in whole or in part, including
illustrations, in any form (beyond that copying permitted by Sections
107 and 108 of the U.S. Copyright Law and except by reviewers for
the public press), without written permission from the publishers.

Designed by James J. Johnson and set in Monotype Dante by
Running Feet Books, Morrisville, North Carolina.
Printed in the United States of America.

Library of Congress Cataloging-in-Publication Data

A companion to Schubert's Schwanengesang : history, poets,
analysis, performance / edited by Martin Chusid.
p.   cm.
Includes bibliographical references (p.) and index.
Contents: The origin and early reception of Schwanengesang /
Walburga Litschauer—The poets of Schwanengesang : Rellstab,
Heine, and Seidl / Martin Chusid—Repetition and correspondence
in Schwanengesang / Edward T. Cone—Texts and commentary /
Martin Chusid—The sequence of the Heine songs and cyclicism in
Schwanengesang / Martin Chusid—On singing Schwanengesang /
Walther Dürr and Martin Chusid—The three styles of
Schwanengesang : a pianist's perspective / Steven Lubin—
A Schwanengesang discography / Richard LeSueur.
ISBN 0-300-07289-9

1. Schubert, Franz, 1797–1828. Schwanengesang (Song cycle)
2. Music and literature.   3. Music—Performance.
I. Chusid, Martin.
ML410.S3C65   2000
782.4'7—dc 21   99-27829

A catalogue record for this book is available from the British Library.

The paper in this book meets the guidelines for permanence and
durability of the Committee on Production Guidelines for Book
Longevity of the Council on Library Resources.

10   9   8   7   6   5   4   3   2   1

For my musical wife, Anita

Contents

Acknowledgments

I am pleased to acknowledge the constant assistance provided by Mrs. Henny Bordwin, President of The American Schubert Institute, who conceived the idea of a comprehensive volume of studies devoted to *Schwanengesang* to be published together with a companion volume of facsimiles of the original autograph. I am also grateful to her, to her husband, Milton Bordwin, and to The American Schubert Institute for providing financial support at a critical stage in the preparation of the two volumes, *'Schwanengesang': Facsimiles of the Autograph Score and Sketches, and Reprint of the First Edition* (New Haven: Yale University Press, 2000) and *A Companion to Schubert's 'Schwanengesang.'*

I wish to thank the staff of the Wiener Stadt- und Landesbibliothek and its director, Hedwig Würtz; the staff of the Gesellschaft der Musikfreunde of Vienna and its director, Otto Biba; Ernst Hilmar of the International Franz Schubert Institute; David Giovacchini of the Harvard University Libraries; the staff of the Interlibrary Loan Service at New York University; the staff of the Music Division of the New York Public Library at Lincoln Center; and especially the graduate students in the Music Department (FAS) at New York University who participated in my seminars on the song cycles of Schubert. It is also a pleasure to thank the editorial staff at Yale University Press, particularly Harry Haskell and Jenya Weinreb, for their numerous and cheerful words of advice.

The dedication of this volume to my wife, Anita, scarcely begins to acknowledge her importance at every stage of this book's long gestation.

Introduction

Schwanengesang, a group of fourteen songs composed to texts by three different poets and named by the Viennese publisher Tobias Haslinger and Ferdinand Schubert, contains some of the greatest Lieder that Franz Schubert ever composed. Yet questions have arisen repeatedly about this publication. Does the fourteenth song, "Die Taubenpost"—the very last song the composer wrote—belong in the collection? To what extent are the songs to be considered a cycle? Can the first thirteen songs really be divided into two separate groups: the seven to texts by Ludwig Rellstab and the six to poems by Heinrich Heine? If so, why did Schubert write the Heine songs as a continuation of the Rellstab Lieder, gathering them all in a single manuscript that is clearly a clean copy and in all probability intended for a publisher? How did Schubert come to know the Rellstab texts? A final query has been raised in recent years: In what sequence should the Heine songs be performed? Although there are few incontrovertible answers to these questions, they are raised in almost every chapter of this book and are especially important for Chapter 5, "The Sequence of the Heine Songs and Cyclicism in *Schwanengesang.*"

In the first chapter, "The Origin and Early Reception of *Schwanengesang,*" Walburga Litschauer, who directs the Viennese office of the New Schubert Edition, presents the extant documents relating to the writing of *Schwanengesang* and reviews the earliest performances of the set. Of special interest are her remarks on the importance of Franz Liszt's transcriptions of the fourteen songs as a means of spreading their fame at a time when public concert life was in its infancy and solo song recitals by individual vocalists were unknown. In the next chapter, the editor examines the lives of the three poets of *Schwanengesang* and the details of their publications primarily up to the time of Schubert's death or shortly thereafter. Special attention is paid to the relationship of each poet to Schubert and to their writings or comments about music. Notably, although the literature on Heine is vast, with much of it of considerable interest, the literature on Rellstab and Johann Gabriel Seidl is limited and, with few exceptions, outdated.

To begin the second part of the book, "Analysis," Edward T. Cone, one of America's most distinguished writers about music, offers a composer's view of the fourteen songs. He emphasizes those features contributing to coherence, and the results are the single most comprehensive essay on the set to date. The next chapter, "Texts and Commentary," includes German texts of the songs as Schubert set them and literal English translations. These translations are not intended for singing; neither syllable count nor metric stress matches the original poetry, and there is no rhyming. As far as possible, however, each line of the translation matches the corresponding line of the German text. In this chapter, the editor coordinates his discussions of individual songs with the analyses of Edward Cone. References to the published literature either introduce different points of view from Cone's or are a springboard for the editor's own ideas. Finally, the composer's sketches, when they exist, and the principal corrections in the autograph are described in some detail.

In order to assist performers, the third part of the book includes a chapter titled "On Singing *Schwanengesang*," by Walther Dürr, a trained singer-scholar who has been the chief editor of the New Schubert Edition from its beginnings and who has edited all the volumes for solo song in that monumental publication. In the writing of this chapter Dürr was assisted by Martin Chusid. In addition, the active performer-teacher Steven Lubin has written "The Three Styles of *Schwanengesang*: A Pianist's Perspective," an original view of Schubert's last period of composition. Lubin also offers a number of observations concerning the differences between the pianos of Schubert's day and our own. He concludes with an affirmative critique of the last song of the set, "Die Taubenpost." The last chapter is a discography compiled and introduced by Richard LeSueur, a music librarian and author who specializes in compilations and reviews of compact discs and who has served as repertoire consultant for several of the world's leading vocalists today (including Jessye Norman, Elly Ameling, and Cecilia Bartoli).

PART I

History

CHAPTER 1

The Origin and Early Reception of *Schwanengesang*

WALBURGA LITSCHAUER

There are contradictory accounts concerning the origin of Schubert's thirteen songs with lyrics by Ludwig Rellstab and Heinrich Heine, which—together with the song "Die Taubenpost," with lyrics by Johann Gabriel Seidl—were published under the title *Schwanengesang*. One of these accounts derives from the poet of the first seven songs, Rellstab, who wrote in his memoirs, *Aus meinem Leben*, that he had transmitted several poems to Ludwig van Beethoven in the spring of 1825, which he later recovered from the deceased composer's estate. In his words, "Some had pencil marks in Beethoven's own handwriting; they were the ones he liked best and the ones he had given Schubert to compose at that time, because he himself felt too unwell. Moreover they are to be found among Schubert's works and some of them have become generally well known."[1] By contrast, Beethoven's factotum, Anton Schindler, maintained that Schubert first received these poems from him after Beethoven's death in March 1827 and that several of them captured his attention because "Beethoven had ear-marked several of them to compose himself."[2] Indeed, Schubert did not begin composing Rellstab's poems until the spring of 1828, which implies that he obtained them only after Beethoven's death. Otherwise it is difficult to explain why he should have begun them so late. Whether the pencil marks in Rellstab's manuscript derived from Beethoven or from Schubert could hardly be verified, as Walther Dürr has suggested, "even if the lost pages were rediscovered some day."[3]

As for the poems of Heine that Schubert used as his textual source for the six songs, they were drawn from the cycle *Die Heimkehr,* which was published in 1826 in the *Reisebilder* and again in 1827 in *Buch der Lieder*. There is a reference to Schubert's use of *Buch der Lieder* in the memoirs of the singer Karl von Schönstein: "When Schubert was still living at Schober's . . . I found he had in his possession Heine's *Buch der Lieder* which interested me very much; I asked him for it and he let me have it, remarking that *in any case he did not need it anymore*. . . . all the above-mentioned Heine songs, which appeared in *Schwanengesang,* are contained in this book, [and] the places where they are to be found are indicated by dog-eared leaves, probably done by Schubert's own hand."[4]

The manuscript version of the two groups of songs (that is, those with words by Rellstab and Heine), dated August 1828, was preceded by various sketches. According to Walther Dürr, it is conceivable that the sketches for the Rellstab songs "reach back to the spring of 1828: the two dated songs on texts by Rellstab not included in *Schwanengesang* [that is, "Auf dem Strom" and "Herbst"] derive from March or April 1828. On the other hand there are the sketches remaining for No. 1 ["Liebesbotschaft"] and No. 3 ["Frühlingssehnsucht"], to be found together with the surviving song fragment "Lebensmuth," which were probably not written until the summer of 1828."[5] In his manuscript Schubert wrote the seven Rellstab and six Heine songs without a title page or other corresponding heading, and without a continuous numbering of the songs.[6]

Only the first song of the autograph manuscript of the final version is given a date: "August 1828." Whether Schubert regarded the thirteen Lieder as a related series of songs must remain an open question. Regardless, in one of his last letters, written on 2 October 1828, he offered the Leipzig publisher Heinrich Probst the Heine songs, together with other compositions, for publication separately. "I have set several songs by Heine of Hamburg, which pleased extraordinarily here. . . . If perhaps any of these compositions would suit you, let me know. . . . Frz Schubert."[7] Probst answered by 6 October: "Of your new compositions, the songs would suit me best, and I would ask you to send them."[8] Nothing came of this correspondence, however. After Schubert's death on 19 November, the complete manuscript of the Rellstab and Heine songs remained in the possession of Schubert's brother Ferdinand, who sold it together with Schubert's last three piano sonatas to the Viennese music publisher Tobias Haslinger for circa 500 florins. After the agreement was concluded, Haslinger planned the publication of the songs in four volumes, of which the first two were to contain the seven settings of the Rellstab poems, the third volume the Heine songs "Der Atlas," "Ihr Bild," and "Das Fischermädchen," and the fourth volume "Die Stadt," "Am Meer," and "Der Doppelgänger."[9] Three days later, on 18 December 1828, Haslinger published a notice in the *Wiener Zeitung* that he "had purchased as his legal property Franz Schubert's last compositions for voice and piano . . . from the estate of the recently deceased, incomparable composer . . . consisting: of 14 still completely unknown songs, with piano accompaniment (composed in August 1828), and three new keyboard sonatas (composed September 1828)."[10]

As may be deduced from this announcement, in addition to the compositions paid for in the agreement of 17 December, Ferdinand Schubert must have subsequently sold to Haslinger a fourteenth song, "Die Taubenpost," which is dated "October 1828." Of the fourteen songs published by Haslinger as *Schwanengesang,* it is the only one written on different paper. It is in no way related to the Rellstab and Heine songs and was clearly added later to the autograph of the song volume for which it now serves as a close.[11]

The appellation *Schwanen-Gesang* (Swan Song) is found for the first time in Haslinger's notice of 31 January 1828 in the *Wiener Zeitung.* According to this appeal for subscriptions, the title selected by Haslinger does not mean a cycle—such as, for example, *Die schöne Müllerin* or *Winterreise*—but merely denotes Schubert's last songs: "Under the above title are offered to the numerous friends of [Schubert's] classic muse, the last blossoms of his noble spirit. They are those musical compositions which he wrote in August 1828, shortly before his departure from this world. Works, which proclaim in the most verifiable manner the professionalism of his richly endowed mastery."[12] In contrast to the earlier agreement with Ferdinand Schubert, Haslinger now announced that the printing of these songs "dedicated to Schubert's patrons and friends" was being prepared in two volumes, not four.

In their anonymously published article "About Franz Schubert," which appeared on 3 April 1829 in the *Österreichisches Bürgerblatt für Verstand, Herz und Gute Laune* of Linz, Josef von Spaun and Anton Ottenwalt referred to the intended dedication by Haslinger: "He [Schubert] wrote . . . about 400 songs, [and] shortly before his death another fourteen completely new ones, which, dedicated to his friends, are being published by Haslinger in Vienna, and among which 'Die Taubenpost' was the last."[13] Then, at the beginning of May *Schwanengesang* was published with neither dedication nor opus number. Moreover, with regard to its totality (that is, all the songs except for *Die Taubenpost*) the title "last composition" is wrong.[14]

In the issue of the Leipzig *Allgemeine Musikalischen Zeitung* dated 7 October 1829 there appeared an appreciation of *Schwanengesang* and *Winterreise* as detailed as it was remarkable. It was written by the editor of that periodical, Gottfried Wilhelm Fink:

Although many others consider . . . *Winterreise* to rank among Schubert's finest offerings, we cannot refrain from awarding our preference by far to the Swan-Songs of the early deceased. We find them more genial, more controlled, more inventive, and more intimately felt. On the whole the poems selected here . . . are much more musical, often fresher because of their clear and poetically expressed contents, and even more beautiful in their form. They [the poems] obviously allowed the composer more lively, yet freer realizations; most desirably, they brought him back from the merely far-fetched, from the pitiless cutting; and then knew how to involve him so continuously that he found neither the time nor the inclination to wander from the proper path of sincere truths onto any uncharted byways. As little as he relinquishes here certain melodic turns, passages, and constant embellishments that had become almost habitual with him, as well as retaining difficult-to-perform accompaniments consisting of descriptive figures carried through to the end, and does so with stabbing modulations; nevertheless, for the most part these stylistic traits derive here far more from the nature of the things, from suitable feelings, so that with sincere sympathy we see the swan swimming, resting under the shadows of the Weeping Willows and on the way to the nether regions, more than we complete the wintry journey with the forsaken wanderer [of *Winterreise*]. And if we do not dwell on affairs that, as matters stand, the new style of composition does not consider worthy . . . so by all means both these volumes should be praised, as they do not contain a single piece that cannot at least be counted as highly successful and beautifully treated. Indeed, without hesitation we may place many of these songs among the most masterly products of Schubert's Muse being sung at any time.

At the very outset "Liebesbotschaft" is extremely graceful, and murmurs of the brook's rustling to the friendly, longing melody singing in constantly hurrying motion to the very end. "Kriegers Ahnung" expresses itself individually but thoughtfully, changing tempos and modulations frequently. "Frühlingssehnsucht" [is] passionate. In poetry and music "Ständchen," No. 4, belongs among the most admirable cantilenas. In addition to the elegant languishing words, the melody has something so sweetly alluring [and] the simple, restlessly demanding accompaniment adorns so appealingly, that it will undoubtedly become everyone's favorite. "Aufenthalt," No. 5, [is] likewise full of character. An irresistible grief sings through the tops of the humming trees, and its deep, soul-stirring lamentation sings in the projecting cliffs. Similarly, in the distance ("In der Ferne") an almost still deeper anxiety, an overburdened heart laments its disappointments and homesickness.

"Abschied," beginning of the second book and at the same time the last poem by Rellstab, is drawn in such lively fashion by poet and composer, that we particularly promise it new friends. After his fashion, the composer has chosen for the subject of his accompaniment the pony "pawing with playful hoofs," and has accomplished it quite successfully.

The accompaniment is anything but easy. At this point we must really not forget that singer and player should rehearse well together if they do not want to ruin thoughtlessly the pleasure in these gifts for themselves and for others. "Der Atlas," No. 8. With this short poem, not especially suitable for musical setting, the composer contrived to do everything possible to initiate H. Heine's poems. As a whole, the remainder of these are well chosen. "Ihr Bild," No. 9, is very simple and painfully deep. "Das Fischermädchen," No. 10, will please. But the following [song], "Die Stadt," grips the strings [of the heart] more deeply, shuddering, as if waves were beating against the shore in the dusky night; and it will penetrate into the deepest recesses of the soul. Equally sensitive and original is the song "Am Meer." The separating [couple] are resting near a fisherman's house; the woman's tears fall heavily upon her white hand; and since he drank those tears, [the man's] body has been wasting away with longing; the unfortunate woman has poisoned him with her tears.—Arousing shudders, "Der Doppelgänger" approaches. The progression of the incomplete chords in the accompaniment, always played in the murky depths, is highly expressive; and the terrifying melody floating above it provides the singer with the utmost in soul-stirring declamation.—The closing song, "Die Taubenpost," is very pleasing melodically, and brilliant in the highly adorned accompaniment, one which demands an assured performance and lasting strength. It will become one of the favorites as soon as it is performed properly.

And so we recommend especially the Swan-Songs to all more serious amateurs, even when in many numbers the music is not always light and entertaining. From them each individual certainly can and will select what is precisely to his taste.[15]

Schubert's friends heard two of these songs for the first time at a Schubertiade that took place at the home of Josef von Spaun. The evening was described in a letter by an Upper Austrian civil servant, Friedrich Ludwig von Hartmann, to his daughter and son-in-law, Anna and Anton von Revertera: "Tuesday, Dec. 23 . . . In the evening I was at Pepi [Josef] Spaun's, where the circle of [Schubert's] friends were gathered and Vogl performed as yet unknown compositions from the months September and October, among them the song composed last before his death: 'Die Brieftaube' ['Die Taubenpost'], one of his most charming; another, however, 'Der Doppelgänger,' is one of the blackest-night pieces to be found among his songs."[16]

Anna Fröhlich, who apparently was present at this Schubertiade, arranged a "private concert," which took place on 30 January 1829, the eve of Schubert's birthday, in the hall of the Music Society, "one half of the receipts for which is to be devoted to the erection of a monument for the deceased composer Franz Schubert, the other half . . . for charitable purposes."[17] As the third portion of the program, "proposed music pieces" were "'Die Taubenpost' of Seidl [and] 'Aufenthalt' of Rellstab . . . performed by Herr Vogl."[18] A published report of the event stated that both songs "were repeated by stormy request. They belong to those [songs] which Schubert composed in the last days of his life, and which . . . are appearing at the Imperial and Royal Privileged Dealer in Works of Art Tobias Haslinger in Vienna. . . . These samples arouse the most intense expectations for the remaining songs of this interesting collection."[19] A repetition of the concert, whose compositions were enthusiastically received by the public, was scheduled for 13 February 1829 but had to be postponed until 5 March because of Fröhlich's illness.[20]

The popularity of the song "Ständchen," which Fink had prophesied would develop into everyone's favorite and which is still a favorite today, can be traced back to its first performance. This took place at a "private musical entertainment" organized on 1 November 1829 by the violinist Ignaz Schuppanzigh; the piece was sung by Ludwig Tietze and had to be repeated at the request of the audience.[21] In April 1838 Franz Liszt, who was twenty-seven years of age, enchanted the Viennese public with a transcription of the song for piano solo: "Songs of Schubert (das 'Ständchen' and die 'Tränen') arranged for piano solo. . . . These were neither variations nor potpourris; they were the simple, glorious songs of the glorious departed, from whose motives the greatest virtuoso scattered graceful, simple, and yet so artistic blossoms on the tear-drenched grave of the beloved, great song-poet. Especially in the first song ['Ständchen'] there was a wondrously magnificent imitative figure of indescribable enchantment; on the whole the interpretation and development of these songs provide gratifying evidence of the understanding, thoughtful, compositional capacity of the celebrated virtuoso."[22]

Liszt arranged more than fifty songs by Schubert for piano solo, among them part of Die schöne Müllerin, half of Winterreise, and the complete Schwanengesang. As can be gathered from a review appearing on 7 December 1839

in the *Wiener Zeitschrift für Kunst, Literatur, Theater und Mode,* at the time
these transcriptions were highly prized and appropriately appreciated: "In
the transcriptions of Schubert Lieder, [Liszt] has created a new genre. Here
is an excellent effort to reproduce the melodic and harmonic beauty of the
new classical Lied as a lyric entity on the piano alone; and to manage this
perfectly, as if with the power of the vocal line and declamation, without
sacrificing in the process any of his pianistic richness. [Liszt's] artistic, characteristic, and tasteful treatment [has] raised these pieces to performance favorites almost everywhere. Now Schubert's immortal songs need remain no
longer the [sole] property of the accomplished singer."[23]

The significance of Liszt's transcriptions was also recognized by Schubert's friends. In 1849, for example, the Tyrolean poet Johann Chrysostomus
Senn wrote in his memoirs that Schubert's songs, "through Liszt, achieved
European fame."[24] The supplement by Anselm Hüttenbrenner to his "Fragments from the Life of the Song Composer Franz Schubert," written for
Franz Liszt in 1854, is also noteworthy. He remarks: "Schubert would, on the
one hand, have derived great pleasure from the fact that several of his finest
songs had been arranged by Liszt's master hand so splendidly for the pianoforte that, in a sensitive performance of them on a grand piano, it is
fairly easy to forgo the words and the vocal part; on the other hand, however, Schubert would have been annoyed by the addition of embellishments
which were not his own. Nevertheless to Liszt, the virtuoso genius, belongs
the unquestionable merit of having demonstrated to the piano-playing
world that the fingers can achieve almost as much as can the throat."[25]

According to Ernst Hilmar, Liszt's transcriptions of Schubert's *Schwanengesang* originated between 1835 and 1838.[26] The arrangements were then
published in 1840 by Haslinger. In the course of his six Viennese concerts of
1838, Liszt not only played the arrangement of "Ständchen" mentioned earlier, but he also accompanied several singers in various Lieder from *Schwanengesang*: on 29 April Ludwig Tietze with "Liebesbotschaft," on 2 May
Benedict Gross with "Ständchen," and on 14 May Benedict Randhartinger
with "Das Fischermädchen."[27]

Transcriptions of *Schwanengesang* were also performed by other pianists
at the time. This can be gathered from, among other sources, a report appearing in the Viennese *Theaterzeitung* of 16 June 1842: "The distinguished
pianist from Prague, I[gnaz Amadeus] Tedesco, has caused a remarkable
sensation in Kiev. . . . He performed Schubert's "Ständchen" enchantingly."[28]
In 1843 Liszt's arrangements of the songs "Ständchen" and "Das Fischermädchen," along with transcriptions for violin and piano by Leopold Jansa,
were published by Haslinger.[29]

It is obvious that in France the songs of *Schwanengesang* to texts by

Heine enjoyed the greatest popularity. In March 1843, Heine stated, in a report titled "Politics, Art and the Life of the People": "Schubert's popularity in Paris is very great, and his name is exploited in the most shameless manner. . . . It is particularly the Heinrich Heine songs, composed by Schubert, which are the favorites here, but the translation of the words is so horrible that the poet was heartily pleased on finding the music publishers to have so few scruples that, suppressing the identity of the true author, they have placed the name of an obscure French hack-writer on the title-page of these songs."[30]

When and for what occasion *Schwanengesang* was first performed in its entirety unfortunately cannot be determined. It is noteworthy, however, that both volumes of the publication served as instructional materials for the first- and second-level girls' vocal classes at the Vienna Conservatory of the Society of the Friends of Music.[31] This was the case probably because Anna Fröhlich, a close friend of Schubert, was active there as a voice teacher.[32] With her efforts on behalf of Schubert's music, Fröhlich counts among those who erected for the deceased composer "the most beautiful monument"—one that, according to the published report of the private concert of 30 January 1829, "will certainly last when the gravestone which covers his bones has long since crumbled into dust."[33]

NOTES

1. Deutsch, *Schubert: Memoirs by His Friends,* 303.

2. Ibid., 319.

3. Dürr, *Neue Schubert-Ausgabe,* series IV, vol. 14a, xxii.

4. Deutsch, *Schubert: Memoirs by His Friends,* 103.

5. Dürr, *Neue Schubert-Ausgabe,* series IV, vol. 14a, xxiii. Unless otherwise noted, all translations are by the author. For the dating of "Lebensmuth" see also Winter, "Paper Studies," 254.

6. Both title and song numbering, however, are to be found in *Die schöne Müllerin* and *Winterreise.* For a physical description of the manuscript and sketches see Chusid, "Introduction" in Schubert, *'Schwanengesang': Facsimiles . . . and Reprint.*

7. Deutsch, *Schubert Reader,* 811.

8. Ibid., 814.

9. Deutsch, *Schubert: Memoirs by His Friends,* 385.

10. *Wiener Zeitung,* no. 293, 1276. Cited in Waidelich, *Dokumente 1817–1830,* 458.

11. See the remarks by Dürr, *Neue-Schubert Ausgabe,* series IV, vol. 14a, xxiv; Chusid, *Schubert's 'Schwanengesang';* and Winter, "Paper Studies."

12. Waidelich, *Dokumente 1817–1830,* 478.

13. Ibid., 515.

14. The description "Franz Schubert's very last composition" is also to be found erroneously applied to the first edition of Schubert's last three piano sonatas. See Litschauer in *Neue-Schubert Ausgabe,* series VII, part 2, vol. 3, xiv. In both cases the descriptions "last work"

and "very last composition" surely derive from commercial considerations on the part of the publishers.

15. Printed in the *Allgemeine Musikalische Zeitung* of Leipzig, no. 40, 7 October 1829, cols. 659–662. Also reprinted in Waidelich, *Dokumente 1817–1830*, 557–558.

16. Litschauer, *Neue Dokumente,* vol. 2, 104.

17. Deutsch, *Schubert Reader,* 851.

18. Ibid.

19. *Monatbericht der Gesellschaft der Musikfreunde des Österreichischen Kaiserstaates,* March 1829. Cited in Waidelich, *Dokumente 1817–1830*, 497.

20. Brusatti, *Schubert im Wiener Vormärz,* 90.

21. Waidelich, *Dokumente 1817–1830*, 563.

22. From a review dated 27 April 1838 in the periodical *Humorist.* Cited in Brusatti, *Schubert im Wiener Vormärz,* 90.

23. Brusatti, *Schubert im Wiener Vormärz,* 107.

24. Deutsch, *Schubert: Memoirs by His Friends,* 335.

25. Ibid., 186.

26. Hilmar, "Kritische Betrachtungen," 118–119.

27. Gibbs, *The Presence of 'Erlkönig,'* 247.

28. Brusatti, *Schubert im Wiener Vormärz,* 144.

29. Ibid., 164f.

30. Deutsch, *Schubert: Memoirs by His Friends,* 412–413.

31. See the "Prize List" in the monthly report for September 1830 published in Waidelich, *Dokumente 1817–1830*, 578.

32. It was undoubtedly because of Fröhlich that the first and second volumes of *Schwanengesang,* and the five published volumes of *Die schöne Müllerin* and *Winterreise,* were all named in the prize list mentioned in the previous note.

33. *Monatsbericht,* March 1829. Cited in Waidelich, *Dokumente 1817–1830*, 497.

CHAPTER 2

The Poets of *Schwanengesang*
Rellstab, Heine, and Seidl

MARTIN CHUSID

The three poets of *Schwanengesang* were all members of Franz Schubert's generation, although each outlived him by several decades. Heinrich Heine was born in Düsseldorf in the same year as the composer, 1797, and he died in Paris in 1856. In 1799 Ludwig Rellstab was born in Berlin, where he died in 1860. Johann Gabriel Seidl was born in Vienna in 1804, and he lived the longest, until 1875. Like Rellstab, Seidl passed away in the city of his birth. Significantly, much of the poetry for which each is best known was written during the 1820s, while Schubert was still alive. Of the three poets, the composer knew only Seidl, although it is conceivable that he could have met Rellstab during the latter's trip to Vienna in 1825. Schubert is known to have attended all the concerts at which Ludwig van Beethoven's late quartets were performed, and Rellstab attended the premiere of the E-flat (Op. 127) and sent a review of the work to the *Berliner allgemeine musikalische Zeitung*. There is, however, no evidence of specific contact between the two. Besides, during that trip the young Berliner was preoccupied with Beethoven.

Rellstab

Ludwig Rellstab, poet for the first seven songs of *Schwanengesang,* is best remembered today as probably the most influential music critic in Berlin during the first half of the nineteenth century. According to a saying that made the rounds of the Prussian capital at the time, "The true Berliner believes first and foremost in the correctness of his first impression; if it was confirmed for him by Rellstab in the *Vossische Zeitung*."[1] Though recognized primarily as a literary figure, Rellstab came from an eminently musical family. His father, Johann Carl Friedrich Rellstab (1759–1813), a student of J. F. Agricola and C. F. C. Fasch, composed music, published it (including a good deal of Mozart), and lectured and wrote about harmony and other musical subjects. He also taught keyboard instruments and singing, and he preceded his son as music critic for the *Vossische Zeitung* from 1808 to his death in 1813.[2] In addition, in 1787 he initiated a public concert series, in which Christoph Willibald Gluck's *Alceste* was first performed in Berlin. Although the series failed after a single season, the elder Rellstab continued to host concerts in his own home. It is a tribute to his musical stature that the most important musicians in Berlin (Vincenzo Righini, Johann Friedrich Reichardt, Friedrich Heinrich Himmel, and Carl Friedrich Zelter) were regular guests in the Rellstab household. Furthermore, the father taught music to Ludwig and his three sisters. One of them, Caroline (1793–1813), became a celebrated soprano at the Breslau Opera, renowned for her portrayal of the Queen of the Night. The other sisters were pianists, and Ludwig, who began playing the piano at age five, is reported to have performed Mozart and Bach concertos at ten.

The young Ludwig, apparently of an independent nature, refused to continue studying music or other humanities (such as classical languages) and instead concentrated on mathematics in preparation for a career in the military. In this he was undoubtedly influenced by the wave of patriotism sweeping the German states during the Napoleonic wars. On 1 April 1815 Rellstab enlisted in the Prussian army, but he was soon discharged because he was underage and had poor eyesight.[3] Later that year, however, he entered a military academy and, because of his mathematical abilities, eventually became an instructor of mathematics in an artillery brigade. In 1818 he received a commission as a lieutenant. That same year Rellstab published, in the periodical *Die Leuchte* of Berlin, a poem, "Elektra," and "Briefe eines Musikfreundes über den Zustand der Berliner Oper" (Letter from a friend of music on the state of the Berlin Opera).[4] By 1820 he appeared to have become disenchanted with the military. Encouraged by some poetic success and by musical friends (Bernhard Klein and especially Ludwig Berger), he left the army to devote himself to literature and music.

In 1816, while still in the service, Rellstab began studying music theory with Bernhard Joseph Klein (1793–1832), primarily a composer of church music written in the style of George Frideric Handel. Klein, who had studied briefly with Luigi Cherubini in Paris, was called the Berlin Palestrina because of his contrapuntal skill. He also composed piano music and wrote more than one hundred songs in a simple, syllabic style. Even earlier,

Rellstab had begun studying piano with Ludwig Berger (1777–1839), a student of Muzio Clementi and an admired interpreter of Beethoven's piano music. Berger, who was one of the most influential pedagogues in Berlin, also taught, among others, Felix and Fanny Mendelssohn, W. Talbert, and A. Henselt. In addition he composed extensively, primarily for the piano but also cantatas, male quartets, and an opera that was never performed, *Orestes,* to a libretto by Rellstab. Berger also produced more than one hundred songs.[5] In 1816 the musician, together with Wilhelm Müller and Rellstab, joined a literary and musical circle in Berlin,[6] and Berger set a group of poems from Müller's *Gesänge aus einem Liederspiel, Die schöne Müllerin.* These were printed as his Op. 11 in 1818, six years before the publication of the more famous setting by Schubert. In April 1819 Rellstab, together with Klein, Berger, and G. Reichardt, founded "Die jüngere Liedertafel," a singing group for which Rellstab is said to have written part music.[7] The organization, participating in the flourishing male choral movement in Germany at the time, included as one of its members E. T. A. Hoffmann. It was established as an alternative to Carl Zelter's older and *abgeschlossene* (closed) choral group.

In 1820 Rellstab, who had become financially independent as a result of an inheritance from his mother, began to enlarge his horizons by studying literature seriously and traveling extensively. It is clear that from the beginning of his career the young man knew how to form personal relationships and how to use every opportunity to his advantage.[8] In this fashion he met many of the most famous literary and musical figures of his time. At Frankfurt an der Oder he studied classical languages and ancient literature with a brother of Leopold von Ranke, and according to his autobiography, *Aus meinem Leben,* he stayed at the home of his friend and teacher Ludwig Berger. "There, in a small attic room, I soon completed a great number of my earliest poems."[9] These may well have included several of the poems set by Schubert. Rellstab also had begun to write plays and librettos, and on a visit to Dresden in 1821 he read his drama *Karl der Kühne* to Ludwig Tieck and his opera libretto *Dido* to Carl Maria von Weber. In his autobiography the poet mentions having read a publication that contained a letter by Weber to the composer's wife about the meeting with Rellstab. "The young Rellstab from Berlin has read aloud to me a grand opera, *Dido;* splendid! Once more there blooms an able opera poet. . . . He also promised to write one for me."[10]

Rellstab continued on to Heidelberg and Bonn, where he attended lectures by August Wilhelm Schlegel and completed his first substantial publication, the cycle of poems *Griechenlands Morgenröthe in 9 Gedichten* (Heidelberg, 1822). He also spent time with Jean Paul in Bayreuth and made the mandatory pilgrimage to Weimar, where he met Johanna Schopenhauer, Johann Nepomuk Hummel, and Bettina von Arnim, and was present when the young Mendelssohn first visited and performed for Wolfgang von Goethe. Although his reception by Goethe was cool—Goethe refused to read his poetry—Rellstab is reported to have visited the aged poet twice more in subsequent years.[11]

Rellstab returned to Berlin in 1823, the year in which his libretto *Dido,* set by Klein, had its premiere (on 15 October), but without success. In 1824 Rellstab became a regular contributor (of reviews of published music, concerts, and operas) to the first serious periodical in Berlin devoted exclusively to music, the weekly *Berliner allgemeine musikalische Zeitung (BAMZ),* founded by the theorist and composer A. B. Marx. For the inaugural issue (7 January) he contributed a poem "Ihr jünger der Göttin," and later that year he supplied both an article, "Rudimentary Thoughts on the Union of Poetry with Music," and the first of a group of musical novellas, *Theodor.* It was about this time that Rellstab financed a publishing company in Berlin administered by Friedrich Laue, a friend from his military period. It was Laue who printed Rellstab's collected poetry, *Gedichte* (1827); later the publisher left to join the Turkish army, causing the literary venture to fail, with considerable financial loss to Rellstab.[12]

Early in 1825 Rellstab's poem "Abschied," later set by Schubert in *Schwanengesang,* was printed in the periodical *Rheinische Flora,*[13] and the young author published two volumes entitled *Sagen und romantischen Erzählungen,* books stimulated by the attractive surroundings of Heidelberg. In March he undertook another trip, this time to Bohemia and Austria by way of Dresden, where he visited Weber again. From Prague and Vienna he sent concert reviews to *BAMZ,* including "On Beethoven's Newest Quartet," Op. 127 in E-flat, a work that he did not like, although he did admit that he may not have understood it. With considerable trepidation, he visited the great composer, carrying personal greetings from Weber and a letter of introduction from Zelter explaining that Rellstab wanted to write a libretto for Beethoven. Some time during his several visits the young man left, or had delivered, eight or ten of his best poems.[14] A letter by Rellstab, undated and with no clear addressee but generally assumed to have been written to Beethoven, is cited by Kreissle von Hellborn, the most important nineteenth-century biographer of Schubert. The contents suggest that this letter may have accompanied the poetry from which Schubert ultimately selected his Rellstab texts:

Most honoured Sir,—I send you herewith some songs which I have had copied fairly for you; some others, written in the same vein, will shortly follow. They have perhaps this novelty about them, that they form in themselves a connected series, and have reference to happiness, unity, separation, death, and hope on the other side of the grave, without pointing to any definite incidents.

I should wish that these poems might succeed so far in winning your approval as to move you to set them to music and that, for this purpose, we should come to terms with a firm conducted on a principle of advancing, as far as possible, the interests of true and the highest art, the composer's inspiration to be considered the first law.

Day and night I am thinking of an opera for you; nor do I doubt of finding a subject which shall satisfy all the claims of a composer, a poet, and the many-headed public,

With the deepest respect,
M. L. Rellstab[15]

Beethoven reportedly told Rellstab that he liked several of the poems and promised to set these, but he never did.

During his six weeks in Vienna Rellstab met many notable musicians of the Beethoven circle, including Carl Czerny and Anton Schindler, as well as such literary figures as Franz Grillparzer, Caroline Pichler, Friedrich von Schlegel, and Ignaz Franz Castelli. Coincidentally, Schubert set songs to poetry by all four authors and wrote his opera *Die Verschworenen* to a libretto by Castelli.[16] Rellstab was also invited to join a high-spirited group of intellectuals who met regularly at an inn located near St. Stephen's Cathedral and who called their meeting place *Ludlumshöhle* (Ludlum's Hell). Musical members of the society included Weber, Hummel, and Ignaz Moscheles. In the following year Schubert was reported to have been on the verge of joining the conclave, but it was disbanded by the police, who were suspicious of "secret organizations."[17]

The visits to Beethoven were obviously the principal reason for the trip to Vienna, and they marked a high point in Rellstab's life. When, shortly before his death, Rellstab wrote *Aus meinem Leben,* he concluded the second of the two volumes with a lengthy chapter describing his visits to Beethoven. From this chapter we learn of Beethoven's physical appearance and poor health at the time, of his almost total deafness by 1825, of his suspicions and unhappiness with almost everyone surrounding him, and of his negative views on the themes of the librettos for *Figaro* and *Don Giovanni.* In response to these remarks Rellstab offered Beethoven as possible operatic subjects *Orestes, Antigone, Belisario,* and *Attila.*[18] But, as with his intended libretto for

Weber, nothing came to fruition. It is clear, nonetheless, that the young man
from Berlin made an excellent impression on Beethoven. When the ailing
composer could not say goodbye—he was preparing to visit Baden-bei-
Wien for health reasons—he left a warm letter for Rellstab:

> As I am on the verge of going to the country, yesterday I personally had
> to make some arrangements, and unfortunately as a result your visit
> [to me] was in vain. Please excuse my as yet very poor health. Since,
> perhaps, I may not see you again, I wish you all conceivable success.
> Think of me in your poetic writings.
>   Your friend,
> Beethoven
> All my love and esteem to Zelter,
> the true guardian of genuine Art. 3 May 1825
>
> [On the reverse side:]
>
> In my convalescence I find myself extremely weak. Be content with
> this small token of remembrance of your friend Beethoven.

Ex. 2.1. Beethoven, Canon WoO 203

There also exists a lightly penciled draft of the remarks on the reverse
side of the letter published separately by Emily Anderson in her edition of
The Letters of Beethoven. She presents the remarks as if they were a letter in
themselves, with the suggested dating of April 1825 but without the canon
to which Beethoven refers; this was missing from the draft. Strangely
enough, she also publishes separately the remainder of the letter of 3 May
but without the remarks on the reverse side, yet with the canon. What is especially noteworthy about the draft is its location "on an empty page of an
undated letter from Rellstab to Beethoven enclosing his libretto for *Orest*."[20]
    Anderson reports that on a portion of the same page is a list of possible
operatic subjects that Beethoven seems to have been considering at the time
for an opera to follow his *Fidelio.* The list is in the handwriting of Johann van
Beethoven, the composer's brother, and includes Sir Walter Scott's *Kenilworth,* a subject that Giuseppe Verdi would consider setting some decades
later.[21]
    The following year Rellstab began his long tenure as principal critic for

the *Vossische Zeitung* (1826–48). Under the pseudonym Freimund Zuschauer (Free-Spoken Observer) he also published a pamphlet *Henriette oder die schöne Sängerin, Eine Geschichte unserer Tage* (Henrietta or the pretty singer, A story of our day) (Leipzig, 1826). It was an attack on the cult surrounding the singer Henriette Sontag, whom Rellstab had first heard in Vienna, and it also ridiculed the British ambassador, whom he called Lord Monday. The ambassador instituted a formal complaint; Rellstab was imprisoned for six weeks, and when he emerged he was a hero. Subsequently the critic returned to prison once more as the result of a second pamphlet: *Über mein Verhältnis als Kritiker zu Herrn Spontini als erste Komponisten und General-musikdirektor zu Berlin nebst einem vergnüglichen Anhange* (About my relationship as critic to Herr Spontini as first composer and general music director in Berlin together with an amusing appendix) (Leipzig, 1827). In this piece Rellstab attacked what he felt to be Gaspare Spontini's abuse of power as well as his imperious manner with musicians and vocalists. Although the king of Prussia, Wilhelm III, admired Spontini's music greatly, after the ruler's death in 1840 royal support evaporated. Audiences mounted hostile demonstrations, and Spontini was forced to resign.

During the year of the pamphlet against Spontini, 1827, Rellstab's most important poetic collection, *Gedichte,* was published in the Prussian capital. It contained all the author's poems set by Schubert (that is, the seven chosen for *Schwanengesang* along with "Lebensmuth," "Auf dem Strom," and "Herbst"). In his book on Schubert Alfred Einstein wrote of Rellstab, "One would scarcely expect the acute critic behind this sensitive wanderer through the world of nature," and there seems to be little doubt that this aspect of Rellstab's poetry (that is, the "sensitive wanderer") appealed to Schubert.[22]

From this point in his career Rellstab increasingly lost interest in poetry. As did his cousin, Willibald Alexis (1798–1871), he began to write historical novels. By far the most successful was *1812* (Leipzig, 1834), a story about Napoleon, whom he idolized. The work had more than thirty editions in the next hundred years and was translated into several foreign languages. Although Rellstab had a knack for satisfying the taste of readers from the emerging middle class, modern critics of his novels find them to have unconvincing plots, cardboard characters, and far too many long, dull stretches. The passages they feel to be of greatest interest usually relate to military events, especially those recalling the author's youth. He also wrote a number of books describing his travels and several biographical studies. A number of these were of musicians, including his friends Berger and Klein. An essay on Carl Maria von Weber was published in the music periodical *Cäcilia* (Mainz, 1828), and Rellstab also wrote an early study of Franz Liszt (Berlin, 1842), one of the relatively few musicians besides Schubert who set his poetry.[23] That Rellstab and Liszt remained friendly for many years is clear from a letter dated 15 July 1855 by the musician to Marie zu Sayn-Wittgenstein, daughter of the Russian princess Carolyne zu Sayn-Wittgenstein, with whom he lived for most of his life: "Since you have seen Rellstab, perhaps through his intervention you might correspond with Varnhagen von Ense. Rellstab's visit will be most pleasant for me for I do not alter my feelings toward those who have shown me kindness and affection."[24]

After Giacomo Meyerbeer replaced Spontini as Prussian *Generalmusikdirektor* in Berlin, Rellstab and C. Birch-Pfeiffer wrote a libretto, based on one by Eugène Scribe, for the new director: *Ein Feldlager in Schlesien* (Berlin, 1844).[25] By virtue of this work, and by translating into German Meyerbeer's *Le prophète* and *L'étoile du nord,* Rellstab helped spread the fame of the Berlin-born Meyerbeer in German-speaking areas of Europe.

Aside from the songs set by Schubert, however, Rellstab's reputation today derives largely from his music criticism. In addition to writing for the *Berliner allgemeine musikalische Zeitung* and the *Vossische Zeitung* of the same city, he wrote for music journals elsewhere (such as the *Neue Zeitschrift für Musik* of Leipzig). He also helped found the short-lived *Allgemeines Oppositionsblatt: Eine Zeitschrift für Literatur und Kunst* (Berlin, 1828–29), and then for twelve years edited *Iris im Gebiete der Tonkunst* (Berlin, 1830–41). But, for all the success his music criticism enjoyed in his own day, reading it today leaves one with the impression that he was neither an original thinker nor a particularly perceptive musician. He most appreciated six past masters: Bach (though with some reservations), Handel, Gluck, Haydn, and especially Mozart and Beethoven (with reservations about *Fidelio,* the Ninth Symphony, and other late works).[26] Of living composers he most liked Cherubini, Ludwig Spohr, Weber, Berger, Klein, and Mendelssohn.[27] He also liked Clementi, John Field, and Hummel. His teacher and close friend, Ludwig Berger, he considered the best of the moderns. Mendelssohn, for whom Rellstab had once written a libretto,[28] actually received mixed reviews despite his relatively high rating. The *Hebrides* Overture, for example, was deemed *matt* (weak) and not particularly original. According to the critic, the principal theme was too much like that of Beethoven's *Pastoral* Symphony. In general Rellstab disliked program music. Field's nocturnes he found to be infinitely preferable to those of Frederic Chopin, and he especially disliked the Polish composer's Mazurkas. For Rellstab they were full of "ear-shattering dissonances . . . tortured transitions . . . cutting modulations

. . . [and] disgusting dislocations" of the melody and rhythm. As might be expected, he vigorously opposed the "new romantics." To this, Robert Schumann retaliated by classing Rellstab among the Philistines in his *Davidsbündlertänze* and *Carnaval*.

As Rellstab was brought up in the North German tradition of songs, including for the most part songs with simple strophic settings, it will come as no surprise that he disliked those of Schubert. His reviews of the Austrian's Lieder, which seem to have been limited to assessments of printed music rather than performances, began with an essay on the ballad "Ein Fräulein scheut von hohem Thurm" (Op. 126). In *Iris* (vol. 1, no. 6) the critic finds in the piece "the depth and tenderness of feeling more than the skill and suppleness of invention." He admits that Schubert expresses the poet's "true, sincere feelings," but believes he does so in an awkward fashion. He concludes by suggesting that Schubert's inability to provide an adequate overall form "almost touches on the laughable."

In the second volume of *Iris* (nos. 39 and 40), he discusses the eight *Ossians Gesänge*: "In his lifetime Schubert has obviously written and published too much. . . . Not a single one of these pieces has a form. In addition to this general failure, there are also many details which are unpleasant [*unangenehm*] as well as extremely far-fetched harmonies which [are] often . . . discordant [*misklingend*]." In a review of Anton Diabelli's publication of the thirteenth and fourteenth parts of Schubert's *Nachlass* (*Iris* 3, no. 19), Rellstab blames the deceased composer for what he perceives to be unhealthy trends in song writing. He doesn't bother to name the Lieder occasioning his tirade, but they are "An mein Herz" (D. 860), "Der liebliche Stern" (D. 861), "Grenzen der Menschheit" (D. 716), and "Fragment aus den Aeschylus" (D. 450). He writes, "the deceased, despite all his achievements, nevertheless has led art on eminently wrong paths [*auf grosse Irrwege geleitet*]. Above all it is from him that the tendency has spread throughout music not just to express the true content of the poem, but also the fortuitous details. . . . [When] one expresses so strongly secondary parts, the totality of the poem often tends to be subordinated." Later in the review he suggests that Schubert's songs could be half as long without losing anything, "and this is the surest indication that there is no formal shape."

In a volume about the reception of music in Berlin before March 1848, Jürgen Rehm identifies, accurately I believe, the Berliner's weakness as a critic: "Rellstab, in aesthetic as in artistic-philosophical matters insecure, accepted the musical principles advocated by Berger and Klein without subjecting them to appropriate investigation."[29] An indication of Rellstab's technical insufficiency may be found in a review he wrote of both the published parts and a four-hand arrangement of Schubert's early string quartet, Op. 120, No. 1. The key signature has three flats, and in *Iris* (vol. 1, no. 7) he describes the piece as in C minor. In fact, all four movements are in E-flat major, and it is the only composite instrumental composition by Schubert in which every movement is in the same key.

Rellstab never reviewed *Schwanengesang,* but he did remark privately about Schubert's settings of his poems. Walther Vetter cites a letter by the Russian author Nikolai Platonovich Ogarev written in 1842: "The poet Rellstab was at the evening meal. An insufferable being. Dry critic. The 'Serenade' is his best work. He maintains that Schubert had botched his verses. An insufferable 'Dummkopf.'"[30]

Heine

Never was nature composed of more diverse elements than those of Henri [Heinrich] Heine: he was at the same time gay and sad, skeptic and believer, tender and cruel, sentimentalist and jester, classic and romantic, German and French, sensitive and cynical, enthusiast and *sang-froid;* everything except boring. To the pure plastic Greek he adds the most exquisite modern sense; this was truly Euphorion, child of Faust and the beautiful Helen.
—THÉOPHILE GAUTIER

Posterity has largely forgotten Rellstab and his poetry, and few musicians, Schubert and Liszt aside, have shown much interest in setting his verses; however, with regard to Heine and his lyrics the reverse is true. According to Philip Miller, who compiled an anthology of poems set to music, Heine inspired more songs than any other single poet, even more than Goethe.[31] Indeed, recent research indicates that since the first publication of *Buch der Lieder* (1827), more than 2,500 musicians have composed about 8,000 settings of Heine's poems.[32] The poet, who was consistently delighted with the interest of composers in his verses and enjoyed socializing with them, once wrote a cycle of forty-four poems, *Neue Frühling* (1831), specifically to be set to music by Albert Methfessel (1789–1865), a musician he had met in Hamburg. Although the violin and dancing lessons that Heine had been given as a child were not particularly successful, he was interested in music all his life. As Barker Fairley suggests in the first chapter of his study *Heinrich Heine: An Interpretation* (a chapter entitled "Song Within Song"), for Heine "song . . . was one of the things his mind turned to, when it turned to writing. The thought of song, the theme of song, inspired him not less surely than the theme of love, with which he often . . . associated it."[33]

Harry, later Heinrich, Heine was born in 1797 at Düsseldorf, then capital of the Duchy of Berg. He was the eldest of four children of Jewish parents. His father, Samson (1764–1828), was a merchant, and his mother, Peira ("Betty") van Gelder (1771–1859), was the daughter of a physician. The Duchy of Berg, occupied by revolutionary French forces in 1794, was ceded to Napoleon in 1806 by the Palatine Elector, Maximilian Joseph, king of Bavaria. As a result, Heine grew up under the liberal Napoleonic Code, which among other things forbade discrimination against Jews. After a short period in a Hebrew school, Harry Heine entered a Catholic elementary school and later a Lyceum, both organized on French models. At the Lyceum he studied rhetoric and learned French, although he never graduated. Instead, in the fall of 1814 he enrolled in a business school. He also absorbed the liberal principles of the French Revolution at the Lyceum and began to develop his lifelong antipathy to German nationalism. He became an ardent admirer of Napoleon, whom he saw as "the incarnation of the French Revolution as a militant and heroic force" and a "modern Prometheus . . . destroyer of Feudal nobility."[34] Recall that Rellstab, too, admired the French leader, no doubt for similar reasons.

During the years 1815–1819, the economically difficult period that followed the Napoleonic wars, Heine tried to become a businessman, first in Frankfurt am Main (September–December 1815), then in Hamburg (1816–19). Both his attempts and his father's luxury trade in silks failed. From that time on, the family of Samson Heine became dependent on Harry's rich uncle, Salomon Heine of Hamburg. This proved to be a painful and at times precarious situation for the young Heine, and to some extent he depended on his uncle to support him for the rest of his life. It was during this phase, however, that he published his first poems, in the periodical *Hamburgs Wächter* (1817), doing so under the pseudonym Sy Freudhold Riesenharf, an anagram for Harry Heine [of] Düsseldorf.[35]

In 1819 he began studying for a law degree at the New University of Bonn, where, in addition to his law courses, Heine also studied with August Wilhelm Schlegel, attending his lectures just a few years before Rellstab. The distinguished poet-scholar's lectures during Heine's stay in Bonn included "The History of Germanic Language and Literature," "The Nibelungenlied, Metrics, Prosody, and Rhetoric," and "Introduction to Romantic Theory." In 1820 Heine wrote three sonnets and dedicated them to Schlegel (published in 1821). The same year he moved on to the University of Göttingen, but he became involved in a duel with a fellow student and was compelled to take a leave of absence. Early in 1821 he traveled to Berlin to continue his law studies. In the Prussian capital the energetic Heine became a student of the philosopher Hegel and participated in a rich cultural and social life, particularly at the salon of Rahel and Karl August Varnhagen von Ense. As Jeffrey Sammons suggests: "Such salons were at the hub of private social life in Berlin. Since they were often presided over by well-married Jewish ladies, they lay partly outside the social caste system and could therefore provide a meeting place for lively minds, whether of the middle class or the aristocracy. Their ambience of mannerly but spirited conversation provided a nurturing shelter for people of modern ideas and spirit, for which public life in Prussia had little use. They were the place to be for a young man from the provinces ambitious for intellectual and literary contacts."[36]

Perhaps as a result of the stimulating environment, Heine began to publish more extensively. In December 1821 a volume of *Gedichte* was printed, and from February to July 1822 there appeared anonymously *Letters from Berlin,* which contained commentary on the court, theater, and opera of the city. In the third of these letters (7 June 1822) Heine mentions Josef Klein (1802–1862), stepbrother and pupil of Bernhard Klein, Rellstab's teacher and friend.[37] Heine and Josef Klein became lifelong friends, and the poet called the musician his Kreisler, after the famous fictional *Kapellmeister* Johannes Kreisler, created by E. T. A. Hoffmann. Josef Klein may have been one of the first musicians to set poetry by Heine to music.

While in Berlin Heine joined the short-lived *Verein für Cultur und Wissenschaft der Juden* (Society for the culture and science of the Jews), a group that confronted the dilemma of how to integrate Jews into German society while they maintained their Jewish identity. The organization, for which Heine taught German culture to youngsters (and reportedly did this well), was dissolved in 1824. Before then, in May 1823, Heine returned to his family, now living in Lüneberg. Had Rellstab not been traveling during this period (1821–23), he and Heine would probably have met in Berlin.

There is evidence, primarily from correspondence, that during his early years in Hamburg (circa 1817) Heine had fallen in love with his cousin Amalie (Molly), daughter of Salomon Heine. She rejected him and in 1821 married someone else. There is also some evidence that in 1823 Heine repeated the painful experience with Amalie's younger sister, Theresa. Most Heine biographers attribute the theme of frustration in love, the principal subject of Heine's early poetry, to these experiences. The truth of the matter is difficult to ascertain with respect to the Elusive Poet,[38] but in any event, it was at this time that the young author began writing the eighty-eight poems of *Die Heimkehr* (The homecoming), the core of *Buch der Lieder* and the section from which Schubert chose the texts for his Heine songs. The *Tragödien, nebst einem lyrischen Intermezzo* (Tragedies [*Almansor* and *Ratcliff*], together with a lyric intermezzo) were published the same year. The first of the dramas, *Almansor,* was performed unsuccessfully that summer in Brunswick. It was during the summer of 1823 that Heine first vacationed on the North Sea coast, an experience that resulted in his writing additional poetry of high quality.

Heine returned to Göttingen during January 1824 to conclude his study of law. In March his *Dreiunddreissig Gedichte* (Thirty-three poems) were published in installments by a periodical in Berlin, *Der Gesellschafter.* Thirty of these were later included in *Die Heimkehr,* of which three would ultimately be set by Schubert ("Die Stadt," "Der Doppelgänger," and "Das Fischermädchen"). It may be useful to note that the order of the poems in the periodical was not the same as in his later publications. "Das Fischermädchen," for example, is the last of the three, no. 12 in this collection, although later it would be the earliest in *Die Heimkehr* (no. 8) of the six poems eventually set by Schubert. Heine scholars have observed at this stage of his career (1824–1827) the poet frequently had groups of his poems published in multiples of eleven: twenty-two North Sea poems, the *Dreiunddreissig [Thirty-three] Gedichte,* the forty-four poems for Methfessel (of which the composer set only one!), sixty-five poems together with a prologue (thus making sixty-six) constituting the *Lyrisches Intermezzo,* and the eighty-eight poems of *Die Heimkehr.* Could this have been a form of homage to Wilhelm Müller's 77 *Gedichte aus den hinterlassenen Papieren eines reisenden Waldhornisten* (Seventy-seven poems from the posthumous papers of a traveling horn player)? Heine admired Müller very much, and he specifically mentions the 77 *Waldhornisten Gedichte* in a letter to the poet from Dessau. It seems noteworthy that in his cycles with poems in multiples of eleven Heine avoids the number seventy-seven, perhaps in order not to compete directly with Müller.

In April 1824 Heine revisited Berlin, and in mid-September he began a walking tour that included the Harz mountains and their silver mines. The trip has been called "the most famous walking tour in the history of German literature."[39] It resulted in *Die Harzreise* (The Harz journey), an unusual blend of travelogue, poetic fiction, and political commentary. Again the poetry was primarily concerned with unrequited love, and it was published in fourteen installments in *Der Gesellschafter* (January and February 1826). During the tour Heine visited Goethe, who was seventy-five and not particularly friendly. As noted earlier, Rellstab had similar experiences when he visited the great poet.

Meanwhile the political situation in Germany was taking a sharp turn to the right. From the year 1819 Prussia began systematically to reinstate restrictive laws against Jews, which had been lifted during the French occupation. The most important of these for Heine was a decree in 1822 that Jews were to be excluded from public academic positions. In order to obtain his law degree and develop a successful career in Germany, on 28 June 1825 Heine converted to Protestantism and took the name Christian Johann Heinrich Heine. This step, which troubled him for the remainder of his life, did lead to the degree of *doctor juris*, granted 20 July. In retrospect, however, the conversion proved futile. He never practiced law and failed in his attempts to obtain a teaching position, first in Munich and then in Berlin. In both situations his liberal political views undoubtedly contributed to his lack of success.

After his graduation Heine again vacationed at the North Sea, this time on the Isle of Nordeney (in the summer of 1825). He repeated the experience again in 1826 and 1827, and once more, memorable poetry resulted. In this instance Heine wrote free verse for the first time in his career, and *Nordsee* I and II became the final sections of *Buch der Lieder*. Although Heine's law degree did not lead to a profession with financial security, his writings did attract considerable attention as well as some modest monetary rewards. He also found his principal publisher for life, Julius Campe, of Hoffmann and Campe of Hamburg, who had developed a small but culturally influential press and who liked such oppositional writers as Heine. Campe republished the successful *Harzreise* in a version closer to Heine's original manuscript than the first edition had been; the work, renamed *Reisebilder* (volume 1 published in 1826), was extraordinarily successful. Early the following year volume 2 of *Reisebilder* was published, and Heine persuaded Campe to print an essentially complete collection of his early poetry, but not without foregoing the usual honorarium.[40] The result, *Buch der Lieder,* a collection of 238 poems, almost all of them previously published (some several times), appeared in October 1827. Walburga Litschauer has suggested (see Chapter 1) that Schubert set the six Heine poems of *Schwanengesang* from *Buch der Lieder* rather than from the first volume of *Reisebilder,* which also included *Die Heimkehr*.

On the day volume 2 of *Reisebilder* was published, 12 April 1827, Heine embarked on a voyage to England. A possible reason for the trip was that he feared repercussions in the German states from the political commentary that formed an integral part of the volume. From the very beginning he liked neither the island nation nor its society, perhaps in part because communication was difficult—he could read but not speak English. Certainly much of his attitude stemmed from the part that the English played in the defeat of his hero Napoleon. He saw the British as the leaders of the anti-French coalition, and to provide the final section of the second *Reisebilder* Heine wrote *Ideen: Das Buch le Grande,* an epic of Napoleon and his army.

According to Michael Perraudin, the *Ideen* was also about Heine himself.[41] While in England the poet received an offer of a position with a prestigious publishing house, Cotta of Munich, as coeditor of the periodical *Neue allgemeine politische Annalen*. He set out for Hamburg in August, but not without pausing en route to enjoy another vacation on the island of Nordeney (August–September). An earlier letter to his friend Varnhagen von Ense in Berlin, dated 29 July 1826, suggests the importance of the seashore to Heine at this stage in his life: "My health is better and better. To be completely restored I need the sea-bathing of this place, and to sail on the waves of the North Sea, which is well disposed towards me now because she knows that I sing her."[42]

In late October 1827 Heine, by now widely read, left Hamburg for Munich, stopping along the way to meet individuals of importance. In Kassel, for example, he visited the brothers Jakob and Wilhelm Grimm of fairy-tale fame. A third brother, Ludwig, was a painter who drew Heine during the visit in a fashion "that makes him look as much like Byron as possible." Lord Byron was an early hero of Heine's, as he was of most European liberals of the time. Other cities visited were Göttingen, Frankfurt am Main, Heidelberg, and Stuttgart, capital of Württemberg, "where Heine was arrested and expelled" because, as he had feared, there was an adverse reaction to the *Reisebilder* on the part of German authorities.[43]

Shortly after assuming his new position in Munich (in late November), he began to scheme to obtain a professorship at the University of Munich. In August 1828 he embarked on a trip to Italy, but before Heine left Munich he was visited briefly by the young Robert Schumann.[44] Along the way he expected to hear that he had received the professorship, but the position never materialized. The success of the two volumes of *Reisebilder* led his publisher Campe to ask for more of the same, and in part Heine's Italian travels were intended to provide the new experiences necessary for the forthcoming books. He had already written about England for his new periodical; he wrote *Reise nach Italien* (Journey to Italy) for a second Cotta journal, *Morgenblatt* (published in December 1828), and later he would also deliver the *Italienische Fragmente* (Italian fragments) to Cotta (published in November 1829). For Campe he wrote *Travels from Munich to Genoa* and *Die Bäder von Lucca* (The baths of Lucca) which were to form *Reisebilder* 3, and *Die Stadt Lucca* (The city of Lucca), part of *Reisebilder* 4. The illness and subsequent death of his father caused Heine to abbreviate the trip, and he returned to Germany in December 1828.

Heine's early poetic achievements, coinciding with the last dozen or so years of Schubert's life, are largely collected in the *Buch der Lieder*. This publication is essentially a combination of the first two volumes of *Reisebilder,* with the writings from Heine's Italian trip appended later. His reputation— both as a gifted poet and, in the eyes of the conservative German govern- ments of the time, as a dangerous, confrontational liberal—was well estab- lished by the end of 1828. At this point it may prove useful to note some similarities between the young Heine and Schubert. Both interrupted their early schooling to prepare for careers in their fathers' professions and did so at about the same age, sixteen. Schubert left the Vienna City Seminary in 1813 and attended a teacher's training school for a year (1813–1814). He then taught in his father's elementary school for two years (1814–1816) before leaving home. Heine, some ten months younger than Schubert, left the Düsseldorf Lyceum in the fall of 1814 to attend business school. From 1815 to 1819 he failed as a bank clerk twice (in Frankfurt am Main and Hamburg) and closed a conspicuously unsuccessful business career of merchandising luxury fabrics in conjunction with his father. As Jeffrey Sammons pointed out, "Heine wanted to be a poet. He associated high dignity and visionary privilege with this calling, and all his life . . . he laid claim to the appellation of poet." Substitute the word *musician* for *poet,* and the same could be said for Schubert. In the same vein, Sammons suggests that Heine was "always more adroitly confident and comfortable in the act of creation than he nor- mally was in the conduct of his everyday life."[45] Again Schubert comes to mind. Furthermore, compared with their great success in writing or setting lyric poetry, neither artist achieved anything comparable in the larger dra- matic forms (opera for Schubert, or plays and novels for Heine).

Turning to the area of artistic influence, it is generally recognized that Goethe provided one of the principal models for Heine's early poetry, and we know that the same towering literary figure provided the primary source of song texts for Schubert, who set sixty-one of Goethe's poems, a number of them twice and others even more times. While discussing re- current borrowings by the poets of Heine's generation, Perraudin sug- gests, "The objects of such borrowing are frequently the works which epit- omize the predominant poetic styles, thus poems from the best-known anthologies of folk-song, or from translated editions of the greats of the past, or by prominent individuals of the preceding generation (notably Goethe)." Later he remarks, "The Heine of the 1820's . . . has a good deal of work which belongs in a tradition of borrowing from Goethe, . . . In fact Goethe became a focus for several of the poetic styles of the epoch, and el- ements from his orientalistic, classical and balladesque work (among oth- ers) were repeatedly used. Probably his most exploited pieces, however, were some of his early, at least approximately experiential love lyrics."[46]

Sammons, who points to specific poems by Goethe as influencing *Buch der Lieder*[47] goes even further:

> Oblique and underground allusions to Goethe, sometimes with a satir-
> ical or contrastive force, abound in Heine's work as a kind of shadow in
> his texts. There is, furthermore, in Heine's career a curious, if perhaps
> partly accidental, *imitatio Goethii,* again an amalgam of analogue and
> contrast. Like Goethe, Heine was a poet who unwillingly took a law de-
> gree. Goethe, too, turned a Harz journey, undertaken, oddly, at almost
> the same age as Heine's, into a literary work. . . . Heine, like Goethe,
> made a journey to Italy and wrote an account of it. Heine wrote a
> *Faust,* and his marriage . . . somewhat resembled Goethe's. At times one
> has the feeling that, in his heart, he sought by divergent route the suc-
> cession to Goethe's standing as the major German writer. [Compare
> this with Schubert's succession, upon Beethoven's death, to the position
> of the leading composer in Vienna!] In this he [Heine] partly suc-
> ceeded, if not in German eyes, then to some extent in those of foreign
> observers.[48]

Closer to the period of *Schwanengesang* was Schubert's interest in the poetry of Wilhelm Müller. By the last year of his life the young Viennese musician had set twenty poems from *Die schöne Müllerin,* all twenty-four poems of *Winterreise,* and "Der Hirt auf dem Felsen" of that author. Heine, too, admired the poet from Dessau and left a striking testimonial of that ad- miration in a missive to Müller seldom quoted in its entirety. The date is 7 June 1826, and the letter was accompanied by a copy of the recently pub- lished first volume of *Reisebilder.* Note the equation of song with poetry and the prominence of Goethe in the final sentence:

> I am mature enough to confess openly to you that the little metre of
> my "Intermezzo," does not only seem a chance resemblance to your
> usual metre, but probably owes its most inward rhythms to your song
> for at the time when I was writing my "Intermezzo," I had just begun to
> know Müller's dear songs. I came very early under the influence of the
> German folk-song, and later when I was a student at Bonn, August
> Schlegel revealed many metrical secrets to me, but I think that it was
> first in your songs that I found the pure sound and the true simplicity
> for which I was forever striving. How pure and how clear are your
> songs, and they are essentially folk-songs. But in my poems only the
> form is in some degree that of the folk-song, and the substance of them
> is that of conventionalised society. Yes, I am mature enough to re-
> peat—and you will find it expressed publically—that I only saw clearly

through reading your seventy-seven poems, how out of the old existing folk-song forms new forms can be fashioned, which are actually of the people, without it being necessary to imitate the old roughness and clumsiness of speech. In the second part of your poems I find the form even more pure and more transparently clear—but, however much I may say of form, it is more important for me to say that, with the exception of Goethe, there is no writer of songs whom I love so much as you.[49]

Although their backgrounds in this area varied greatly, another potential point of contact between Heine and Schubert is music. Heine's mother, according to letters written in her youth, played flute, and the poet took violin and dancing lessons as a boy. More important, throughout his life Heine claimed that Rhenish folklore and folk music had made a strong impact on him during his youth. The following letter to Ferdinand Österley (14 August 1825) touches on several aspects of the subject of Heine and music and was written during his first visit to the island of Nordeney:

I often go for a walk on the beach and ponder the marvelous tales of the seamen. The most entrancing of all is the story of the "Flying Dutchman," whom sailors see in a storm driving past with full sails: and then he launches a little boat to send to the passing ship all sorts of letters with which nothing can be done, because they are addressed to people long since dead. Often I think of the dear old story of the fisherboy who listened on the beach to the nightly dances of the sea nixies, and after went through all the world with his fiddle, and delighted and enchanted all men by playing for them the melody of the nixey waltz. A dear friend of mine told me the story once at Berlin when we heard the playing of just such a wonderworking boy, Felix Mendelssohn-Bartholdy.[50]

The first sentence is the earliest reference Heine is known to have made to the subject that would later become the most famous segment of the fragmentary novel *Aus den Memoiren des Herren von Schnabelwopski*, the legend of the Flying Dutchman. This was Heine's version of the story, with the unique ending that Richard Wagner used for his opera.[51] In addition, Wagner's opera *Tannhauser* is, perhaps, indebted to Heine's medieval poem with the same title.[52] The famous ballet by Adolphe Adam, *Giselle*, owes its theme of the Willies, ghosts of brides who died before their wedding nights, a story retold in Heine's essay *Elementargeister* (elemental spirits),[53] and both César Cui and Pietro Mascagni wrote not particularly successful operas based on Heine's tragedy *William Ratcliff*.[54] Heine also wrote scenarios for two dance ballets, *Die Göttin Diana* and *Der Doktor Faust,* neither of which was ever performed.[55]

The reference to Mendelssohn is of interest inasmuch as Heine undoubtedly heard the gifted young musician when the poet was in Berlin and Mendelssohn (1809–1847) was twelve or thirteen years of age. Furthermore, the composer, who wrote "On Wings of Song," one of the most popular of all settings of Heine's poetry,[56] was clearly more than casually acquainted with the poet. Witness the following excerpt from a letter from Mendelssohn to the poet and close friend of Heine, Karl Immerman, dated 11 January 1832 and written from Paris: "I seldom see Heine, because he is entirely absorbed in liberal ideas and in politics. He has recently published sixty 'Frühlings Lieder' [Spring Songs]. Very few of them seem to me either genuine or truthful, but these few are indeed wonderful. Have you read them? They appeared in the second volume of 'Reisebilder.'"[57]

In some ways, however, it is the story of the fisherboy who became successful playing the nixie waltz that intrigues most in the letter to Österley. Barker Fairley, in *Heinrich Heine: An Interpretation,* argues that music consistently stimulated Heine's imagination. He suggests in fact that "Heine is so full of music that he often hears it where there is none."[58] Not only did the poet call his most famous collection *Buch der Lieder* (Book of songs), but the central position in the very first poem of the collection is devoted to "düstrer Lieder, düstern Melodien" (gloomy songs, gloomy melodies). Music drew him to musicians as well. Already mentioned was his friendship with the minor composers Josef Klein and Albert Methfessel, and Heine wrote an Encomium as well as the cycle of forty-four poems for Methfessel to set. It was in Paris during the 1830s and 1840s, and after his own reputation had grown enormously, that he met composers of the stature of Frédéric Chopin and Franz Liszt. Until the end of Heine's life, Hector Berlioz was a particularly close friend, whose wedding the poet attended. The literary composer constructed a chapter of his famous *Memoirs* as a letter to Heine, and later in the book he devoted a section of another chapter, "The Scale of My Works," to a letter from Heine together with his own response.

Considering Schubert's distinct predilection for setting poems about music or with references to music—and some of these settings are among his best—it may prove instructive to ask why Schubert did not set any of the many musically oriented poems in *Buch der Lieder.* From *Die Heimkehr* among others he set No. 23, resulting in the song "Ihr Bild," and No. 24, now known as "Der Atlas." Why did he pass over No. 22, "Die Jungfrau schläft in der Kammer," a poem dominated by music?

The maiden slept in her bedchamber,
Trembling, the moon gazed in;
Outside were singing and playing,
As if waltz melodies.

"I will look just once from the window
To see who breaks my rest."
A skeleton fiddles before her,
And sings like one possessed.

"To dance with me you promised,
And you have broken your vow.
Tonight is a ball in the churchyard,
Come out and dance with me now."

The music bewitches the maiden;
From her home she goes forth;
And follows the bony fiddler,
Who sings as he scrapes his bow.

He fiddles, and hops and dances,
And rattles his bones as he plays;
His skull nods grimly and strangely,
In the clear moonlight's rays.[59]

No. 51 of *Lyrisches Intermezzo*, the section preceding *Die Heimkehr* both in *Reisebilder* 1 and *Buch der Lieder*, begins "Vergiftet sind meine Lieder" (Poisoned are my songs). The second poem of *Die Heimkehr* is the famous "Die Lorelei," set with such great success by Friedrich Silcher. In this poem it is the siren's song that brings "Am Ende Schiffer und Kahn" (the boatman and his boat to their end). As these three poems suggest, and they are typical, for Heine music is a powerful, magical, often terrifying, and potentially destructive force. Was he influenced in this by E. T. A. Hoffmann (1776–1822)? According to Sammons, Heine "greatly admired Hoffmann in his student days."[60] The author-composer-caricaturist was still alive and living in Berlin when Heine arrived in the Prussian capital in 1821, and Heine possibly met him. In any case, Fairley points out that in Heine's "account of E. T. A. Hoffmann in *Die romantische Schule* we are told that . . . Wenn Hoffmann seine Toten beschwört und sie aus den Gräbern hervorsteigen und ihn umtanzen: dann zittert er selber vor Entsetzen, und tanzt selbst in ihrer Mitte, und schneidet dabei die tollsten Affengrimassen" (when Hoffmann conjures his dead and they climb from their graves and dance around him: then he shakes with terror, and he himself dances in their midst, and in so doing affects the wildest apelike grimaces).[61] This is remarkably suggestive of the *Totengerippe* (skeleton) in *Die Heimkehr* No. 22, cited above. To be sure, Heine outgrew his Hoffmann phase, but not until he had completed *Buch der Lieder*. According to Siegbert Prawer, in July 1827 the poet wrote to a friend, "Leave Hoffmann and his ghosts which are all the more horrible because they take their stroll in the market place and behave just like one of us. . . . I give you the example of how to pull yourself out of these depths by your own hair."[62]

Music was quite another matter for Schubert. Yes, it had great power and it was magical, but in his songs it was consistently a positive force—one that either provided pleasure or offered a refuge, or at least assistance in meeting the pain and disappointments of life, and even solace in death. Witness the intensely moving "Des Baches Wiegenlied" following the young miller's suicide in *Die schöne Müllerin*.

But what about the many poems of Heine without music, those that are concerned with unrequited love? Certainly most Heine commentators agree that "with only a handful of exceptions, the nearly 240 poems of *Buch der Lieder* are about unrequited love."[63] And, to be sure, this was a major concern of Schubert. Whereas it is most obvious in the Müller cycles, it is also important for *Schwanengesang,* including four of the Heine songs. But I believe that Schubert chose his Heine poems carefully. I do not agree with those commentators who lament the fact that Schubert found the poetry of Heine so late in his life. As I read the poems of *Buch der Lieder* and try to imagine Schubert's reactions to them, Mendelssohn's comments about the "Frühlings Lieder" keep coming to mind. I think that Schubert, like Mendelssohn, found the vast majority of the Heine poems he knew to be fundamentally uncongenial; that he was repelled by Heine's destructive, rejectionist wit; that he realized the immense difficulties of setting to music Heine's "sting in the tail," that unpredictable reversal of meaning at the end of so many of his poems. The only one of the six Heine songs Schubert composed in which the final lines change the meaning of the Lied is "Am Meer." And here I believe that Schubert deliberately chose to underplay the "sting" in his setting in favor of the ambiguity of the relationship between the protagonist and his beloved—the ambiguity he so convincingly suggests by the abnormally positioned (inverted) augmented-sixth chord resolving to a tonic in root position rather than to a dominant or dominant substitute (tonic in second inversion) at the beginning and end of the song. I also think

that Schubert understood far better than is usually assumed Heine's fundamentally anti-romantic view of poetry and the deep cynicism barely masked
in many superficially romantic poems set by other composers—the cynicism revealed, for example, in the deliberately trite language of "Du bist wie
eine Blume." In his study of *Buch der Lieder* Prawer writes, "Just as it would
be hard to think of another collection of ostensible love-poems in which ha-
tred and contempt so nearly outweigh love, so it would be hard to find another collection of poems in which so much talk of natural objects is coupled with so little first-hand observation of nature."[64] Both these attributes
of Heine's poetry were, I suggest, decidedly uncongenial to Schubert. Although I disagree with Prawer's implicit criticism of Heine's descriptions of
the sea in the *Nordsee* poetry—I find them strong and convincing—elsewhere in the poetry I think his comments about nature are to the point.

There are other points of divergence. Schubert was hardly the most
orthodox of Catholics, but one wonders what he thought of No. 66 of *Die
Heimkehr,* with its comic tone and first verse: "Mir traumt: Ich bin der liebe
Gott" (I dreamt: I was the beloved Lord). As Prawer suggests, "Heine throughout his life liked to treat God as a fellow author."[65] Heine's extreme (uncon-
trollable?) ego and destructive wit must have disturbed the innately modest
Schubert considerably.

As far as I know, Schubert is mentioned by Heine only twice in his writings and correspondence, both times positively. On 18 November 1830,
Heine wrote to the pianist, theorist, and composer Eduard Marxsen, later
to become a teacher of Brahms: "Klein's settings please me very much. It
appears that shortly before his death Schubart [*sic*] also composed very
good music for my songs, which unfortunately I do not know yet."[66] Heine
also reported on the popularity that Schubert's songs, especially the Heine
songs of *Schwanengesang,* had achieved in Paris during the early 1840s (see
Chapter 1).

Less than three years after Schubert's death, in May 1831, Heine felt compelled to leave Germany and settled in Paris for the rest of his life. The
forces at work—the Metternich-contrived censorship and the danger of ar-
rest—were basically the same for Schubert and his circle. In fact, they were
felt as early as 1815 by the small group of Schubert's friends developing their
aesthetic principles at the Viennese City Seminary.[67] For Heine the pressures
began to build with the Carlsbad decrees of 1819, which instituted censorship and close supervision of universities. Similarly, the free exchange of
ideas in Schubert's circle was increasingly hindered, and the circle itself de-
teriorated steadily during the last decade of his life. In an area related to
song, I suspect that Schubert the opera composer and his librettists had an

especially difficult time finding operatic subjects that would be both of interest to them and acceptable to the censors. From the time of his *Reisebilder* but particularly after his emigration, both in France and in Germany Heine increasingly became a symbol of political freedom and liberalism.

For idealistic reasons, at one point Heine became a friend and supporter of Karl Marx, and he remained so until he realized that his own poetry would become one of the first casualties of the communist revolution. His later writings, such as *Deutschland, ein Wintermärchen* (Germany, a winter's tale) and *Atta Troll, a Midsummer Night's Dream,* inspired several generations of writers, and not only in Germany and France. Luciano Zagari argues, for example, that the fantastic fable *Re Orso* (King Bear) by Arrigo Boito, composer of the opera *Mefistofele* and Verdi's last and greatest librettist (his librettos include the revision of *Simon Boccanegra, Otello,* and *Falstaff*) "would be unthinkable without Heine's *Atta Troll,*" also a fable about bears.[68] In the words of Nigel Reeves, "Heine so imbibed the cultural climate of his age, he was so steeped in the German intellectual tradition, so sensitive to the spiritual changes of the present, that his work is a focus-point for nineteenth-century European Cultural History."[69]

As a result of illness, for the last eight years of his life Heine was confined to bed. He called it his "mattress grave." Yet he continued to write to the day of his death, and Ernst Pawel, in *The Poet Dying: Heinrich Heine's Last Years in Paris,* says that Heine "dealt with his dying in a way that transcended mere courage and gave it a meaning few men have been able to wrest from it."[70]

Seidl

Both the poetry and the life experiences of Johann Gabriel Seidl, poet of "Die Taubenpost," provide the strongest possible contrast with that of the controversial, perpetually dissatisfied émigré and rebellious genius, Heine. At least in the period known as the *Vormärz* (that is, before the revolutions in March 1848) Seidl was successful as author, teacher, and government official, and he could well qualify as a model, almost a caricature, of the *gemütlich* (genial), conservative Biedermeier poet-schoolteacher-bureaucrat. It seems particularly appropriate that his poem "Gott erhalte, Gott beschütze" should have won a competition in 1853 and, combined with Haydn's music, should have become the Austrian national anthem.

Unlike Rellstab or Heine, the Viennese-born-and-raised Seidl knew Schubert personally. He also wrote more lyrics set by the composer than either of the other two, for a total of fifteen.[71] Five of these appear to have been transmitted from the poet in manuscript.[72] He was also close enough to the composer to write an elegy, "Meinem Freunde Franz Schubert: Am Vortage seines Begräbnisses" (My friend Franz Schubert: On the day before his burial), published in the leading cultural periodical of Vienna, the *Wiener Zeitung für Kunst, Musik, Theater und Mode*.[73] Had Schubert lived long enough, he would have become an uncle by marriage to Seidl's son, who married Ferdinand Schubert's daughter. Furthermore, during the last year and a half of his life Schubert oversaw the publication of three groups of songs set to Seidl texts: Op. 80, Op. 95 (the *Four Refrain-Lieder*, dedicated by the composer to the poet), and Op. 105. Together with "Die Taubenpost" these account for all twelve solo songs set to Seidl poetry (Seidl also wrote the lyrics for three male quartets by Schubert).

Perhaps the most striking difference between Heine and Seidl was in their political and social attitudes, a difference that had a profound effect on their writings.[74] Seidl, who grew up in Metternich's Austria, was the son of a court lawyer, and he traveled little. The son knew only the environs of the Austrian capital—about which he wrote a poetic tourist guide, *Wiens Umge-bungen* (Vienna's surroundings, 1826)—and the southeastern provinces of his country—about which he published a volume called *Wanderungen durch Tirol und Steiermark* (Travels in the Tyrol and Styria, 1840). As a result, Seidl was thoroughly conservative, "a strict adherent of absolutism."[75] He wrote many patriotic poems (such as a set of twelve Lieder, *Gott, Kaiser und Vater-land*) and, in addition to other governmental tasks, served as a *Buchzensor* (censor of books) from 1840 until censorship was abolished in 1848.

There is a possibility that Seidl met Rellstab during the latter's trip to Vienna in 1825, inasmuch as the Viennese poet was also a member of the group meeting at the *Ludlumshöhle* mentioned by the Berliner in his autobiography. There is, however, no evidence that Seidl ever met or corresponded with Heine.

Seidl, the son and grandson of lawyers, was born in Vienna on 21 June 1804; he was, therefore, more than seven years Schubert's junior. An only child, sickly and shy, he attended St. Anne's Normal School and in November 1813 matriculated at the Akademisches Gymnasium. This was an advanced secondary school affiliated with the university, and the same educational institution that Schubert had attended but left earlier that year. The musician's voice had changed, and although he could no longer sing in the Royal Chapel Choir, a scholarship was available to him contingent on more dedicated devotion to mathematics and Latin, undoubtedly at the expense of music. Schubert refused. Seidl, in contrast, was a precocious student, especially in classical languages. His poetic gifts were recognized and encouraged early by Anton Rössler, an instructor at the school who gave him lessons privately as well. In 1819 he enrolled for the usual two-year program in philosophy at the university, where he studied with, among others, Johann Ferdinand von Dienhardstein, who later became director of the Burgtheater, Vienna's principal venue for spoken drama.[76] Two of Seidl's fellow students at the time were the poets Ludwig Halirsch and the Hungarian Nicolaus Lenau, whose poem "Don Juan" inspired Richard Strauss's orchestral work of the same name. The lectures that Seidl attended were in the areas of classical philology, aesthetics, and classical literature. Under pressure from his father, he undertook the study of jurisprudence in 1822.

Meanwhile, in 1820, barely sixteen, he began to publish poetry in Austrian and German periodicals. His first poem was a hymn, "An die Sonne" (To the Sun), in the style of Friedrich Gottlieb Klopstock, and it was printed under the pseudonym Emil Ledie in the short-lived periodical *Cicada*. His father died in October 1823, leaving the family penniless, and the young man had to support his mother, her sister, and himself. He undertook the task energetically, writing extensively and teaching privately in the homes of wealthy Viennese businessmen, reportedly for five and six hours a day. In one of those homes he met Therese Schlesinger, likewise of good family and likewise destitute, who was employed as governess and household administrator for a wealthy relative. Six years later they married.

As an author Seidl was both prolific and multifaceted, writing poetry, stories, reviews of theater and concert life, topographical and other essays, and translations—often adaptations—from French, English, and Italian dramas, farces, and sentimental comedies. He also wrote about music. When Weber's *Euryanthe* was first performed in Vienna (in the fall of 1923), Seidl wrote of it twice: "After Hearing *Euryanthe*" for the *Theaterzeitung* and "The Composer of *Euryanthe* and *Freischützen* [sic]" in the first volume of his *Dichtungen*. During 1824 Schubert seems to have agreed to set a comedy by Seidl and Ludwig Halirsch called *Der kurze Mantel* (The short cloak), based on a popular dramatic fairy tale. Apparently the composer changed his mind, and Seidl wrote:

> Vienna, 1st July 1824
> Valued Sir and Friend,
>   In Heaven's name make haste with *Der kurze Mantel*. Demmer, who rules the roost now that [Wilhelm] Vogel has been dismissed, will give it as his first autumn production and clamours for the music.—Money is sure to come now. . . . New forces we shall have as well. . . . It now all depends on you. . . .

Do not let yourself regret your promise; the theatre, after Vogl's fall, now seems to regain some credit, and much is to be expended on the outward appearance of the [Short] Cloak.

Reply soon and reliably to your

J. G. Seidl[77]

Seidl's greatest success resulted from his poetry, which occupied the larger part of his first publication of collected writings, *Johann Gabriel Seidls Dichtungen* (Vienna, vols. 1–2 published in 1826 vol. 3 in 1828). To obtain an accurate picture of the publication history of both Heine's and Seidl's literary works, we should consider briefly two related types of contemporary publications: belletristic journals and annual culturally oriented almanacs.[78] According to Perraudin, after 1815, although "censorship [was] a conditioning factor on the cultural productions of the whole of the Biedermeier period . . . after two decades of war . . . the educated classes turned without needing much official encouragement to predominantly apolitical pursuits." And this, combined with "the sentimental predilections of the age," led to the growth of "an extensive belletristic press." Among these journals was *Der Gesellschafter* of Berlin, which, as we saw, printed much of Heine's early work, as well as that of Seidl,[79] who was also an early contributor to the Dresden *Abendzeitung*.[80] Somewhat earlier (April 1818), the *Abendzeitung* had printed "the first foreign criticism of any work by Schubert."[81] In Vienna *Die Allgemeine Theaterzeitung* published several items by Seidl, including in 1822 an early version of "Nachtgesang im Walde," which Schubert later set for four voices and four horns.[82]

These journals, while published frequently (several times a week), "were insubstantial things, generally a single sheet, folded once to give four 10 × 8 inch sides, closely (and badly) printed in double columns, and augmented occasionally by a two- or four-side *Beilage*. . . . Their content . . . was mainly poetry, *Novelle*-length fiction, and occasionally dramatic extracts in serial form, also anecdotal *Korrespondentenberichte* from other German [and Austrian] cities, lengthy theatrical reviews [including opera], and even longer, often serialized literary ones."[83] However, as Perraudin stresses, "The principal subject of the reviews in the belletristic journals was a final, and in fact arguably the *most* characteristic, literary phenomenon of the age, the so-called literary almanacs or belletristic anthologies. . . . The frequency and tone of such reviews show that the almanac's appearances were altogether perceived as the high points of the literary calendar." These almanacs, printed in the fall of the year preceding their date, to take advantage of the Christmas season, were particularly important for Seidl during most of his life. Not only was a good proportion of his literary output first printed in them—Hans Max may not have been exaggerating when he suggested that "there was hardly an almanac to be found that was not adorned by an offering from Seidl"[84]—but the young poet was also active as editor of the *Taschenbuch* ("pocketbook," a frequently used name for the almanacs, indicating their small format) *Aurora* for some thirty years (1828–58).[85] Wolfgang von Wurzbach reports that Seidl was also editor at different times for the almanacs *Veilchen, Iduna,* and *Freund des schöne Geschlechts* (Friend of the fair sex), where versions of several poems from one of his best collections of lyric poetry, *Lieder der Nacht,* appeared.[86] Apropos music, it was in the Viennese almanac *Aglaja* for 1828 that Seidl's poem "Nach Beethovens Begräbnisse" (After Beethoven's burial) appeared.[87] For the second issue of *Aurora* that Seidl edited (1829), the poet wrote a novella entitled *Theresa* and a poem "Reschen," a lower-Austrian-dialect form of Theresa. This was the year Seidl and Theresa Schlesinger married. According to Wurzbach, it was about this time that Seidl began writing his "Flinserln," the Austrian dialect poetry in which he remained unexcelled in the nineteenth century and which contributed greatly to his popularity in Austria.[88] The poem "Reschen" describes Theresa in dialect as "the black-eyed maid with the nut-brown hair." At about the time Seidl was preparing this issue for press, in the summer of 1828, Schubert wrote a short letter to the poet:

> Most highly esteemed Herr Gabriel!
> Enclosed I send you back these poems, in which I could discover absolutely nothing poetic or useful for music. I take this occasion to enquire at the same time whether you have my music to your poems "Widerspruch" (Contradiction) and "Wiegenlied" (Lullaby) in your possession, in which case I beg you to send them to me as soon as possible, since I wish to publish them.
>
> Yours reverentially,
Vienna, 4 August 1828
Franz Schubert[89]

Whether he received the music back from Seidl or not, Schubert submitted the songs to the Viennese publisher Josef Czerny, and they appeared as Nos. 1 and 2 of Op. 105 on the day of the composer's funeral (21 November 1828). No one, however, seems to have asked the question, why did the poet have the music in the first place? Although I have yet to see corroboration, Wurzbach states that Seidl had a "prächtige" (splendid) tenor voice and was capable of singing in concert.[90] Perhaps he asked Schubert for the songs because he wanted to sing them. Yet Seidl is never mentioned as attending any of the dozens of musical events described in the documentary sources, the *Schubert Reader* or *Schubert: Memoirs by his Friends;* he doesn't appear in the famous sepia drawing by Moritz Schwind, "Schubert Evening at Spaun's;"[91] and Otto Erich Deutsch specifically says that Seidl was "never among the guests . . . at Ignaz Sonnleithner's musical soirées."[92] Nor was he ever identified as a member of either of the two Schubert literary circles described by David Gramit or Walther Dürr and Arnold Feil.[93] Seidl was too young to participate in the group at the Vienna City Seminary that Josef von Spaun led and which consisted primarily of students from Linz (1814–19). But he should have been a prime candidate for the second Schubert circle, a looser, younger reading group, with less focused (perhaps less liberal) attitudes that was active in the second decade of the century.[94] Yet he is never mentioned.

The contents as well as the salutations at the beginning and end of the letter to Seidl imply that the by-now-well-established composer did not regard the younger poet too highly. Deutsch has suggested that Schubert's "Most highly esteemed Herr Gabriel," and the "reverentially," were probably ironic.[95] There is another document linking Seidl and Schubert. On the occasion of the publication of a set of songs to Seidl texts by the minor composer, poet, and critic Friedrich August Kanne, the young poet placed an announcement in the Viennese journal the *Theaterzeitung* for 22 August 1826: "A special interest may attach to these compositions because many of these poems have been composed also by Fr. Schubert, B. Randhartinger, Fr. Lachner and others; to be engraved and published shortly and thus offering a comparison that will be both interesting and useful."[96] Thus both in his letter to Schubert about *Der kurze Mantel* and in this announcement we find Seidl trying to derive benefit from his relation to Schubert and the latter's renown as a composer of vocal music.

Seidl appears in another promotional event particularly atypical of Schubert. The publisher of the *Four Refrain-Lieder* (Op. 95), Thaddäus Weigl, included the following note in his announcement of 13 August 1828 in the *Wiener Zeitung:*

FOUR REFRAIN-SONGS
by Johann Gabriel Seidl
set to Music for One Voice with Pianoforte Accompaniment
and most amicably dedicated to the Poet by
FRANZ SCHUBERT

The public has long cherished the wish to have, for once, a composition of a merry, comic nature from the pen of this song composer of genius. This wish has been gratified in a surprising manner by Herr Schubert in the present four songs, which in part are truly comic and in part bear in them the character of ingenuousness and humour.[97]

Except for "Bei dir allein," the songs are not especially good Schubert. Was the idea to advertise the songs as Schubert's only "merry, comic" songs Seidl's or the publisher's? It would not have been out of character for the notion to have been Seidl's.

Returning to the letter Schubert wrote to Seidl on 4 August 1828, the question remains whether Seidl, who had just become editor of *Aurora,* could have obtained the music for "Widerspruch" and "Wiegenlied" from Schubert because he hoped to publish them as a supplement in a forthcoming issue of the periodical. There was certainly a precedent for this. Schubert's song "Widerschein" first appeared in the autumn of 1820 as a *Beilage* (supplement) to an almanac for 1821, *Taschenbuch zum geselligen Vergnügen* (Pocketbook of social pleasure) of Leipzig.[98]

It is hardly surprising that when the artist Josef Teltscher, a friend of Schubert's, painted a portrait of Seidl in 1829, he showed on the piano several songs by Schubert set to the poet's verse: "Der Wanderer an den Mond," "Im Freien," and "Die Taubenpost."[99] During the same year Seidl received his first governmental appointment, as a professor at the state *Gymnasium* in the small town of Cilli in southern Styria, now a part of Slovenia. Roman ruins in the area incited Seidl to take an interest in archaeology and numismatics, subjects about which he began to write. He continued with his poetry, producing *Bifolien* (1836), his most highly regarded work, which had five editions by 1855.[100] His years in Cilli were happy ones: he raised a family, did a bit of traveling in the region, continued writing and editing, and made new friends, including a poet from Graz, Karl Gottfried von Leitner. Coincidentally, Schubert had set nine of Leitner's poems, almost all of them in the last year of his life, including the splendid song "Winterabend" (D. 938).

Seidl's "happy exile," as he characterized his eleven years in Cilli, came to an end as the result of one of his new areas of interest, numismatics, and a false report in 1840 that he had died. This report brought him to the attention of the Viennese Court. His name was already known there, as he had dedicated the successful collection of poetry *Bifolien* to his patron, Archduke Johann. Having been awarded the position of third curator of the Coin and Antiquities Cabinet at a modest salary, Seidl discovered that the return to Vienna with a large family (wife, two children, mother, and aunt) was a financial disaster. This helps to explain his acceptance of the thankless additional position of *Buchzensor* and, following the abolition of censorship

in 1848, his subsequent securing of a teaching position in Vienna. The rest of
his life was not particularly happy. His poetry had gone out of fashion,
many literary friends resented his position as censor, and he was insensitive
to political and social progress. As Wurzbach remarked, he ignored the new
era, and it ignored him.[101]

But even during the height of his popularity, the 1830s, not everyone
praised Seidl. In his two-volume *Poetry and Poets in Austria in the Year 1836*,
Julius Seidlitz writes positively. He likes the *Lieder der Nacht*, which "contain
many outstanding poems," and he is also partial to the *Bifolien*. Although he
has difficulty deciding which set is better, he is convinced that Seidl's lyric
poetry is "more original, more sensitive, warmer than the Ballads."[102] In
contrast, at about the same time (between 1836 and 1840) there appeared an
anonymous and distinctly less favorable view of Seidl in a small volume entitled *Austrian Parnassus*. It begins with a physical description: "Heavy, good
natured physiognomy, actually quite skilled lyricist, stereotypically genial
[*gemütlich*], mediocre prose, contributor to all the journals and publisher's
almanacs, overrated, weak, without much spirit, professor in Cilly in lower
Styria, privileged patriot." The author then lists and describes some works:
"*Bifolien—Georginen* etc. (weak, dubious geniality). Lyric poems (among
them good ones). Lieder (many of them set to music). *Novellen* (tedious),
journal articles (insignificant)."[103]

There is no mention of the highly original dialect poetry, which would
probably not have interested literary critics at the time. But the negative
view is remarkably prescient of attitudes held by modern critics. It is also
of interest for the remark about the numerous settings to music of the
Lieder. In addition to Schubert, Randhartinger, Lachner, and Kanne, mentioned by Seidl himself, Robert Schumann, Carl Loewe, Meyerbeer, and a
host of minor Austrian composers have set poetry by Seidl. Perhaps the
most noteworthy of the Austrian composers from Seidl's own generation to
set his verses is the extraordinarily popular theater composer Adolph Müller
(1801–1886), who wrote some four hundred songs, many published by
Haslinger.[104] Another is Johann Vesque von Püttlingen (pseud. J. Hoven,
1803–1883), who was, according to Reinhold Seitz, "among Austrian song
composers . . . perhaps the most significant in the period between Schubert
and Wolf." He wrote approximately three hundred songs, including all
eighty-eight Lieder of Heine's *Die Heimkehr*.[105]

Among Seidl's other activities relating to music may be mentioned his
translation and adaptation of the Scribe-Delavigne libretto for Daniel
François Esprit Auber's *Maçon* as *Der Maurer und der Schlosser* (first performed
1 August 1826, Kärntnerthor Theater; published Vienna, 1827); he wrote the

texts for Franz Lachner's cantata *Die vier Menschenälter* (published Vienna, 1831, and performed in Vienna and other cities) and the same composer's "Liederspiel" *Heirat durch Heirat*. He also adapted Shakespeare's *Tempest* as a libretto for an opera by Philipp Jakob Riotte (1776–1856), *Der Sturm oder die Geisterinsel* (performed successfully at Brünn, September 1833) and wrote an explanatory text for Beethoven's ballet *Die Geschöpfe des Prometheus* (performed unsuccessfully in Vienna, 1841 and 1853, but performed successfully at Munich, 1856, and published there without date).[106]

On the whole Seidl's song texts have aroused mixed reactions. In an early review that included Schubert's songs of Op. 80 ("Der Wanderer an den Mond," "Das Zügenglöcklein," and "Im Freien"), a reviewer, perhaps G. W. Fink, wrote in the Leipzig *Allgemeine Musikalische Zeitung*:

> The poems are pretty; but for the purpose of musical composition one could wish for a more careful linguistic finish and desire at least that they should be free of false accents and make *fewer words* on that which they express; all of which has made the avoidance of all that is long-winded and monotonous not a little difficult for Herr S., since he wished to remain praiseworthily faithful throughout all the verses, not only to the melody, but also . . . to the . . . accompaniment, particularly in 2 and 3. He has achieved this avoidance, so far as it was possible under the circumstances; but the singer and the pianist must put much variety into their delivery, if the faults are not to show through somewhat in the last number.[107]

More recently John Reed notes Seidl's "conventional sentiment and arch humour." While discussing *Das Zügenglöcklein,* he makes a point that could apply to a number of Schubert's settings of the Austrian's poetry: "The melodic and harmonic variations reach out beyond the pious sentiments of the poem to a deeper humanity and compassion."[108] Similarly, Dietrich Fischer-Dieskau refers to the "conventional poetry" of "Die Taubenpost" and advises shortening "Wiegenlied," surely a criticism of the poet as much as, if not more than, of the composer. In his extensive recording of the Schubert songs for Deutsche Grammophon, the great singer follows his own advice on "Wiegenlied."[109]

Unlike Rellstab, who wrote little poetry after his single volume of *Gedichten* (Berlin, 1827), Seidl never gave up his deep attachment to lyric verse. Near the end of his life he lamented his declining poetic powers in two short verses. In 1860 he wrote:

> Was ich fühlt' im jungen Busen,
> Hüllt' ich lebhaft einst in Verse;

Treulos zeigen, ach, die Musen
Mir, dem alten, jetzt die Ferse.

[That which I used to feel in my young breast,
At one time in lively fashion I wrapped in verse;
Alas, the muses show themselves to be faithless
Now they leave me, the aged one, behind.]

And shortly before his death he wrote:

Auf meiner langen Fahrt durchs Leben
Hatt' ich so manches aufzugeben.
Doch einen Verlust verschmerz' ich nie,
Abhanden kam mir—die Poesie.[110]

[During my long journey through life
I've had to give up so much.
Yet one loss I've never gotten over,
I have lost—my Poetry.]

Of the three *Schwanengesang* poets discussed, Heine was by far the most important and the most imaginative, and he was also the most interesting as an individual. It is not surprising, then, that the six settings of his verses by Schubert should result in a number of the most imaginative songs the composer ever wrote. Nevertheless, the generally more relaxed poems by Rellstab and Seidl led Schubert to write songs that contrast nicely with the more intense and more concise Heine Lieder. The resultant group of fourteen songs, though hardly a cycle in the traditional sense, does have cyclic elements.[111] And over the years the songs have proved to be remarkably satisfying as a group to many performers and their audiences.[112]

NOTES

1. König, *Ludwig Rellstab*, 4.
2. The twelve-year-old Ludwig is reported to have written an essay, corrected by his father, for that journal. Goedeke, *Grundrisse*, vol. 14, 750.
3. Houben, "Einleitung," ix.
4. Goedeke, *Grundrisse*, vol. 14, 749, refers to "Elektra" and the "Briefe eines Musikfreundes."
5. Rellstab, *Ludwig Berger*, 116.
6. Youens, "Behind the Scenes," 3–22.
7. Rellstab, *Ludwig Berger*, 102.
8. König, *Ludwig Rellstab*, 2–3.

9. Rellstab, *Aus meinem Leben,* vol. 2, 11. See also p. 8.

10. Ibid., vol. 2, 44.

11. Houben, "Einleitung," xii.

12. Ibid., xiii.

13. In no. 18 (30 January 1825), 69. Goedeke, *Grundrisse,* vol. 14, 749.

14. See Litschauer, Chapter 1 of this book.

15. Kreissle von Hellborn, *Life of Schubert,* vol. 2, 134.

16. Rellstab also mentions meeting the actors Heinrich Anschütz, Karl Schwarz, and Emilie Neumann. *Aus meinem Leben,* vol. 2, 221.

17. See Eduard von Bauernfeld, "Alexander Baumann and the 'Baumann's Höhle,'" in Deutsch, *Schubert: Memoirs by His Friends,* 241. Deutsch also indicates the source of the group's colorful name: a popular dramatic fairy tale with that title, written by Adam Gottlieb Oehlenschläger and first performed in 1817 at the Theater an der Wien. Ibid., 245. See also pp. 223–224 and 293 and Hanson, *Musical Life,* 58–60.

18. Rellstab gave his libretto *Orestes* to Ludwig Berger, who never set it. The subject of Belisario was set some years later by Donizetti, and in 1846 Verdi wrote an opera based on Werner's *Attila,* which would have been Rellstab's source as well. It was one of Verdi's most successful early operas.

19. *Aus meinem Leben,* vol. 2, 265–266.

20. Anderson, *Letters of Beethoven,* vol. 3, 1190–1191 and 1190 n. 2.

21. Ibid. *Kenilworth* is on a short list of subjects, including *King Lear* and *Manon,* to be found in Verdi's first volume of *copialettere,* although the list was omitted from the publication *I copialettere,* ed. G. Cesari and A. Luzio (Milan, 1913; reprint, Bologna, [1968]). Microfilms of the manuscripts for all Verdi's and Giuseppina Strepponi Verdi's *copialettere* may be consulted at the Archive of the American Institute for Verdi Studies at New York University.

22. Einstein, *Schubert,* 308.

23. Among the handful of poems by Rellstab that Liszt set to music was "Herbst," which he set twice as "Es rauschen die Winde." See Snyder, *Index of Lieder,* 356. Liszt avoided setting any of the *Schwanengesang* poems and certainly never knew of Schubert's setting of "Herbst," which was first published in 1895, well after the Hungarian musician's death in 1886. In addition to his close friends Berger and Klein, other composers who set poetry by Rellstab included Heinrich Marschner ("Die Aufenthalt") and Schubert's close friend Franz Lachner ("Ständchen"). See Miller, *Ring of Words,* 262, 264.

24. Liszt, *Letters,* 66. Von Ense and his wife, Rahel, were friends of Heine.

25. The same opera was produced under the name *Vielka* in Berlin in 1847. Its music was used by Meyerbeer for his opéra comique *L'étoile du nord* (Paris, 1854), and Rellstab translated the new work into German as *Nordstar.*

26. Rehm, *Zur Musikrezeption,* 91–93.

27. Rellstab, *Aus meinem Leben,* vol. 1, 296.

28. The secular cantata *Begrüssung, Festmusik zum Fest des Naturforscher,* also called the "Humboldt" Cantata; performed in Berlin, 1828.

29. Rehm, *Zur Musikrezeption,* 83.

30. Vetter, *Der Klassiker Schubert,* vol. 2, 357 n. 44.

31. Miller, *Ring of Words,* xx.

32. Metzner, *Heine . . . Bibliographie,* vol. 1, 11.

33. Fairley, *Heinrich Heine,* 2.

34. Sammons, *A Modern Biography,* 33.

35. Ibid., 59.

36. Ibid., 82.

37. See the letter cited below from Heine to Edward Marksen (18 November 1830) about his delight at the settings of his poetry by Klein and Schubert. Deutsch (*Schubert: Memoirs by His Friends,* 390) identifies Klein as Bernhard Joseph. It is possible, however, that Heine meant Bernhard's younger stepbrother Josef, a close friend of the poet's.

38. This is the title of an analytical study of Heine's poetry by Jeffrey L. Sammons (*Heinrich Heine: The Elusive Poet*). Both here and in his later *Heinrich Heine: A Modern Biography* Sammons stresses the difficulty in pinning down personal biographical data about the poet.

39. Sammons, *A Modern Biography,* 98.

40. A good discussion of the frequently rocky relations between Heine and Campe is to be found in ibid., 118–124.

41. Perraudin, *Poetry in Context,* 101.

42. Heine, *Memoirs,* 181.

43. Sammons, *A Modern Biography,* 133–134, with the drawing of Heine reproduced facing p. 142.

44. Gerald Abraham, "Robert Schumann," *New Grove,* vol. 16, 832. Mentioned also in Massin, *Franz Schubert,* 1262 n. 2.

45. Sammons, *A Modern Biography,* 47–50, 60, and 86. Concerning the period in which Heine wrote *Ideen: Buch le Grand,* which Sammons believes to be the best work Heine had done to that point in his career (that is, until *Nordsee* 3), he remarks, "Once again we see him [Heine] more at home in his creativity than in his external circumstances." Ibid., 128.

46. Perraudin, *Poetry in Context,* 2 and 16.

47. Sammons, *Elusive Poet,* 34–36.

48. Sammons, *A Modern Biography,* 102–103.

49. Heine, *Memoirs,* 123. Regarding the relationship of Heine and Müller, see Nollen, "Heine and Wilhelm Müller," as well as a chapter with the same name in Perraudin's *Poetry in Context,* and Reeves, *Poetry and Politics,* 43–54.

50. Heine, *Memoirs,* 159–160.

51. Wagner admitted this in the first edition of his autobiography, *Mein Leben,* "although in later years, after Wagner became irritated with Heine in particular and Jews in general, he tried to belittle Heine's achievement." Sammons, *Elusive Poet,* 319.

52. Heine's poem was published in *Salon* 3 (July 1839). Sammons claims that with Heine's parodistic version of the medieval poem "Tannhäuser," "for the second time [Heine] provided the inspiration for a Wagner opera." *A Modern Biography,* 217. Ernest Newman, in *The Wagner Operas* (New York, 1949), only suggests that Wagner "must have been acquainted" with a passage by Heine that hails the "charmingly told" story of Tannhäuser and Venus "as worthy to stand by the side of *The Song of Songs*" (63–64).

53. Sammons, *Elusive Poet,* 335.

54. Sammons, *A Modern Biography,* 70.

55. These scenarios are discussed extensively in the chapter "The Masked Dancemaster" in Sammons, *Elusive Poet,* 335–348.

56. See S. S. Prawer's analysis of both the song and the poetry, which begins his valuable monograph on the *Buch der Lieder,* 11–12.

57. Mendelssohn, *Letters,* 186–187.

58. Fairley, *Heinrich Heine,* 28.

59. Translation mainly from *Heinrich Heine: Poems and Ballads,* trans. Emma Lazarus, 104–105.

60. Sammons, *A Modern Biography,* 194.

61. Fairley, *Heinrich Heine,* 36, provides an English translation together with the original German. I have altered the translation considerably.

62. Prawer, *Buch der Lieder,* 14.

63. Sammons, *Elusive Poet,* 82.

64. Prawer, *Buch der Lieder,* 27. Sammons, in *Elusive Poet,* puts this idea another way: "Heine was a creature of the city and had little direct and genuine response to nature" (455).

65. Prawer, *Buch der Lieder,* 21.

66. Deutsch, *Memoirs,* 389.

67. Gramit, *Intellectual and Aesthetic Tenets,* 147–154.

68. Zagari, "Permanence in Change," 89.

69. Reeves, *Poetry and Politics,* 191.

70. Pawel, *The Poet Dying,* 194.

71. They include twelve solo songs, of which one exists in a version for solo tenor and chorus, "Widerspruch" (D. 865, Op. 105, No. 1), and three male quartets: "Grab und Mond" (D. 893), "Nachthelle" (D. 892) with tenor solo as well as quartet, and "Nachtgesang im Walde" (D. 913) accompanied by four horns. The other eleven solo songs are "Der Wanderer an den Mond" (D. 870, Op. 80, No. 1), "Zügenglöcklein" (D. 871, Op. 80, No. 2), "Im Freien" (D. 880, Op. 80, No. 3), the *Four Refrain-Lieder* (D. 866, Op. 95) consisting of "Die Unterscheidung," "Bei dir allein," "Die Männer sind méchant," and "Irdisches Glück," as well as "Wiegenlied" (D. 867, Op. 105, No. 2), "Am Fenster" (D. 878, Op. 105, No. 3), "Sehnsucht," (D. 879, Op. 105, No. 4), and the final song of *Schwanengesang,* "Die Taubenpost."

72. Scholchow, *Die Texte,* could find no published sources for the four *Refrain-Lieder* and "Die Taubenpost" that date from Schubert's lifetime.

73. Facsimile in Waidelich, *Dokumente (1817–1830),* 1826–1827. Also reprinted in Wolfgang von Wurzbach, ed., *Johann Gabriel Seidls ausgewählte Werke,* vol. 2, 96–99.

74. For a self-incriminating description of Seidl's conventional attitude toward women and women poets, see Susan Youens' chapter on Gabriele von Baumberg in *Schubert's Poets and the Making of Lieder.* Youens cites or paraphrases extensively from Seidl's poem "Einer jungen Dichterin" (To a young poetess): "Throw your pen and half-written sheet away . . . leave off concocting verses." Instead, Seidl suggests to the young lady, "Life itself will be your poetry; to love, to serve, your versification."

75. Wurzbach, *Seidls . . . Werke,* vol. 1, lxxvii.

76. Schubert set Dienhardstein's poem "Skolie" (D. 306) and wrote the music for his "Hymn on the Birthday of the Emperor" (D. 748).

77. Cited from Deutsch, *Schubert Reader,* 357–358. Deutsch, in his notes, reports that this was Seidl's first stage piece and that it was performed eight times at the Theater an der Wien with music for each of the three acts by a different composer, none of them Schubert, although "the MS in the Vienna City Library still bears the remark 'The music by Franz Schubert.'"

78. This discussion is largely drawn from the section "Heine's Literary Environment" of Perraudin's *Poetry in Context,* esp. 195–202.

79. Ibid., 6 and *passim* for Heine; Goedeke, *Grundrisse,* vol. 9, 109 and *passim* for Seidl.

80. Scholchow, *Die Texte,* vol. 2, 653.

81. Deutsch, *Schubert Reader,* 87.

82. Goedeke, *Grundrisse,* vol. 9, 107, and Deutsch, *Schubert Reader,* 631–632. Other important belletristic journals of the times included the *Zeitung für die elegante Welt* of Leipzig and Cotta's *Morganblatt für gebildete Stände.* Perraudin, *Poetry in Context,* 196. Several others in Germany and Bohemia publishing early versions of Seidl's *Lieder der Nacht* included the *Abendzeitung* of Dresden and *Der Kranz* of Prague. Goedeke, *Grundrisse,* vol. 9, 109.

83. Perraudin, *Poetry in Context,* 196–197.

84. Max, "Eine biographische Skizze," xi.

85. Wurzbach, *Seidels . . . Werke,* vol. 1, xxix.

86. Ibid., xxix–xxx, and Goedecke, *Grundrisse,* vol. 9, 109.

87. Ibid., 109. See also Deutsch, *Schubert Reader,* 168, for more information on *Aglaja.*

88. Wurzbach, *Seidls . . . Werke,* vol. 1, xxxi and *passim.*

89. Norwood and Green, "A New Schubert Letter," 340–341.

90. Wurzbach, *Seidls . . . Werke,* vol. 1, xxiii.

91. Reproduced in *Schubert Reader,* facing p. 768 with key printed on p. 784.

92. Deutsch, *Schubert: Memoirs by His Friends,* 282.

93. Dürr and Feil, *Franz Schubert,* 10–13. See also Gramit, *Intellectual and Aesthetic Tenets.*

94. This group is well described in Gramit, *Intellectual and Aesthetic Tenets,* chaps. 4 and 6.

95. See Norwood and Green, "A New Schubert Letter," 341 n. 4. Was the irony perhaps associated with the conventional piety often to be found in Seidl's writing?

96. Deutsch, *Schubert Reader,* 549.

97. Ibid., 798.

98. Ibid., 152, with a reproduction of the first page of the song on p. 157.

99. Ibid., 958. These were among the most popular of Schubert's Seidl songs at the time. The composer had originally intended to program "Der Wanderer an den Mond" at his private concert on the anniversary of Beethoven's death (26 March 1828). Instead he substituted "Fischerweise." Ibid., 752–753. Einstein, in *Schubert,* 261, reports the contemporary popularity of "Im Freien" but adds, "Present day taste finds [the song] insipid." See Chapter 1 for a discussion of some early performances of "Die Taubenpost."

100. Wurzbach, "Johann Gabriel Seidel," 167.

101. Wurzbach, *Seidls . . . Werke,* vol. 1, xxxii, xxxv, and lxxvii.

102. Seidlitz, "Johann Gabriel Seidl," 67–72.

103. Anon., *Oesterreichischer Parnassus,* 38.

104. Peter Branscombe, "Adolf [Adolph] Müller [Schmid]," *New Grove,* vol. 12, 767–768.

105. Seitz, "Johann Vesque von Puettlingen," *New Grove,* vol. 19, 686. In his article in *Musik in Geschichte und Gegenwart* Seitz says "between Schubert and Brahms" (vol. 13, col. 1567). The setting of *Die Heimkehr* was published in Vienna in 1851 according to Seitz in *Musik in Geschichte und Gegenwart.* In *New Grove,* Seitz reports the setting of only eighty-five of the eighty-eight Lieder. I suspect a misprint in *New Grove.*

106. Wurzbach, "Johann Gabriel Seidl," 179–180.

107. Deutsch, *Schubert Reader,* 719, italics mine.

108. Reed, *Schubert Song Companion,* 87, 479.

109. Fischer-Dieskau, *Schubert . . . Songs,* 282 and 288.

110. Wurzbach, "Johann Gabriel Seidl," 164.

111. Almost without exception the songs deal with a young man who is ultimately frustrated in love. See Chapter 5, especially Rellstab's description of the cyclic implications in the group of poems he left for Beethoven to set.

112. Perhaps the most obvious illustration of this statement is the large number of vocalists who have recorded the fourteen songs of *Schwanengesang* as a unit; see the discography (Chapter 8).

PART II

Analysis

CHAPTER 3

Repetition and Correspondence in *Schwanengesang*

EDWARD T. CONE

It is a truism that musical design depends—largely if not primarily—on repetition of one sort or another. Whether immediate or eventual, exact or altered, complete or fragmentary, strictly contained or freely extended, the reiteration of musical ideas promotes the comprehension of their organization into recognizable patterns. Some repetitive designs for complete movements may be easily classifiable as generic "forms." Others may depart considerably from conventional norms or even resist all attempts at such classification. But when broadly interpreted, the concepts of statement, variation, development, and reprise are basic to our understanding of traditional Western music—and perhaps of all music.

The influence of analogous concepts on the organization of poetry is not so obvious; yet it is real. Poetry, too, makes statements, varies and develops them, recapitulates them. Whereas the repetitive elements in music may be melodic, harmonic, or rhythmic, those in poetry may be metrical, verbal, imagistic, or conceptual. Like musical repetition, which can be narrowly motivic or broadly thematic, poetic repetition can apply to mere phonemes or individual words, on the one hand, or to lengthy refrains, on the other. In more general terms, dramatic characters, narrated events, and even abstract ideas can be treated repetitively.

When a poem is set to music, the extent to which the repetitive patterns of the music are coordinated with those of the poetry crucially affects both the musico-poetic form and the expressive content of the song. Where the patterns of the two media correspond, they reinforce each other. Where they differ, each may seem to function independently. If that is actually the case, the result, even if musically beautiful, is an incompletely realized song. More interestingly, however, the apparently contrasting patterns of the two media can influence each other, encouraging alternative interpretations of the words and new articulations of the music.

Those concerns point to a more suggestive categorization than the traditional dichotomy of strophic versus "through-composed" song.[1] For that classification is not comprehensive. Is a da capo aria, or a song in sonata-form, through-composed? Yet neither is strophic. I suggest that we assign them to a third category: songs whose music exhibits a design, such as a conventional generic "form," that is explicable in absolute musical terms.

It is among examples of the last type that striking examples of non-correspondence might be expected, owing to the abstract and, from the verbal point of view, arbitrary nature of purely musical design. Yet musical repetition in successful songs of this category justifies itself poetically—either by underlining obvious conceptual or imagistic themes or by suggesting the kind of reinterpretation cited above. Sometimes perfect correspondence occurs, occasioned by the simultaneous reprise of words and music. Once, of course, that was entailed by the standard forms of the Renaissance chanson and the Baroque aria. Later composers, lacking those conventions, sometimes created opportunities for such correspondence—and for musical recapitulation—by imposing their own verbal repetitions.

If we accept this new category as valid, we can then subsume both members of the traditional division under a single rubric: a type of song that explicitly depends on correspondence between words and music. In the strophic song the natural vehicle for that correspondence is the stanza. The resulting repetitions may be purely conventional, as in much folk and popular song. Or a composer may choose the strophic form in order to emphasize the uniform emotional tenor of a poem, as exhibited not only in its invariant metrical pattern but also in its periodic verbal recurrences. The through-composed song, by contrast, does not rely on periodicity. It seeks opportunities for correspondence in the narrative or rhetorical structure of the poetic text. It matches the motifs and themes of the poetry, their repetitions and contrasts, with parallel constructions of its own. True, in so doing it may approach the strophic norm. In that respect it is met—from the other side, so to speak—by the modified strophic song that, under the influence of poetic meaning, at times forsakes stanzaic reiteration. There is, after all, no rule commanding adherence to one extreme or the other, and there are intergrades of all kinds. That is another reason why these songs may all be considered together in a single category—call it Type A—as opposed to my group of more abstractly designed songs, which would then constitute Type B.

It might be argued that the strophic pattern is really the vocal analogue of another conventional instrumental form, the theme and variations. From that point of view, my line of demarcation between Types A and B would seem to be erased. But the variation-form differs from other abstract patterns such as the sonata-form in that it is not self-limiting. There is no principle within the definition of the form itself to prevent a series of variations from going on and on: there can always be another one. Some theorists have characterized the fugue as a process rather than a form; the same can be said, perhaps with even more justification, of the variation-set. Here again my Type A would seem to be a valid category, for through-composition is also a process rather than a form.

My reason for insisting on the new bifurcation is that it reveals an interesting point about *Schwanengesang.* Of the Heine songs, all but one belong to Type B. A glance at the poems suggests a possible explanation. Four of the six consist of three brief stanzas, and the predominance of that verse-form may have suggested to Schubert a cycle in which the deceptive simplicity of Heine's texts would be matched by the comparable simplicity of short ternary (or, where appropriate, binary) musical designs. That, at any rate, is the plan Schubert adopted, whether or not by premeditation. Consequently, only one song, "Der Doppelgänger," resists Type B classification.[2]

The poems by Rellstab, in contrast, contain from three to six stanzas: one poem each of three and six stanzas, two of four, and three of five. Their settings are diverse, ranging from the almost exactly strophic to the completely through-composed. Again, with one exception, these songs belong to a single category, Type A. Only "Aufenthalt" exhibits a form that can be accurately described in conventional generic terminology (in this case as a *Bogen,* or arch).[3]

Let us begin with a discussion of the Rellstab examples. Of the seven, "Frühlingssehnsucht" adheres most closely to the strophic norm. That choice was almost inevitable here, for the five stanzas of the poem exhibit a unique pattern: four dimeter lines rhyming *abab,* then three tetrameters, *ccc,* and lastly a short fragment consisting of a single word or phrase, which Schubert invariably repeats. Four of those refrain-like tags pose questions; the last is a joyful answer. The obvious rhythmic parallelism is emphasized by the persistent use of present participles; they act as a grammatical motif connecting the several stanzas. There are other verbal connections as well. Stanzas 1 and 3, for example, are related by slant-rhyme ("mild" and "Gold") and by locution ("Wie . . . begrüssend" and "Wie . . . begrüssendes").

Those correspondences would necessarily be reflected by a setting like Schubert's, which admits variation from strophic reiteration only in the final stanza. But Schubert goes further, calling attention to the opening rhyme scheme. He sets the first four short lines in a quasi-sequential pattern that matches both their balance as a whole and the parallelism of their rhymes (mm. 13–20). He then goes further by repeating the entire quatrain, this time setting each pair of lines identically (mm. 23–30). Even if one failed to catch the rhymes the first time through, now they leap to the ear!

That recognition is certainly a result of the reduplication, but was that Schubert's purpose in adopting the device? Or was his intention primarily musical—to establish his key by means of four balancing phrases before proceeding with a striking modulation to flat VII? In Schubert's songs we should expect such reasons to support each other as they do here; and they do so with respect to a further textual reduplication—that of line 7 (mm. 41–49). That expansion of three tetrameters into four (lines 5, 6, and 7) balances the original doubling of four dimeters into eight. Of the four new phrases thus accommodated, the first pair is, as before, roughly sequential (lines 5 and 6); the second pair matches the duplication of line 7 with repetitive melody. In these respects the second half of the stanza seems to be modeled on the first, but there are important differences. Its two sequential phrases modulate, leading to a fermata on flat VII. Its second pair of phrases subtly vary the expected repetition, moving harmonically from I to iii. At that point the questioning refrain enters, recalling the preceding fermata by a half-cadence on V of flat VII. Finally, the piano's reinterpretation of that chord as IV initiates a retransition to the tonic—and the following stanza.

The second half of the stanza thus balances the phrase structure of the first half but complicates its tonal orientation. In the first stanza, that progression matches the poetic move from the lyrical picture of the opening lines to the rhetorical questioning that succeeds it. The music closely follows that gesture. The first question, "Wie habt ihr dem pochenden Herzen getan?" in line 6, is underlined by the first move to flat VII and the fermata there. The modulatory repetition of the following line, "Es möchte euch folgen auf luftiger Bahn!," emphasizes the vagaries of the "Bahn." Finally, the questioning induces another pause at the searching half-cadence of the refrain, "Wohin?" (made even more tense by the sudden pianissimo). It is tentatively answered by the return to the tonic of the second stanza.

A rationale that applies to one stanza may not apply equally, or at all, to the others. Thus it is possible that Schubert, once having composed the opening stanza, found himself constrained to repeat it because of the relentless poetic pattern. A superficial reading of the song might confirm that suspicion, but it would fail to take into account an important principle governing the aesthetic of successful strophic songs. Text and music are constantly interpenetrating, each giving the other new meanings in successive stanzas. On the one hand, repeated music can reveal unsuspected textual connections; on the other, diverse texts can suggest new interpretations of the same music.[4] In the present case, the fermata after line 6, which punctuated a rhetorical question in the first stanza, serves different purposes in those that follow. In the second, it gives the listener time to gaze at the reflection in the water, while the ensuing modulatory repetition mirrors the protagonist's imaginary journey. In stanza 3, the fermata extends the smile of the sun, in contrast to the hero's tears that follow. Those tears suggest a reinterpretation of the music for line 7. Heretofore the poetry, and therefore the music, has moved directly toward the questioning refrain, so that the passage in iii, D minor, sounds transitional. This time the words suggest that the refrain ("Warum?") is an afterthought; hence D minor receives cadential (and tearful) weight as a strongly contrasting tritone away from the surrounding A flat. In stanza 4 the mood brightens again. Is it too far-fetched to interpret the fermata this time as a different kind of break—the bursting of the buds ("die Knospe bricht") as the music breaks off? This time the duplicated line 7 seems uniquely balanced between the major I and the minor iii. Its first statement refers back to the satisfaction of the plants: they have found what they wanted. The repetition points anxiously toward the beloved: "*They* found what they needed, but what of you?"

The resolution comes, of course, in the final stanza. One might ask: How, if the poetic form is as powerful as I have insisted, could the composer find another appropriate setting? To tell the truth, he didn't, for the final variant departs only slightly from its model. The "Klage und Schmerz" of its opening quatrain are reflected in a minor version of the original melody, moving from B-flat minor to its relative major; the turn to the beloved is of course indicated by a return to the major. Once more the fermata punctuates a question. Once more the fifth line moves from I to iii. Yet this time, oddly enough, the D minor sounds exultant. That is partly because of the newly soaring vocal line, partly because of the contrast of the present I–iii in B-flat major to the previous i–III in B-flat minor. Last of all, the refrain, no longer a question, forsakes the flat VII in favor of a positive major IV–minor IV–V[7]–I. So the song, in spirit if not in letter, remains stubbornly strophic.

One further repetitive detail should be mentioned before leaving "Frühlingssehnsucht." That is a device that recurs so frequently in Schubert's songs that it may sound like a mannerism, almost a musical tic: the interpolation, within a phrase or between phrases, of a pianistic echo of the vocal line.[5] Yet it is not a mere cliché, as the composer demonstrates here. If, as I have come to believe, the persona of a song such as this can best be considered as a single figure, a poet-composer who is equally responsible for words, vocal line, and accompaniment,[6] then instrumental interpolations of this kind can be construed as continuations of the protagonist's thought— unspoken ideas articulated in purely musical terms. Thus the two-measure unit that follows the first pair of vocal phrases extends their thought by echoing, both melodically and harmonically, their cadence (mm. 21-22). But the corresponding passage after the second pair is divergent (mm. 31-32). Its rising third is derived from the first interpolation, and it prepares for the phrases to come. In this way an echoing tag—a pianistic rumination, so to speak, on the content of the preceding passage—has been transformed into an expectant forecast. The result upsets a regularity that might otherwise prove monotonous, for the strophe superficially appears to exhibit an oddly rigid parallelism:

> 4 + 4 + extension of 2 mm.
> 4 + 4 + extension of 2 mm.
> 4 + 4 + extension of 1 m. with fermata
> 4 + 4 + extension of 4 mm.

But if we take the second interpolation as anticipatory, we hear a fresh burst of energy that interrupts the relaxation of the first two pairs of phrases and continues through the third pair—until the fermata enforces a pause for breath:

> 4 + 4 + 2,
> 4 + 4,
> 2 + 4 + 4 + $\widehat{1}$,
> 4 + 4 + 4.

In the last stanza, the second interpolation supports a different strategy. Neither an echo nor an anticipation, it links the stanza's questions in a single interrogative gesture that culminates in the last fermata—to be answered by the resounding major peroration.

The echo plays an even more decisive role in "Ständchen." This song, too, begins with a strophe exactly repeated—but only once. For Schubert divides the five stanzas of Rellstab's poem into two strophes of eight lines each plus a four-line conclusion. In the strophes, each pair of lines yields a four-measure vocal phrase followed by a two-measure echo. Even more clearly than in "Frühlingssehnsucht," those echoes represent a continuation of the thought of the poet-composer—the "unitary vocal-instrumental protagonist that is coextensive with the persona of the actual composer of the song."[7] That is suggested at the outset by the four-measure prelude that introduces the persistent accompaniment figure. Obviously the title (which means "serenade") is to be taken literally, and the song represents a serenader accompanying himself—perhaps on an idealized guitar—while he sings, and while his thoughts echo his words.

Those echoes undergo an interesting development. In the first instances, authentic cadences on i (D minor) and III (F major) are duly repeated, both melodically and harmonically. The echo enriches its model each time, adding an inner part that parallels the melody in sixths and thirds. This new line is important, for it is soon to be taken over by the voice. That occurs after the third phrase, when for the first time the echo is heard over a harmonic alteration. The plagal cadence of the phrase (again on III) is replaced by an authentic one, and the voice, although now carrying the inner line, reinforces the cadence by completing a descent to the (temporary) tonic (mm. 21–22). What was originally merely an enhanced echo is thus transformed into a confirmation. The development is carried even further after the following phrase, which, returning to the original tonic, converts it into D major. Again two measures—in range now far from a simple echo—replace a plagal cadence with an authentic one; and again the voice parallels the accompaniment—although more freely. Indeed, at this point the voice retains the lead, even though the piano motif is octave-doubled. Together, the two parts complete the return to the tonic and intensify the turn toward major.

The codetta that follow is typically Schubertian in its alteration of B flat to B natural, effecting a haunting mixture of major and minor. The entire passage (mm. 29–36) is a kind of double echo, transforming the cadences of the two preceding phrases and at the same time preparing for the strophe to come. For when the original melody reenters, it closes a circle—a chain of derivations that may only now become apparent (Ex. 3.1a).

That series of motivic transformations ensures that the second strophe is not just a conventional copy of the first, for its principal theme appears in a new light. Moreover, the duplication demonstrates how musical correspondence can actualize an identification merely implied by the poetry. Where the first strophe referred to the protagonist's own song—"Leise flehen meine Lieder"—the second introduces the image of nightingales. Its domination of Rellstab's third and fourth stanzas is what especially justifies Schubert's paired setting. The nightingales, too, "flehen" the beloved; indeed, they speak for the lover: "Flehen sie für mich." The musical connection between the two strophes reinforces the verbal link, ef-

Ex. 3.1. "Ständchen"

fecting a metaphorical identification of the avian singers with their human interpreter.

The music of the unpaired concluding stanza abandons strophic limitations and enters the region of the through-composed. With no time for breath, much less for the expected codetta, the serenader bursts forth anew. The piano imitates his first four measures, not with a passive echo but with a true canon, as if the protagonist is pushing his own limits by means of his accompaniment. Harmonically, he really does so, arriving at a cadence that is tonally new: V_5^6–i in B minor (vi of D major), while his melody extends a gesture familiar from the outset (Ex. 3.1b). When at last he pauses, after the longest vocal stretch of the song (mm. 49–66), the accompaniment subtly underlines his breathlessness. For the echo to which it now reverts is too short-winded to encompass the usual phrase-member of two measures. It refers only to the last measure of the vocal phrase (m. 66), which it reiterates twice over the weakest of cadences—a iv $\frac{6}{4}$–i that merely extends the preceding harmony. Perhaps that double repetition reminds the singer of another derivation. The last line of the stanza, "Komm, beglücke mich!" magically transforms its predecessor, revealing its origin in the conclusion of the two preceding strophes (Ex. 3.1b).

The renewed strength of that passage does not last. It soon gives way to a descending line that, again blending minor with major, prepares for one more transformation. The last "beglücke mich!"—now imitatively following its accompaniment—provides yet another source for the codetta that returns to conclude the serenade (Ex. 3.1c). Perhaps because the protagonist has exhausted the strength of B natural in the preceding outburst, the coda preserves only the B-flat version in a final echo of the entire song.

The resemblance of strophic pattern to variation-form is attested by "Abschied." Of its six stanzas, the first, third, and fifth are set to identical music, in the tonic, E-flat major. The second and fourth are likewise identical; their music is a strict variation, in the subdominant, of the original model. The last stanza is also a variation, although a more freely developing one that begins in flat VI and modulates to the tonic. Like "Frühlingssehnsucht," the poem cries out for some sort of strophic treatment, for each of its five-line stanzas is introduced in the same fashion: by a line that opens and closes with an exclamatory "Ade." To this refrain Schubert adds one of his own, for he concludes every stanza by a repetition (verbal, not musical) of the fifth line, followed by a return (again only verbal) of the first line.[8] (In his last stanza, Schubert repeats both the fourth and fifth lines of verse.) Throughout the song the "Ades" are linked musically as well as verbally. Although not identical, they all exhibit the same iambic rhythm and the same rising melodic contour. Beginning and concluding each stanza, they bind all five together in the portrayal of a journey in progress—a picture supported by a steadily trotting accompaniment that persists throughout with a rhythm of unbroken eighth notes.

At the same time, the unvarying pace is emphasized by the rhythm of the melody. Schubert's seven-line stanzas exhibit an isorhythmic construction within a symmetrical frame:

Only in the last, deviant stanza is the close linkage broken by a two-measure interlude, but even this stanza adheres to a similar rhythmic pattern.

There is a poetic correspondence that justifies Schubert's use of alternating strophic models in "Abschied." The odd stanzas, which adhere to the tonic version, refer to the hero himself, to the friendly maidens of the town, to a specially remembered window—all peculiarly personal references. By contrast, the second and fourth stanzas, which adopt the subdominant version, refer to the natural world—to grove and stream, to sun and stars. The last stanza, despite the hero's earlier assurances of his cheerfulness, sounds a note of regret, "Ade, ihr Sterne, verhüllet euch grau!" Introduced by a piano interlude that refers for the first time to the tonic minor, its flat VI links the stars with the fading light of the window.[9] This tonal excursion continues through the first two lines of the stanza. It is set off from what follows by the previously mentioned two-measure interpolation, which further extends its harmony—perhaps representing a slight weakening of the hero's resolve. If so, the ensuing return to the tonic is motivated by his renewed courage ("Darf ich hier nicht weilen"). His music is still strongly influenced by the flat VI. The modulation first touches on that chord's relatives, minor iv and minor i, before the reduplication of lines 4 and 5 gives it a chance to revert to the major through natural VI, IV, and ii. Here a version of the corresponding passage in the preceding odd stanzas, duly followed by the return of line 1, produces a final sense of resolution, both musical and moral.

Of all the Rellstab poems, "In der Ferne" displays the most extreme metrical uniformity. Each of its three stanzas consists of four couplets, written in a persistent dactylic dimeter—with occasional substitutions, such as amphimacers, for the first of the two dactyls. There is a persistent syntactic motif as well, for twenty of the twenty-four rhyme-words are present par-

ticiples. Such invariance almost demands strophic or quasi-strophic treatment. Schubert's first stanza, in B minor, accordingly serves as a model that
the succeeding stanzas vary—the second following its source closely, the
third, in the tonic major, moving further afield. Finally that stanza, verbally
repeated, yields a still more freely composed concluding section.

Schubert's model matches the rhythmic motif of the poem with one of
its own. Each of the eight poetic lines is set to the same two-measure rhythmic pattern,

or a close variant thereof:

Only when the composer extends the poetic stanza by repeating its eighth
line does he relinquish the formula. But that phrase, which expands two
measures into five, is achieved by stretching the second measure of the basic
motif:

can be heard as

Schubert's second and third stanzas adhere closely to the isorhythmic model. Only the repetition of the third stanza departs from the persistent pattern. Both its fourth and eighth lines, embodying two diverse deceptive cadences, expand the usual two-measure group into four—producing
the only masculine endings in the song:

But they, too, give way to the pervasive motif, which returns in one more
stretched variant to support the by-now-obligatory repetition of the eighth
line:

It is worth noting here that the mysterious prelude, whose semitone
parallel octaves have been suggested as the source of the famous parallel

chords at "Mutterhaus hassenden" and "Busen, der wallende,"[10] also fore-casts the device of stretching. Each time it appears, introducing stanzas 1, 2, and 3, its conclusion expands

$$| \; \flat \; \quad \bar{\;} \quad | \quad \text{into} \quad | \; \flat. \quad \quad | \; \flat. \quad \quad \quad |,$$

effecting a written-out ritardando.

Phrase expansion is not Schubert's only means of parrying the monot-ony threatened by the isorhythm. Every stanza is articulated at least once by a measure of piano echo. Of the divisions thus effected, the most startling is the one common to the first two stanzas. Each of them interposes such a measure after only two lines—four measures—and emphasizes the articu-lation by a fermata. The resulting phrase structure—five measures, i–v, an-swered by seventeen measures, V–i—certainly points up the contrast be-tween the generalization of the poem's first two lines and the illustrative details that follow. The same scheme is less appropriate when applied to the second stanza, as the composer seemed to realize. For although in the first stanza the phrase after the fermata begins anew, in the same register as be-fore (m. 13), the corresponding phrase in the second stanza continues the rise of the vocal line and proceeds to mount much higher than before (mm. 42 ff.). A performance might therefore underplay the fermata this time in the interest of a more continuous period.

Whereas the first two stanzas employ the same punctuation by echo for two different sets of words, the third stanza and its repetition contrast two different types of articulation for the same poetry. The first version, after opening in B major, turns with increasing harmonic complexity toward the minor for lines 5 and 6. This couplet contains the first specifically personal reference in the poem, an allusion to the loved one whose rejection pre-sumably sent the hero on his journey. That reference, together with the cou-plet's momentary abandonment of the motivic participle (at "Schmerze, ach!" and "Herze brach—"), must have impelled the composer to interrupt the melodic flow with two measures of echo, one after line 5 and one after line 6. The autograph suggests that those were inserted after the composi-tion of the vocal line but before the completion of the accompaniment.[11] (An earlier couplet with a similar rhyme, lines 7 and 8 of stanza 1, conveys no personal message and receives no distinctive musical treatment.) By in-dividuating lines 5 and 6, the echoes serve a formal purpose as well. They underline the proportions of the stanza:

lines 1–4:	8mm.
line 5 + echo:	$6\begin{cases} \text{2 mm. + 1} \\ \text{2 mm. + 1} \end{cases}$
line 6 + echo:	
line 7:	$8\begin{cases} \text{2 mm.} \\ \text{2 mm.} \\ \text{4 mm. (+1 m. interlude).} \end{cases}$
line 8:	
line 8 rep:	

Note that it is the expected stretching of the repeated line that brings the last phrase into balance with the first and permits a return to the B major of the stanza's opening.

The second version substitutes periodic for symmetrical balance in its attempt to confirm the solace suggested by the turn to major. Its antecedent phrase is tentative. Derived from line 7 of the preceding version, it admits echoes after both the first and second lines before achieving a continuous approach to its cadence—a surprisingly deceptive one on V^6/vi (m. 100). But the consequent gains new courage. The echoes no longer interrupt the melody; they have been replaced by a freely imitative counter-melody (Ex. 3.2). As a result we are almost deceived by a picture of integration and acceptance—only to be startled by another deceptive cadence, one on lowered VI (m. 111). It opens the way for a return to the tonic minor. What follows is based once again on the formula of the repeated line 8, presented in a new variation. Accepting the lowered VI as an applied dominant, it introduces a Neapolitan sixth that leads inexorably to a powerful conclusion. This time the final line takes no part in the attempted balance of the stanza. It is the hero's isolation, not his consolation, that is confirmed.

The remaining three Rellstab songs stray from the strophic norm in the direction of through-composition. They may be compared with respect to their employment of literal reprise. "Kriegers Ahnung" is completely through-composed, returning only briefly to its opening material; "Liebesbotschaft" contains a functional recapitulation; while "Aufenthalt" moves still further toward a reprise-controlled abstract form.

In "Kriegers Ahnung" only the piano introduction receives a reprise. The four stanzas are diverse both in musical materials and in tempo, but they are unified by the persistence, on various levels, of a single motivic gesture. That is the alternation of the dominant of the prevailing C minor with its upper neighbor, G–A flat–G. Sometimes the motif is incomplete, and sometimes it is elaborated as G–A natural–A flat–G or G–A flat–A natural–G. The last is the form in which it is first heard in mm. 1–7 of the introduction (Ex. 3.3a). Here it is confined to an inner voice, but as the introductory material continues, forming the accompaniment of stanza 1, the motif is stated

Ex. 3.2. "In der Ferne"

more clearly. It is heard in the bass of mm. 13–15, which constitute an elaborate echo of the preceding vocal line (Ex. 3.3b). Not until the following phrase, however, is the motif actually brought into the open. Now voice and piano simultaneously present it in its simplest form, *G–A flat–G*, but they go further, elaborating it by inversion into a double neighbor, *G–A flat–G–F sharp–G*. (That move was adumbrated in the introduction by the bass of m. 5.) The unrelieved doubling of voice and bass draws special attention to words that no doubt reveal the poetic significance of the motif: "Mir ist das Herz so bang und schwer." That significance is further emphasized in the peculiar echo that follows, half vocal and half instrumental. Unlike the preceding echo, this one is exact, but the voice, omitting the first measure, joins the piano only for the second, "so bang, so schwer" (Ex. 3.3c). The passage thus isolates the key words that identify the prevailing mood of the song. At the same time, it offers convincing evidence of the identification of vocal and instrumental personas. The piano gives voice to that portion of the protagonist's thought that remains unspoken. (It is interesting that Schubert utilized two versions of the repeated line. The first time, he wrote, correctly, "so bang und schwer"; the second time, more forcefully, yet without apparent textual justification, "so bang, so schwer.") The somber tone continues in the concluding line of the stanza, "Von Sehnsucht mir so heiss." It, too, is repeated—textually but not musically. That extension affords an opportunity of expanding the double neighbor simultaneously in voice and piano as they proceed to the half-cadence at m. 25 (Ex. 3.3d).

The first stanza ends with a fermata on V, a harmony to be picked up again by the last stanza; but meanwhile stanzas 2 and 3 have exploited the two neighbors, *A flat* and *A natural*. Stanza 2, introduced by a deceptive cadence, V–VI, develops the pervasive *A flat* as a key. Its major mode and its livelier tempo (*Etwas schneller* in contrast to *Nicht zu langsam*) celebrate the warrior's loving memories. His fears are temporarily in abeyance, and the

Ex. 3.3. "Kriegers Ahnung"

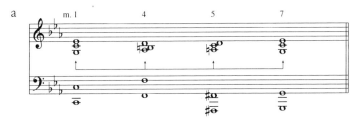

power of the persistent motif is accordingly minimal. Again two lines of text are chosen for repetition, in this case the second and fourth. Musically, the stanza consists of two almost identical halves, in which the reiterated lines are marked by descending stepwise sequences. But the two sequences arrive at contrasting melodic goals: the first on *A natural* (harmonized, in A flat, with major VI, m. 35), the second on *A flat* (harmonized with IV, m. 41). I hear in that opposition a veiled reference to the *A natural–A flat* of the motif. Can the entire stanza be construed as embodying a transposition— from *G–A flat–G* to *A flat–A natural–A flat*?

Be that as it may, the contrast of *A flat* and *A natural* is heightened in the next stanza, in which the warrior's thoughts return to his actual situation. The *D flat* (IV of A flat) that concludes stanza 2 is rewritten for stanza 3 as *C sharp*, the dominant of F-sharp minor—which, as *G flat*, functions as a minor Neapolitan in F minor. That relationship is revealed by a wrenching modulation that brings *A natural* and *A flat* into shocking relief (mm. 52–53). It underlines the total loneliness expressed in the repeated third line ("ganz allein"). That loneliness deepens into despair in the repeated fourth line, which is set to a definitive cadence in F minor.

In the final stanza (*Geschwind, unruhig*) the overt deployment of the motif in both simple and elaborated forms characterizes the return to C minor. That is effected by reversing the *G–A flat* that introduced the central portion of the song. F minor now reverts to subdominant status, and iv^6–V^7 initiates an *A flat–G* alternation that is reiterated, first in the piano bass, then in the voice as well. The insistence on the motif is abetted by the almost complete repetition of the first line, both verbally and musically—for this stanza, like all the rest, duplicates two lines of text. The piano then reinterprets *A flat* as *G sharp* in a move toward A minor—a reference to the expanded motif (mm. 67–68). That modulation proves to be abortive, however, for the second extended phrase opens in C major as the hero's thoughts turn once again to his beloved. His "Herzliebste, gute Nacht!"— the repeated fourth line of the stanza—moves gently through A-flat major (flat VI, m. 83), to come to rest in F major (IV, m. 87).

Now the poem is finished—but not the song. The alteration of *A natural* in the cadential F major to *A flat* (m. 88) motivates a repetition of the entire stanza. It is modified in such a way as to elaborate the neighboring motion still further in the harmonic development of the first phrase (Ex. 3.3e). This time the second phrase, although moving to flat VI as before, omits the modulation to IV and proceeds through a German sixth to i$^6_4$, which summons the return of the piano introduction. That move accompanies a double repetition of the warrior's farewell. Its reversion to the opening tempo and its characteristic rhythm recall the hero from his dreams of major possibilities to the reality of the tonic minor. The portentous music that previously underlay his anxieties (his "Herz so bang, so schwer") now darkens the implications of his final "gute Nacht!" He is going to sleep, yes, but he will soon be going to his death, and here the voice brings into the open the motif as it was covertly stated by the introduction (Ex. 3.3f). At this point the listener may realize that the progress of the entire song can be described, not too fancifully, as the elaboration of a huge neighbor framed by the I–V of the opening section and the i$^6_4$–V–i of the conclusion (Ex. 3.3g).

Ex. 3.3. (*continued*)

"Liebesbotschaft" consists of four stanzas: A (I–vi), B (IV), C (ii major–III), A (I–vi). Each of the first three stanzas is distinguished by its own phraseology and pattern of internal repetitions, and the reprise is completed by a new phrase leading to the tonic.

The introduction sounds superficially like a conventional statement of key and accompaniment figure, but its unusual five-measure span is to prove influential later on. The twelve measures of the first stanza set its eight short lines of verse in parallel fashion, two by two, producing four phrases. In each, two lines of sung text occupy two measures, followed by a single measure of pianistic echo. The regularity of the design, however, is relieved by the diversity of the echoes. No two are alike, and only the third is literal. The protagonist, as it were, imagines the brook as playfully reflecting his own thoughts.

The next stanza lacks echoes, but it achieves a complement of twelve measures by repeating lines 5–8. The first two pairs of lines are set identically, and the music of the repeated lines 5–8 is very similar to its model. So the pattern that emerges is:

Lines 1–2:	2 mm.	*a*
Lines 3–4:	2 mm.	*a*
Lines 5–8:	4 mm.	*bc*
Lines 5–8:	4 mm.	*b'c*

As a counterpoint to that repetitive pattern, however, another is simultaneously presented. That is based on a motivic detail that appears six times. Its

Ex. 3.4. "Liebesbotschaft"

first statements (mm. 19 and 21) decorate the cadential measures of each *a*. By performing the same function for each *c* (mm. 25 and 29), the motif emphasizes the 2 + 2, 4 + 4 phrase structure. But it is also applied to the first measure of each *b* (mm. 22 and 26)—a choice that is not as capricious as it seems, for it connects the concealed slant-rhyme of "Busen" (line 4) and "Rosen" (line 5). Indeed, all the instances of the motif are syllabically related: "Gar*ten*," "Bu*sen*," "Ro*sen*," "Kuhl*ender*" (Ex. 3.4). Only "Blumen" in the very first line is not so treated, possibly because of its proximity to the cadentially important "Garten." At these moments the voice, so to speak, is fancifully imitating itself, and at the end of the stanza it is doubly echoed by two measures of piano interlude.

The first two stanzas are linked by rhythmic pattern. Every pair of lines in the first exhibits the same two-measure rhythm:

and every pair of the second can be heard as a variation of that formula. The opening phrases of the third stanza, while adhering to the same model, augment it to four measures:

The second half of the stanza reverts to the original pace. Its four lines are set as one continuous phrase, again of four measures. The stanza closes with a repetition of those lines (verbal, not musical) that stretches the final measure into two, turning four measures into five, thus expanding the

stanza's sixteen measures into seventeen. The last measure becomes, by elision, the first of a four-measure transition to the final stanza.

That stanza, a musical reprise of the first, accordingly produces twelve
measures as before. But now the final two lines of poetry are repeated to
music that adopts both the augmented rhythm and the stretched cadence of
the preceding stanza. Once again we hear sixteen measures expanded into
seventeen. This time, however, the grouping is not three 4's plus 5, but four
3's plus 5. Once again the cadential measure is elided, introducing the regularity of an eight-measure coda.

As the preceding analysis suggests, what is interesting here is the way
the stanzas, despite their diversity of melody, use a recurring rhythmic formula to preserve a sense of strophic periodicity. The return of the opening
music thus seems natural. It is further justified—and probably occasioned
—by the poetic links between the first and last stanzas. Their second quatrains mutually rhyme, and their final lines exhibit similar constructions:
"Bringe die Grüsse / Des Fernen ihr zu," and "Flustre ihr Träume / Der Liebe
zu." (In his perceptive analysis of this song, Thrasybulos Georgiades points
out another important poetic-musical link. The augmented rhythm of the
repeated "Flustre ihr Träume" in the fourth stanza recalls the similar
rhythm of "in Träume versenkt" in the second.)[12]

In "Liebesbotschaft," then, the poetically invoked musical recurrence in
the last stanza is not a mere reprise; it makes explicit the latent strophic nature of the entire song. That explanation does not apply to the more thor-
oughgoing abstract formalism of the remaining Rellstab example, "Aufenthalt," where the symmetry of a complete arch-form, ABCBA', is even
extended to encompass an almost identical introduction and coda. The arch
was no doubt motivated by Rellstab's own reprise of the first of the poem's
five stanzas. But the recapitulation is not only poetically invoked; it is also
musically required.

Each stanza consists of four short lines, rhyming *abcb*. Schubert clearly
articulates the stanzaic divisions by piano interludes, yet the whole song
seems driven by a single impulse that originates in the ominously expressive
introduction. There the piano initiates a triplet rhythm that persists without
break until it terminates in the coda, which, like the introduction, buttresses
the arch. Schubert expands each stanza by verbal repetition—the first and
third in extenso, the second in part.

If the final reprise is poetically enjoined, the purely musical one that precedes it, that of section B, is at least poetically invited—by the parallelism of
stanzas 2 and 4. In each, the word "wie" initiates a simile; in each, the word
"ewig" intensifies the protagonist's grief. Schubert's setting of the earlier

Ex. 3.5. "Aufenthalt"

stanza dwells on the latter word. Instead of repeating all four lines, he focuses on the crucial word and the lines that embed it:

> Wie sich die Welle
> An Welle reiht,
> Fliessen die Tränen
> Mir ewig erneut,
> Fliessen die Tränen
> Mir ewig, ewig erneut,
> Fliessen die Tränen
> Mir ewig erneut.

He adds musical support to this verbal gesture by a subtle motivic correspondence among the repetitions of the word "ewig." In the fourth stanza,
which is musically almost identical to the second, "ewig" is attached to the
word "bleibet," which this time receives the musical stress (Ex. 3.5).

The recall of B, rhetorically justified though it is, cannot terminate the
song because of its dominant orientation. The four stanzas traverse an arch
that is incomplete both thematically, ABCB, and tonally, i–v–III–v. The completion in both respects is effected by the return of the opening section in
accordance with Rellstab's demand. This time the correlation of the music
with the poetry is made more precise. The music of the original statement
only partially responded to the stark rhythmic and syntactic parallelism of
the poetry:

> Rauschender Strom,
> Brausender Wald,
> Starrender Fels . . .

Now the participial phrases are set isorhythmically:

(varied only by the length of the note of resolution). Moreover, when the
repetition of the stanza is climactically altered in such a way as to require

musical expansion, the resulting textual duplication increases the sum of isorhythmic motifs to seven. Only the eighth and last participial phrase (once more "Brausender Wald") is given special treatment. It is set to an expansive phrase that enables the voice to approach its cadence by intoning the melody of the introduction. So when that theme is echoed by the piano coda, it sounds like a reverberation from the "Starrender Fels" of the hero's "Aufenthalt." In retrospect, that conclusion motivates the introduction. Together, they frame the song musically, while symbolically depicting the stark scene that inspires the poem.

It is interesting, and perhaps not coincidental, that "Der Atlas," the first of the Heine songs (according to the standard ordering), likewise ends with a verbal and musical return of the opening, producing in this case a typical three-part form. Unlike the reprise of "Aufenthalt," this one is the composer's own idea. In going out of his way to turn the poem's two stanzas into three, was Schubert thereby announcing for the Heine group the program to which I have previously alluded as a possibility: the adopting of the ternary pattern as a norm? As I have noted elsewhere, the motif that opens "Der Atlas" is deployed throughout the Heine set (Ex. 3.6a).[13] Thus it is not impossible that Schubert wished to unify this cycle still further by a formal pattern. In any case, each of the first four Heine songs exhibits a version of the familiar ternary design.

In "Der Atlas" the ultimate return of the first two lines constitutes only the most extensive of the many verbal repetitions to which Schubert subjects Heine's poem. I find that treatment justified by the poet's own rhetoric, which depends on constant verbal linkages within and among lines:

> "Ich unglückselger Atlas! . . . glücklich sein, unendlich glücklich,"
> "Eine Welt, / Die ganze Welt . . ."
> ". . . muss ich tragen, / Ich trage Unerträgliches, . . ."
> ". . . das Herz in Leibe. / Du stolzes Herz, . . . stolzes Herz,"
> ". . . ja gewollt." / Du wolltest . . ."
> ". . . unendlich elend, . . . bist du elend."

Schubert's textual reduplications produce the space needed to build a convincing musical structure—one equally based on insistent repetition. Its principal material is the pervasive motif noted above—let us call it x. Announced (for the cycle as a whole as well as for this song) by the octave bass of the introduction, x proceeds to generate a vocal melody, calling forth an answering phrase y (Ex. 3.6b). A modulation from the tonic (G minor) to a distant form of the mediant (B major) now leads to the contrasting second

Ex. 3.6a.

Der Atlas

Ihr Bild

Das Fischermädchen

Die Stadt

Am Meer

Am Meer

Der Doppelgänger

stanza. So far, the vocal melody has been freely doubling the bass, but now it strikes out more independently as the protagonist turns to address his "stolzes Herz." At the same time, a pulsing reiteration of *x*—a symbol of the heart?—continues to control the bass line. A return to the tonic heralds the reprise. It is by no means literal, for it temporarily sets voice and piano at odds. Continuing to assert its independence, the voice recalls a version of *y* against the piano's insistence on *x* (Ex. 3.6c). Not until the answering phrase are the two united as before, perhaps because the hero only belatedly remembers that the "stolzes Herz" which he was excoriating is, after all, his own. Now voice and accompaniment coincide once again, as if to synchronize thought and feeling for a last climactic outburst.

The next three songs of the cycle are likewise in simple ternary form. Since their poems consist of three stanzas each, they can be set straightforwardly, without the necessity of a textual reprise. Their stanzas correspond to the respective divisions of the musical form. But how well does that form,

Ex. 3.6b. "Der Atlas"

with its conventional thematic recapitulation, answer the rhetorical demands of each poem?

In "Ihr Bild," the tightly knit song-form accurately reflects the shifts of attention in the poem:

A: i–I   The lover, gazing at his beloved's portrait.
B: VI   The beloved, seemingly alive.
A: i–I–i   The lover's reaction.

The thematic contrast is slight. In particular, one melodic element, appearing in various guises, underlines the emotional trajectory of the poem: the portrait, smiling and weeping, evokes the lover's weeping response (Ex. 3.7a).

Particularly noteworthy are the distinctive ways each phrase is echoed. The initial period contrasts a minor antecedent with a major consequent. At the close of the antecedent, its two measures of dominant cadence are ruminatively repeated by the piano bass. But the corresponding measures of the consequent phrase are echoed only indirectly, so to speak. The piano interlude confirms the turn to major, but instead of exactly repeating the cadential measures of the melody, it ponders them further by offering an alternative accompaniment (Ex. 3.7b).

Ex. 3.6c. "Der Atlas"

Ex. 3.7. "Ihr Bild"

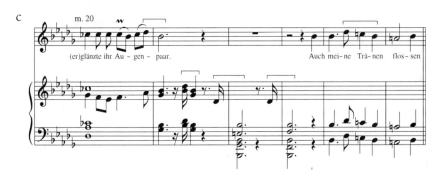

The importance of that gesture will become clear in the reprise. In the central section of the song-form, the echo is reduced to a simple descending third after each of the two phrases. The second of those constitutes the subject of a retransition to the tonic of the opening. At the same time it reveals another subtle motivic connection, one that closely links the tears of lover and beloved (Ex. 3.7c). The reprise holds one surprise in store, produced by the irregular echo noted above. This time it is in minor, in stark contrast to the immediately preceding vocal phrase. Clearly, Schubert means for us to take the last lines of the poem literally. The lover's phrase in major, previously associated with the "geliebte Antlitz," now supports his refusal to accept his loss: "ich kann es nicht glauben / Dass ich dich verloren hab!" Only during the piano postlude does he awaken, or awaken to reality, and admit the truth. The echo, as before, could serve as an accompaniment for the previous words silently rehearsed—but this time in minor. That mode isolates the clause and reverses its meaning: "[Ich weiss] dass ich dich verloren hab!'"

Even more obviously adaptable to the ternary mold is the poem of "Die Stadt." In the first and last of the three stanzas, the poet views the fateful town; in the second, he describes the boat ride that brings it into sight. In Schubert's version the journey is characterized by a monotonously reiterated musical gesture: the pianistic elaboration of a diminished seventh over an octave tremolo. This famous arpeggiation seems to arise from nowhere to create an atmospheric prelude, it recurs as the accompaniment of the central contrasting section, and it dies away to nothing in a postlude.[14] Despite its connections with other songs in the cycle (see, for instance, Ex. 3.10h), in its immediate context it is unprepared and unresolved, as if depicting a journey that has no beginning and no ending.

The overall pattern of the song can accordingly be shown as b–ABA–b. But that schematization does not indicate the contrast between the first and third stanzas. Both of them are declaimed against an almost isorhythmic chordal accompaniment, but the pianissimo of a misty dusk in the first is replaced by the forte-fortissimo of a sunrise in the third. The melody, also, is varied. Its two cadences, on iv (m. 10) and i (m. 14), are circumspectly approached by stepwise motion in the first stanza; in the third both are intensified by upward and downward leaps—the only occurrences in the song of vocal intervals greater than a third. Their parallelism suggests a symbolic relation between the illumination of the sun ("Leuchtend vom Boden empor") and the acute realization of loss ("Wo ich das Liebste verlor") (Ex. 3.8). Equally as striking is the alteration of a normal supertonic sixth to a Neapolitan in order to create a special accent: "Und zeigt mir *jene* Stelle" (m. 32, my emphasis). The rays of the rising sun have fallen on just *that* place, with its associations of loss and grief.

Among the ternary songs, "Das Fischermädchen" is unique in that its digression is simply a varied transposition of its principal statement—from A flat to C flat. Perhaps that was Schubert's way of reconciling the strophic demands of three similar and closely related stanzas with the three-part design established as a norm by the song's neighbors in the cycle. At any rate, the second stanza sounds more like a development—a section of thematically controlled contrast—than like the second member of a parallel group of three. That impression is to some extent due to the key chosen for the stanza: flat III, the relative major of the tonic minor. A comparison of that indirect relationship with the much closer tonic-subdominant connection

Ex. 3.8. "Die Stadt"

between the stanzas of "Abschied" suggests why the latter falls much more easily into the strophic class.

The central section presents not only contrast in key but also alterations of melodic detail. One of those was no doubt occasioned by considerations of the vocal tessitura. Although the high B *double flat* required in m. 42 by an exact transposition of m. 21 would not exceed the limit elsewhere established (in "Frühlingssehnsucht"), it would seem excessive for the song's prevailing lightness of mood (Ex. 3.9a). In contrast, the high G flat avoided by an octave displacement in m. 32 was obviously not thought to be out of range, for it is precisely the note that replaces the unusable B *double flat*. Indeed, it was perhaps the prominence of the G flat throughout the last phrase of the stanza that persuaded the composer not to employ it during the first phrase. More than that: as a result, the original stanza and its transposition, despite their divergence of key, are similar in the way each gradually extends the upper range of the voice (Ex. 3.9b). Tonally distant yet melodically close: Is that combination a symbol of the protagonist's attempt to draw nearer to the fishermaiden?

The controlled coordination of contrast with similarity is also at work when that crucial G *flat* introduces the most interesting among the variants of the second stanza. At mm. 39–40 the composer avoided the high A *flat* required by the transposition of mm. 18–19, using a free inversion of the melodic figure that is striking because of its leap of a seventh. The result is probably the most difficult vocal passage and certainly the most dissonant measure in the song (Ex. 3.9c). Evidently the word "sorglos," sung at that point for the second time, is not to be accepted without suspicion. But perhaps the lover is doing his best to be convincing, for the descending seventh of "doch sorglos" recalls a rising seventh from the end of the first stanza, as "Hand in Hand,/Wir kosen . . ." (Ex. 3.9d). In the same way, it looks forward to the corresponding passage in the last stanza, where many a pearl ". . . ruht/In seiner Tiefe . . ." If the maiden can conquer her doubts, the couple,

Ex. 3.9. "Das Fischermädchen"

hand in hand, without care, will presumably enjoy the pearls of the lover's heart.

What remains the same in all three stanzas is the phrase structure. Combining the techniques of echo and variation, the composer has doubled the length of a normal eight-measure period. The resulting form reflects the importunity of an impatient lover as successive repetitions increasingly concentrate the passages they follow, moving from pianistic reiteration to vocal variation. First, a four-measure antecedent phrase is partially echoed by a piano interlude of just half its length. Those two mea-

sures, although almost parenthetical, are nevertheless prophetic of what is
to come. For the four-measure consequent receives in its turn a complete
repetition (vocal as well as instrumental), an emphatic variant that extends
the entire period by half its length (exactly so, if we count only the vocal
measures). Finally, that variation is itself extended by half when its two cadential measures undergo their own elaboration. Thus in tabular form:

Period:

antecedent: 4

(echo): $8\begin{cases} & \end{cases}$ $(2 = \frac{1}{2} \text{ of } 4)$

consequent: 4

Var. of consequent: $4 = \frac{1}{2} \text{ of } 8$

Var. of cadence: $2 = \frac{1}{2} \text{ of } 4$

"Das Fischermädchen," then, absorbs a strophic pattern into a ternary
form. "Am Meer" shows how a quasi-strophic pattern can be accommodated to a large binary form. (Since I treat this view of the song in detail in
another essay, what follows is largely a synopsis of that discussion.)[15] From
one standpoint, "Am Meer" can be considered as a huge period, framed by
the mysterious chords of the famous prelude and postlude. The antecedent
and the consequent of the period respectively embrace the first two and the
last two of the four poetic stanzas. The two large sections are closely parallel, consisting of four phrases each—two per stanza. In each case, the first
pair of phrases constitutes a smaller period in itself, set off from what follows by an echo in the piano. The second pair consists of a contrasting modulatory phrase answered by one that returns to the mood and the key of the
opening. Only here do we find a distinction between the two halves of the
song, a discrepancy that motivates my qualification of the strophic pattern
as "quasi." In the first instance the final phrase moves to a half-cadence that
returns, again after an echo, to the opening. The parallel phrase of the second half progresses to a full cadence, which is confirmed by a return to the
chords of the introduction.

How well does this reading of the musical form correspond with the
structure of the poem? Superficially, at least, quite accurately, as the following
outline indicates. (In it, the numerals refer to the poetic stanzas; the capital letters to the larger musical sections; the lower-case letters to the phrases.)

Antecedent			Consequent		
1. A	(aa')	The two silent lovers.	3. A	(aa')	The man's response.
2. B	(b)	The storm-driven gull.	4. B'	(b)	His stormy life.
	(c)	The weeping woman.		(c')	His memory of her tears.

Yet the narrative suggests an articulation more subtle than exact bifurcation. Logically, the first three stanzas belong together: they recount a crucial incident in the past. The final stanza deals with its subsequent effects on the hero's life. That contrast implies a different musical grouping—not AB–AB' but ABA–B'. The binary period yields to a ternary song-form with coda. Such a coda, returning to the central contrast of the song-form, is unusual but not unique.[16] A performance projecting that interpretation—say, by dwelling on the full cadence of the returning A—could introduce an element of surprise at the recall of B. It could thereby intensify the expressiveness of the musical material of the coda, much as the words at that point throw ironic light on the sentimental story. The symbolism of the restless gull is at last made clear, and the nature of the woman's tears is revealed. Schubert's poison may not be so bitter as Heine's, but it is powerful nevertheless. It is the poison of regret, of remorse.

One further detail may be construed as supporting my possibly idiosyncratic interpretation of "Am Meer" as ternary form. Each of the three primary sections—A, B, and A—is followed by a measure of echo in the piano. In that way the cadential structure is outlined as I–V–I. But the returning B receives no such echo. Instead, it is followed directly by the recurrence of the introductory motif—here, as originally, stated twice. The final section is thus distinguished from its three predecessors, for its cadence is not confirmed. It dissolves into the mysterious postlude, which, like its source in the prelude, echoes itself.

In an odd way, then, "Am Meer" conforms doubly to the rubric I have suggested for the Heine songs. It embodies not one but two generic forms. And although the ternary version follows the dramatic course of the poem more closely, the binary version projects an underlying musical balance. For that reason it suggests that Schubert's protagonist has arrived at a state of acceptance unavailable to Heine's. Perhaps the two readings can be reconciled in a single performance—one in which the recurrence of the storm in the coda is an unexpected outbreak, yet is again succeeded by calm. This time it leads to a perfect cadence recognizable not simply as the conclusion of the coda but also as an answer to the half-cadence of the song's midpoint. But if that rendition is not feasible, never mind: there can always be another performance.

"Der Doppelgänger" remains the one Heine song that refuses to submit to my classification. By way of compensation, its form suggests a multiplicity of possible interpretations, all referring to Type A. Does the song consist of a series of strophic stanzas, a theme with variations, or a through-composed continuum? Probably it is best described as a passacaglia or chaconne that finally breaks out into a freely composed peroration. The combination of forward motion and circularity in its ostinato matches the hero's own advance and hesitation as he approaches a confrontation with his past.

At every level, the music forecasts the image of doubleness that emerges at the climax of the poem.[17] At the outset, the four-measure introduction exhibits several dimensions of duplication. To begin with, the outer voices double each other in parallel octaves around a constant pedal on the dominant F sharp; indeed, the entire chordal texture is doubled (Ex. 3.10a). Then, the descending half step of the first pair of measures is exactly transposed in the next pair (Ex. 3.10b). More than that, those two measures present a melodic and harmonic retrograde inversion of the first two (Ex. 3.10c). Schubert's hero is haunted by the concept of doubleness from the beginning.

When the voice enters, the piano repeats its four measures, but it extends them to produce what will be the eight-measure chordal ostinato of the chaconne. But that extension at the same time conceals another duplication: its bass is a slightly varied form of the introductory motif (Ex. 3.10d). In the last two measures of the ostinato, the upper line abandons the bass in preparation for the introduction of a new pianistic voice. That enters when a dominant seventh, sustained for two further measures, supports one more reduplication: an echo of the vocal line (mm. 13–14). Meanwhile, that melody has also contributed to the process, for its two halves freely mirror each other, motif by motif—abba (Ex. 3.10e).

Duplication now arises on a higher level, as that entire ten-measure section, which covers half of the first stanza, is repeated for the second half of the stanza (mm. 15–24). The repetition is exact in the piano and only slightly varied in the voice. It is succeeded by an even more comprehensive duplication, when the pattern of two complete ostinati is repeated for the second stanza (mm. 25–42). That repetition, however, is compressed. As the hero draws nearer to his goal, the ten-measure units of ostinato plus echo are reduced to nine, the echo being suppressed in favor of a one-measure extension of the final chord (mm. 33 and 42). That chord is expressively modified each time by an alteration of the dominant seventh. The first time, with C *natural* replacing C *sharp* in the bass, it becomes a French sixth; the second time, through the intrusion of G *natural*, a climactic German sixth—marking the first occasion in the entire song when the omnipresent F *sharp* is forsaken. The approach to the climax is of course shared by the voice. Unlike the static melody of the first stanza, that of the second steadily rises. As before, the second half of the stanza is a variation of the first—but this time a variation that increases the tension. Instead of the high F *sharp* that was

Ex. 3.10. "Der Doppelgänger"

the goal of the first phrase (over the French sixth), it substitutes a G (over the German sixth).

The final section of the song is heralded as the German sixth resolves back into the French. *F sharp,* and with it the dominant function, is restored, in preparation for a complete tonic minor triad. Here, at the confrontation of hero and Doppelgänger, the music apparently gives up the ostinato and its insistence on duplication. But does it? The passage begins (m. 43) with a static two-measure fragment in the voice, followed immediately by a varied repetition. The piano supports this reduplication by a steady rise, effected by two successive inversions of the initial half-step motive. Now the voice, too, begins to rise, expanding the range of its motif in two more variations (mm. 47–50). The harmony is based on a shocking modulatory shift to sharp iii, D-sharp minor, supported by full triadic sonorities, i–V. Here the piano reverts twice to a descending form of the half step, *D sharp–C double sharp*—the most immediate and boldest reiteration in the entire song (Ex. 3.10f). Surely the hero and his double are face to face! A wrenching German sixth (this time on *G*, m. 51), effects a return to the tonic B minor by way of a resolution on i$^6_4$. In so doing it recalls the earlier German sixth on *C*, copying both its striking sound and its half-step resolution *G–F sharp*. An equally important connection is heard in the voice, whose high *F sharp* over the i$^6_4$ of m. 52 at last resolves the climactic *G* of m. 41. In so doing it initiates a vocal phrase that emerges at last on a tonic supported by a perfect cadence.[18]

The third stanza, then, is not bifurcated like its predecessors. The accompaniment, remarkably enough, can be analyzed as a huge expansion of the four primary measures of the ostinato. After the tonic of m. 43, its first goal is D-sharp minor, whose dominant, *A sharp*, enters strikingly in a middle voice in m. 47 and, as a root, in the bass of m. 48. From then on, the upper voice rivals the bass in prominence. It transforms *C double sharp* into *D natural*, which now initiates a doubling of the vocal descent to *C sharp*—thus completing the *B–A sharp–D–C sharp* motif of the ostinato. But this time the line continues, in both voice and piano, to the tonic. There an elision occurs, as the cadence overlaps one last statement of the four primary measures (Ex. 3.10g).

It is important to recognize that the final vocal phrase is the only one in the song that is not stated twice. True, it is doubled by the piano—but conventionally, in standard accompanimental fashion, by full chordal harmony. It can be said, in fact, that those measures—mm. 52–56—constitute the only normal phrase in the song. For the protagonist is experiencing an epiphany—an acceptance of his earlier self and a comprehension of the power of emotions long buried but still very much alive. It is a recognition not unlike the one realized by the hero of "Am Meer"—presumably the same man. Perhaps that is the reason for the recollection of that song in the heart-stopping alteration of the fourth chord of the ostinato in m. 59. Replacing *C sharp*, *C natural* is the root of a major triad that leads to a plagal cadence in B major. Lawrence Kramer discusses in detail the relation of that chord to the *C naturals* of mm. 32 and 41.[19] Richard Kramer looks further back. For him the C–B within "Der Doppelgänger" recalls the approach to the song from its two predecessors in the cycle.[20] He accepts the putative placement of "Die Stadt" between "Am Meer" and "Der Doppelgänger," but I find the progression through the songs more convincing in the traditional ordering (Ex. 3.10h). That produces a stark tonal contrast between "Am Meer" and "Der Doppelgänger" that is briefly but vividly recalled by the intrusion of C major into the final cadence of the latter.

The traditional succession can make sense poetically as well as musically, in a narrative that binds the three songs together as the utterances of a

Ex. 3.10. (*continued*)

g

h

"Die Stadt"   "Am Meer"   "Der Doppelgänger"

single protagonist. Two poems in which he describes the present frame one in which he narrates the past. Thus the hero, approaching (by water) the town of his youth, is reminded of a fateful day by the sea long ago. That memory induces him to seek out the house associated with his lost love. So in these three songs, at least, I find ample justification for retaining the old order.

With relief we turn to "Die Taubenpost," even though it is usually assumed that the song was not intended by Schubert as a postlude. There is no documentary evidence that the composer wished this lonely setting of a Seidl poem to be associated with his Rellstab and Heine cycles. As a result critics have tended to treat it with neglect or condescension. Thus Maurice Brown: "*Die Taubenpost,* Schubert's last song, belongs neither in body nor in spirit to either the Rellstab group or to the Heine group of songs; for all that it can inspire an affectionate response in the Schubertian."[21] I find such a dismissal too peremptory. When I used the qualified phrase "usually assumed," I meant to leave open the possibility that Schubert might, after all, have written the song as an addendum to the two conjoined cycles. In the absence of definite evidence to the contrary, it is this possibility that I wish to explore.

Compare "Die Taubenpost" with the last of the Rellstab set, "Abschied." Both songs convey a mood of lighthearted sentimentality; so if "Die Taubenpost" succeeds the Heine set, the entire cycle divides neatly into two halves with similar conclusions. Moreover, in that case the final song of each half is preceded by a contrasting group—three songs of great emotional intensity, to be relieved by the following détente. Pursuing the question further,

I wonder whether it is pure coincidence that a cycle commencing with a song entitled "Liebesbotschaft" now ends with one whose last words are "die Botin treuen Sinns." Indeed, both poems deal with messengers of love: in the first instance, an actual brook; in the second, a metaphorical carrier pigeon.

"Die Taubenpost" is of special interest in connection with the formal classification I have tried to establish. Again, it is somewhat similar to "Abschied," but the resemblance is superficial. The earlier song, despite its alternating key scheme, fits easily into the varied strophic model. "Die Taubenpost" combines strophic, ternary, and through-composed elements in a unique design. In broadest terms, the song consists of four sections, ABA'C, a configuration that suggests a three-part form followed by a coda or expanded by a through-composed development. But the final section sounds like neither alternative. That is because of its unusual relation to the verbal text. Whereas the three preceding sections comprise two poetic stanzas each, section C sets the one remaining stanza twice, the second time as an obvious variation of the first. Moreover, each version ends with a refrain that has already been made familiar at the close of both A and B. That consists of a vocal echo that is both verbal and musical. Accompanied by a characteristic phrase in the piano, it turns a deceptive cadence into an authentic one (for example, in mm. 20–23).

The persistence of that tag encourages one to hear the ternary sections as quasi-strophic (as in "Das Fischermädchen"), but there are signals conflicting with that interpretation. Section A begins with a repeated four-measure phrase; its original statement cadences on the tonic (G major), but its reiteration turns to major III (V of vi). That occasions two measures of pianistic elaboration until the second stanza restores the tonic with an eight-measure period followed by the two-measure tag (mm. 16–25). It is true that section B likewise opens with a repeated four-measure phrase, but its first statement is in G minor, cadencing on V. Its repetition repeats the progression, this time in G major. Thus, whereas the two phrases opening section A began similarly but led to contrasting cadences, those of section B lead from modal contrast to similar cadences. Moreover, the period is succeeded not by a short piano interlude but by a plunge into flat III, a key that persists throughout the section. So when the final phrase of B (mm. 42–47) reverts to a melody identical with its parallel in A (mm. 20–25), it sets up a kind of cognitive dissonance: thematic similarity but tonal contrast.

In general, the harmonic complexity of the second pair of stanzas (section B) accords well with the protagonist's mixed emotions. After the first section's laudatory description of the carrier pigeon, attention now turns to its arrival at the beloved's house. The protagonist imagines the bird's secret gaze, the "scherzend" exchange of greetings, and the bestowal of his "Träne" —shifts in mood underlined by a musical setting that binds the two stanzas together without a break.

A modulation returns us to G major and the slightly varied reprise, as the poem reverts to praise of the pigeon. The final stanza now follows immediately. That is surprising because of the pattern previously established: five measures of piano introduction, four measures of interlude separating B from A, four more preceding A'. But the interlude expected after that reprise fails to materialize. The piano takes over again only at the very end of the song, where five measures of coda balance those of the introduction. Thus section C enters as a continuation of A'. Verbally, the connection is effected by the word "treu," which links the sixth and seventh stanzas. Musically, the tonic of the cadence (m. 71) is extended through a new four-measure phrase, arriving at a new cadence on IV. Only now does the voice pause, in preparation for a striking departure from the smooth melodic style that has hitherto prevailed. Retaining the familiar framework of an eight-measure period plus a two-measure echo, the vocal line is articulated in a unique way. It is broken into fragments separated by one-measure rests—a reflection of the choppy sentence structure of the two concluding lines. Schubert's reiteration of the rhetorical question "Kennt ihr sie?" produces a six-measure palindrome that hovers around the supertonic (major, then minor) before it is resolved by the familiar two-measure cadence with its echo. In this way the two lines are stretched to fill the ten-measure space heretofore occupied by a complete stanza (mm. 77–86).

The harmonic excursions of the last stanza venture even further during its varied repetition, which, like its model, follows its predecessor without a break. This time the extended cadence moves through the minor subdominant to rest on flat VI, a subtle reminder of the flat III that concluded section B. At the same time, the alteration of *E natural* to *E flat* and the ensuing return of *E natural* motivate a new conclusion for the final stanza, one that emphasizes *E natural*. By a tiny variation of detail, it exultantly confirms the identification of the pigeon as "die Botin treuen Sinns" (Ex. 3.11).

Is it just by chance that Schubert produced in this last song an example that resists classification? As I have shown, "Die Taubenpost" incorporates, within an extended ternary design, techniques of strophic articulation, of harmonic variation, and of continuous through-composition. I like to think that the composer, whether consciously or unconsciously, was producing in

Ex. 3.11. "Die Taubenpost"

Schwanengesang his *Die Kunst des Liedes*. If so, "Die Taubenpost" can take its place as a final summary, a cheerful demonstration of his mastery of the craft.

NOTES

1. See, for example, Richard Capell: "Schubert's forms of song are two, the strophic, and the 'durchkomponiert' or, as we might say, continuous, cyclic, onrunning." Capell, *Schubert's Songs*, 66.

2. J. H. Thomas insists that "twelve of the fourteen songs in *Schwanengesang* are of modified strophic type." See Thomas, "Schubert's Modified Strophic Songs," 85. His definition of "modified strophic," however, seems to me too broad to be of discriminatory value.

3. My source for the original poetic texts is *Franz Schubert, Die Texte,* ed. Maximilian and Lilly Schochow.

4. I discuss these possibilities at greater length in an essay titled "'Am Meer' Reconsidered: Strophic, Binary, or Ternary?" In *Schubert Studies,* ed. Brian Newbould (Aldershot: Ashgate, 1998), 112–126.

5. I borrow the term "echo" from Richard Kramer. See his *Distant Cycles,* 108.

6. See Cone, "Poet's Love or Composer's Love?," 177–192.

7. Ibid., 182.

8. In his refrains, Schubert is following cues given by the poet, who ends each stanza with an indefinite "Ade . . . " That is explicitly completed only in the last stanza by a repetition of its opening line. Did Rellstab imply similar endings for the other stanzas as well?

9. J. H. Thomas finds in Schubert's songs a number of instances where flat VI is "associated with the idea of night." See "Schubert's Modified Strophic Songs," 91.

10. See Kerman, "A Romantic Detail," 56–57.

11. See R. Kramer, *Distant Cycles,* 108–109.

12. Georgiades, *Schubert, Musik und Lyrik,* 355–356.

13. Cone, *Composer's Voice,* 40. To the examples adduced there (from "Der Atlas," "Das Fischermädchen," "Ihr Bild," and "Der Doppelgänger") I might add one concealed in "Am Meer," mm. 14–17 and 35–38.

14. Walther Dürr describes the realistic tone-painting here: "In the scenario everything is susceptible of a 'poetic' interpretation: diminished-seventh arpeggios refer to the moist breath of wind, regularly accented chords to the strokes of the oars, tremolos in the bass to the unsteady gliding of the boat." See Dürr, "Schubert's Songs and Their Poetry," 21.

15. Cone, "'Am Meer' Reconsidered." See note 4 above.

16. Compare, for example, Beethoven's *Bagatelle* Op. 126 No. 4. See Cone, "Beethoven's Experiments in Composition: The Late Bagatelles," 97–98.

17. For an extended discussion of this "doubleness," involving both words and music, see Richard Kurth's interesting essay "Music and Poetry, a Wilderness of Doubles: Heine-Nietsche-Schubert-Derrida."

18. Richard Kramer hears the high vocal G of m. 41 resolved by the bass of m. 52 (see Kramer, *Distant Cycles*, 131–132). I find more audible the resolution that preserves both register and vocal color. No doubt both connections are at work.

19. L. Kramer, "The Schubert Lied," 221–222.

20. R. Kramer, *Distant Cycles*, pp. 128–132.

21. Brown, *Schubert*, 306.

CHAPTER 4

Texts and Commentary

MARTIN CHUSID

Such is the spell of your emotional world that it very nearly blinds us to the greatness of your craftsmanship.—*Franz Liszt on Schubert*

In this chapter the individual songs of *Schwanengesang* are treated in the order they are found in the manuscript at the Morgan Library: seven Lieder to texts by Rellstab, six to texts by Heine, and the single setting by Seidl, "Die Taubenpost." Each discussion is preceded by the original German text of the poem, together with an English translation.[1] The translations are not intended for singing; I made them as literal as possible, for the most part providing a line-by-line correspondence. After each poem there follows a brief consideration of the sketches, if available, together with remarks on some of the more important corrections in the autograph. When pertinent there is also a reference to Edward Cone's analysis of the song in Chapter 3. Other topics discussed depend on the nature of the song and both the extent and quality of the literature it has evoked. Generally speaking, there has been far less serious discussion of the Rellstab songs and of "Die Taubenpost" than of the Heine songs. Of these, "Der Doppelgänger," "Die Stadt," and "Ihr Bild" have attracted the most attention. The citations in this chapter are of two sorts. Many are crucial to the subject discussed and appear in the body of the text. Those less critical references that still merit attention are gathered in a section called "From the Literature" following the main discussion of each poem.

By way of introduction I should like to raise some issues often neglected in writings about Schubert's Lieder. First, few commentators remark on the composer's skill at editing the poetry he set. It isn't surprising that Schubert was sensitive to what would (or would not) sound well when sung and that he made changes in many of the verses he used. But it is less inevitable that almost invariably these changes also improved the poetry. Heine, for example, uses the word "Doppel*t*gänger," with the explosive *t* in the middle. Schubert instead chooses the more euphonious "Doppelgänger." For good acoustical reasons his spelling has since become the title of both song and poem, although that version of the word never appears in Heine. (Schubert's title is used because the poet provided no titles for the eighty-eight poems of *Heimkehr* from which the six in *Schwanengesang* were chosen.) The only other change Schubert makes in the six Heine poems he set is to alter "starrte" to "starrt" in the first stanza of "Ihr Bild" (see my discussion later this chapter of this not-so-trivial alteration). In those poems of Rellstab and Seidl he set, Schubert often went beyond altering the spelling or the endings of words. He sometimes changed them completely. The new words are not only more singable, they usually improve the sequence of verbal stresses of the verse. In stanza 5 of "Die Taubenpost," for example, Seidl ends the first line "im Wachen *und* Traum." In spoken and sung German the final *d* of "und" is another explosive *t* sound, as in "Doppeltgänger." Schubert's "im Wachen *im* Traum" is far smoother and sings beautifully. Furthermore, there is no loss in comprehensibility, and there is a distinctly improved rhythmic flow to the final accent of the line of "Traum." An appreciable number of such changes are to be found in Schubert's settings of Rellstab's poems as well, especially the setting of "Abschied."

The second issue to be raised concerns the degree of independence of the music in an art song. For a composer such as Schubert, who was an instrumentalist before he began to sing and who remained an instrumentalist all his life, the music of most of his songs has a high degree of internal logic and will have a purely musical effect on listeners who do not necessarily understand or pay much attention to the words. The factors contributing to this effect are sometimes referred to as the musical design. How important this aspect of vocal composition may be is illustrated by a letter in which Schubert refused a request from Leopold von Sonnleithner to write a vocal ensemble piece for a concert. He said that there was no way of guaranteeing that he would find an appropriate musical form for the composition.[2]

Another area of considerable interest, and in English-speaking countries an area of some controversy as well, is the idea that for musicians brought up in the tradition of major-minor tonality (that is, from about 1680 to today, but especially during the eighteenth and nineteenth centuries), individual keys often have specific affects or associations. Beethoven, for example, described B minor as a "black" key.[3] While analyzing "Auf der Donau," Walther Dürr writes, "It appears that [in this song] Schubert is governed by

distinct affects that are peculiar to individual keys." He continues, in a more
general vein, "Today it is scarcely contested that Schubert allowed himself
to be governed by such [key] affects."[4] In *The Schubert Song Companion* John
Reed puts the same idea another way: "Schubert's instinctive awareness of
the emotional colour of individual keys is an essential part of his genius for
finding the best musical form for a particular text. No student of the songs
can be unaware of the emotional potential in his hands of B minor or A
minor."[5] Reed then goes on to list what he believes to be the characteristics
of each key, followed by a list of Schubert's songs in that key. On his list for
the key of G major are two Lieder from *Schwanengesang*: "Liebesbotschaft,"
which begins the cycle, and "Die Taubenpost," which ends it. Reed describes
G major as "an essentially lyric key associated with love and serenity." An ex-
amination of the more than fifty songs in G major on his list suggests another component almost always present: nature and the countryside that
Schubert loved so well.[6] These often refer to flowing water, as in "Liebesbotschaft," or birds, as in "Die Taubenpost."[7] Another frequent feature of
Schubert's songs in G major is a distance from the beloved (in "Liebesbotschaft" again, and in "An die Entfernte"), or that longing (*Sehnsucht*) so
central to the meaning of "Die Taubenpost." In this regard see also Schubert's setting of Goethe's poem "Sehnsucht." What differentiates the G-major
songs from so many others Schubert wrote about longing or separation is
that the poems set in this key are never accompanied by a sense of betrayal
or frustrated love. The only G-major songs in the song cycle *Die schöne Müllerin*, for instance, are early; they occur well before the maid reveals her
preference for the hunter. It is perhaps not coincidental that there are no
G-major songs in the cycle *Winterreise*, where the betrayal of the protagonist
is made clear from the outset. Finally, Felicitas von Kraus described Schubert's songs in that key as "almost without exception perceptions of nature
and love."[8]

Two other pairs of songs in *Schwanengesang* share keys. "Kriegers Ahnung" and "Die Stadt" are in C minor but otherwise do not particularly resemble each other. In contrast, two songs in B minor—"In die Ferne" and
"Der Doppelgänger—have much in common. As Richard Kramer observes
about these songs,

> B minor is made an element of expression in both the Heine and Rell-
> stab songs, shrewdly positioned in each set, aligned with the poetic in-
> stance of greatest anguish. The key itself acquires topos-like status. . . .
> Whatever *B minor*—in all its specificity and as some abstraction tied in
> with the tonal system and the repertories of music that endow the keys

with their complexity of association and character—can have meant to Schubert, the key itself invades his expressive vocabulary, informing, however subconsciously, all those aspects of the music that, conversely, define the key for us. To put it more aggressively, in the conceiving of the song, the poetic idea and the idea of key belong to the inchoate creative impulse from which the song will emerge.[9]

Although Kramer avoids providing an actual description of the character of the key, others do not. Recall that Beethoven labeled it "black." John Reed provides not only descriptive words or phrases, but also the specific songs in B minor that suggested them: "physical and mental suffering ('Der Leidende,' 'Philoktet'), loneliness ('Einsamkeit'), alienation and derangement ('Der Doppelgänger,' 'Der liebe Farbe')."[10] Walther Dürr, while discussing the B-minor song "Der Unglückliche," suggests related ideas: "lamentation, agitation, awaiting death."[11] These terms, particularly Dürr's, would also seem to fit well the blackest song in *Winterreise*—its conclusion, "Der Leiermann"—when it was in its original key, as well as "Klage" (first line: "Trauer umfliesst mein Leben" [Sorrow floods my life]), likewise in B minor. In her remarks on "Der Doppelgänger," Brigitte Massin also refers to the key of B minor: "For Schubert it is the tragic and despairing key."[12]

Another topic of importance for the composer of vocal music is whether he chooses to reuse portions of the text, and if he does, why? Or, as songs with words, phrases, or lines repeated are far more common than those without, perhaps we should reverse the question and ask: If he does not, why not? This is a particularly relevant query for the Heine songs, where four ("Ihr Bild," "Die Stadt," "Am Meer," and "Der Doppelgänger") do not repeat text. In general, textual repetition is a sign that a composer is solving a problem of musical design.[13] In this regard see Edward Cone's discussion of "Frühlingssehnsucht" and "Der Atlas" in Chapter 3.

The Rellstab Songs

The exact source of the poetry for Schubert's initial group of songs in *Schwanengesang* is not clear (see Chapters 1 and 5). We know, however, that the composer set nine poems by Ludwig Rellstab as songs for voice and piano and a tenth for voice, piano, and horn, "Auf dem Strom," a composition performed at Schubert's successful private concert on 26 March 1828, the anniversary of Beethoven's death. Seven of the solo songs constitute the Rellstab portion of *Schwanengesang*, and an eighth, "Lebensmuth," appears to have been originally planned as the opening song of this group but was discarded.[14] Schubert's setting of the remaining Rellstab poem, "Herbst," is compared below with "Aufenthalt," the fifth Lied in *Schwanengesang*, with which it shares a number of musical characteristics.

Except for Thrasyboulas Georgiadis' analysis of "Liebesbotschaft,"[15] Rufus Hallmark's detailed study of "Auf dem Strom,"[16] and Richard Kramer's chapter "In der Ferne" on the seven Rellstab songs of *Schwanengesang* in his book *Distant Cycles*, the Schubert literature has tended either to overlook or treat superficially the Rellstab settings. By far the most substantial analyses of these songs are to be found in this volume. See especially Chapter 3 by Edward Cone, whose remarks are referred to often in the following commentary.

Liebesbotschaft

Rauschendes Bächlein,
So silbern und hell,
Eilst zur Geliebten
So munter und schnell?
Ach, trautes Bächlein,
Mein Bote sey Du;
Bringe die Grüsse
Des Fernen ihr zu.

All' ihre Blumen
Im Garten gepflegt,
Die sie so lieblich
Am Busen trägt,
Und ihre Rosen
In purpurner Gluth,
Bächlein, erquicke
Mit kühlender Fluth.

Wann* sie am Ufer,
In Träume versenkt,
Meiner gedenkend
Das Köpfchen hängt;
Tröste die Süsse
Mit freundlichem Blick,
Denn der Geliebte
Kehrt bald zurück.

[Message of Love

Rustling brook,
So silvery and bright,
Do you hurry to my loved one
So lively and swift?
Ah, dear brook,
You be my messenger;
Bring her greetings
From the distant one.

All her flowers
Tended in the garden,
Which so sweetly
She wears at her bosom,
And her roses
In crimson glow,
Brook, refresh them
With cooling waves.

When at the bank
She sinks into dreams,
Thinking of me
She hangs her head;
Comfort the sweet one
With friendly gaze,
For her beloved
Soon will return.

*In the first edition of Rellstab's *Gedichte* (Berlin, 1827), this word is "Wenn."

Neigt sich die Sonne   As the sun sets
Mit röthlichem Schein,   With reddish blaze,
Wiege das Liebchen   Rock my darling
In Schlummer ein.   Into slumber.
Rausche sie murmelnd   Murmering, rustle her
In süsse Ruh,   Into sweet repose,
Flüstre ihr Träume   Whisper her dreams
Der Liebe zu.   Of my love.]

For the first poem of his Rellstab group, Schubert chose an optimistic one redolent with images of a benevolent nature and untroubled love. As in his cycle *Die schöne Müllerin,* which also begins cheerfully, and particularly his song "Wohin?" here, too, a brook appears as a trusted friend. A manuscript with sketches of "Liebesbotschaft" and "Frühlingssehnsucht" at the library of the Gesellschaft der Musikfreunde, however, begins with an all-but-complete song, "Lebensmuth." Had Schubert retained his setting of "Lebensmuth," a cheerful song in B-flat major, as the first Lied of his Rellstab set, the parallel with the opening of *Die schöne Müllerin* would have been even stronger:

"Das Wandern," B-flat major   "Lebensmuth," B-flat major
"Wohin?," G major, $\frac{2}{4}$ meter   "Liebesbotschaft," G major, $\frac{2}{4}$ meter

For a discussion of the way Schubert's musical structure follows the stanzaic division of the poem (four stanzas, four sections: ABCA'), see Chapter 3. There is an additional element of interest. The most distant tonal movement in the song occurs in the setting of the third stanza, section C. Here Schubert moves to, stresses, and concludes in B major, tonally speaking a considerable distance from the tonic, G major. The final verse of that stanza reads "Kehrt bald zurück." As the preceding line makes clear, the subject is the protagonist, who "soon will return." This is followed by the final stanza, which begins with the same music as the first and is also in the tonic key, G. Did Schubert intentionally design his return so that the tonic key "Kehrt bald zurück?" Was this, in effect, a musical play on words?[17] Certainly the tonal return from B to G is carried out quickly; during the short retransition the tonicized B-major triad (mm. 48–49) is immediately followed by the dominant and tonic chords in G major (mm. 50–51). There is no intervening harmony, nor are there any intermediate passing tones. Compare the speed of this return with those of "Aufenthalt," "Der Atlas," and "Das Fischermädchen," in each of which a return from B or C-flat major is made to the tonic key for the final section, but with considerably more harmonic motion than here.

In addition to his choice of key, Schubert uses an impressive array of musical devices to suggest the pastoral setting of the poetry. First, note the constant thirty-second-note motion in the keyboard part (generally accepted as an analogue for the flowing brook). Second, echoes, most often an out-of-doors acoustical phenomenon, are heard repeatedly in sections A and A', once again played by the piano.[18] Pairs of horns, the quintessential outdoor instruments, are suggested by the succession of harmonic intervals— major sixth, perfect fifth, and minor third, the so-called horn fifths—in the left hand of the pianist at several points in the song, such as the echo measures 6 and 54. Double pedals in the lowest part of the prelude and elsewhere (mm. 18–21) recall the drone accompaniment of another rustic instrument, the bagpipe. These and other pedals (for example, in mm. 12–17, 18–21, and the postlude) tend to slow the harmonic rhythm, suggesting the relaxed pace associated with life in the country. Recall the similar use of a slow harmonic rhythm in Beethoven's *Pastoral* Symphony.

To reflect the more static quality as the beloved "im Träume versenkt" (sinks into dreams, stanza 3), Schubert applies rhythmic augmentation to the vocal line. That is, the dactylic succession of eighth note followed by two sixteenths, typical of the song as a whole, now becomes quarter note and two eighths.[19] This is coordinated beautifully with a turn to the minor mode following the cadence of section B in C major, to help set off the crucial stanza of the poetry, the third. In this stanza we learn of the reciprocated love of maiden and protagonist, and it closes with his promise to return.

A particularly noteworthy feature of section A and its return as the fourth section, A', is the emphasis melodically on the pitch *b*, the mediant of G major. Whether Schubert planned it consciously or not, the stress on this note serves to foreshadow the most important tonal area of the third section (and stanza), B major. Does the attention paid to the pitch and key of B in "Liebesbotschaft," and such other songs as "Aufenthalt," prepare our ears for the key of what is generally accepted to be the climactic Lied of the Rellstab group, "In der Ferne," B minor-major?[20] Perhaps not by itself, but there are also subsidiary tonal centers of B (= C flat) of importance in the Rellstab set; namely, its dominant (F sharp = G flat) and subdominant (E) appear in other songs and reinforce the tonal association (see also Chapter 5)

Remarks on the Sketch

Although it appears to have been written first, the sketch for "Liebesbotschaft" is compositionally the most advanced of the three remaining sketches for *Schwanengesang*. (The others are for "Frühlingssehnsucht" and

"Die Taubenpost.") Unlike most sketches, this one contains almost no significant deviations from the vocal line of the published "Liebesbotschaft," and the rhythmic motion of the piano part (arpeggiated thirty-second notes) is already set in the first two notated measures. To be sure, the exact pitches of these two keyboard measures were changed later. Furthermore, Schubert laid the sketch out on the page as if he were preparing his autograph. He prepared to use all three staves for every measure, although there is little written on the bottom two, those intended for the piano part. In addition, he leaves an entire brace empty at the beginning of the song for the still-to-be-written prelude. A manuscript arrangement of this sort has been called a "skeleton score." The sequence of events is generally as follows. The most important melodic material (the entire vocal part together with at least the melody of the more important instrumental interludes, as here) is entered first, perhaps from an earlier draft. Then the composer fills in any part of the text omitted previously, and the missing instrumental portions. Finally he adds the tempo, dynamic, and articulation marks, making any necessary alterations and corrections along the way. When this final stage has been completed, the autograph emerges, and the skeleton score has disappeared—unless, as in this case, the composer has for whatever reason abandoned the skeleton score (in effect the incomplete autograph) or portions thereof. Because the written evidence usually vanishes, it is understandable that remarkably little has been written about this important compositional phase until quite recently.[21]

There are two accidental omissions of measures in which the keyboard virtually echoes the voice part, one in the sketch (m. 8) and the other in the autograph (m. 11); both were later corrected by Schubert. The double omission suggests the possibility that at one time there was an early version of the song, perhaps only in the composer's mind as he studied the poetry, in which there were no echoes at all. Singing the vocal part without the echoes, in fact, makes perfectly good musical sense. Yet the regularity of the resultant rhythmic segments is far less interesting than the frequent three-bar phrase units in the final version. In addition, this hypothetical version of the song loses a portion of its pastoral character (the echoes and the suggestion of the horns).

From the Literature

There is a valuable analysis of "Liebesbotschaft" in the book *Schubert: Musik und Lyrik,* by Thrasyboulas Georgiadis. Among other things, he stresses the importance of the doubled note values (rhythmic augmentation) at mm. 32 – 39 and 64ff. In both instances the text refers to dreams. Schubert has brilliantly suggested a new and slower time frame that matches perfectly the reduced activity of the dozing maiden. Specifically the composer augments the two-bar melodic units with their eighth- and sixteenth-note rhythms into four-bar phrases of quarters and eighths.[22]

Georgiades also observes that the second half of Schubert's setting of each long line of text is rhythmically a mirror image of the first.[23]

Because of the exceptions he cites (mm. 38 and 56) and many he doesn't mention (such as the entire third section), I find this observation less useful than others he makes. More to the point, Georgiades notes the predominance of the inherently interesting three-bar rhythmic units in sections A and A', as well as the complete absence of interludes within the setting of stanzas 2 and 3. Finally, he presents a tonal diagram of the song in which two successions of keys or tonicizations by falling thirds are important. In the first (mm. 1–39), the overall harmonic progression is G major–E minor–C major–A minor–F major. In the second (mm. 40–65), it is B major–G major–E minor–C major. With respect to his diagram, Georgiades notes Schubert's use of every scale degree (with the seventh lowered), although observing that the fifth degree, *D*, appears only as the dominant chord in the principal key (mm. 51 and 67). It should be remarked, however, that the pattern of falling thirds suggested by Georgiades is not between equivalent tonal areas. The regions of A minor, F major, and the second C major (m. 64) are extremely brief. In fact they carry little more weight than the tonicized D minor (mm. 26–27) or G-sharp minor (suggested but not confirmed in mm. 44–45) within longer contrasting tonal areas.

Other noteworthy remarks about "Liebesbotschaft" include Alfred Einstein's statements that "the Rellstab songs . . . underline something new: the conversational role of the piano accompaniment. 'Liebesbotschaft' could well take its place in *Die schöne Müllerin* were it not for this new emphasis which transforms it into a concert piece."[24] Felix Salzer included analytical reductions of the song in the second volume of his influential study *Structural Hearing,* unfortunately without commentary or conclusions.[25] Finally, J. H. Thomas, also noting the downward progression of thirds mentioned by Georgiades, believes this "helps to give cogency" and suggests "The balance between control of tonality, accompaniment and freedom of melodic invention creates a song of great lyric, even rhapsodic quality."[26]

Donald Tovey appears to have been the first author to have observed that Schubert set the vocal part of the beloved's dreamy mood in stanza 3 in a tempo twice as slow as the rest of the setting. He focuses, however, on the fact that the *Bächlein*, the keyboard accompaniment, continues with the previous tempo, and he draws a conclusion from the effective combination of the two: "Schubert the song writer is as great a master of movement . . . as Mozart or Beethoven."[27]

Kriegers Ahnung

In tiefer Ruh liegt um mich her
Der Waffenbrüder Kreis;
Mir ist das Herz so bang und
    schwer,
Von Sehnsucht mir so heiss.

Wie hab'ich oft so süss
    geträumt*
An ihrem Busen warm!
Wie freundlich schien des Heerdes
    Gluth,
Lag sie in meinem Arm!

Hier, wo der Flammen† düstrer
    Schein
Ach! nur auf Waffen spielt,
Hier fühlt die Brust sich ganz
    allein,
Der Wehmuth Thräne quillt.

Herz! Dass der Trost Dich nicht
    verlässt!
Es ruft noch manche Schlacht.—
Bald ruh' ich wohl und schlafe fest,
Herzliebste—Gute Nacht!

[Warrior's Premonition

In deep repose around me lies
The circle of comrades-in-arms;
My heart is so fearful and
    heavy,
I burn with such ardent desire.

How often have I so sweetly
    dreamed
Upon her warm bosom!
How friendly shone the hearth's
    glow,
As she lay in my arms!

Here, where the dark luster of the
    flames
Alas! Plays only upon weapons,
Here my heart feels utterly
    alone,
Tears of melancholy spill forth.

Heart! Let solace not
    forsake you!
Many a battle yet calls.—
Soon I'll rest well and sleep deeply,
Dearest beloved—Good night!]

*In Rellstab's *Gedichte*, "geruht."
†In ibid., "Flamme."

Edward Cone indicates that Schubert's formal approach in this song is through-composition, with a reprise of the prelude in the final section (see Chapter 3). He also suggests the presence of an important half-step figure underlying and unifying the Lied (G–A flat–G). A discussion of the poem's meaning (that is, that the "warrior's premonition" is of his own death) may be found in Chapter 6.

My discussion will take as its point of departure the idea that in his mature songs, especially those of the three great cycles, Schubert frequently tends to equate the minor mode with reality, which is usually unpleasant, often painfully so. See, for example, "Gefror'ne Thränen," "Der Stürmische Morgen," or "Der Leiermann" from *Winterreise*. At the same time, the composer often associates the major scale with various types of escape from that reality: in *Winterreise*, examples include memories of past happiness (as in "Der Lindenbaum"), pleasant dreams (as in "Frühlingstraum"), or illusions (witness "Tauschung," which actually means "illusion," and "Die Nebensonnen").[28] Death, the ultimate release from reality, is often viewed benevolently in Schubert's songs,[29] and it is often set in the major mode; sometimes this occurs in brief references, whereas other instances involve complete songs (such as "Das Wirtshaus" (from *Winterreise*), symbolically an inn or rest house for the dead, that is, a cemetery). The most famous example is the passage in which Death speaks during Schubert's almost instantaneously popular song "Death and the Maiden."

Perhaps the best single group of illustrations for this thesis is to be found in *Die schöne Müllerin*, where six of the twenty songs are in minor. Five of these are near the end of the cycle, beginning at the point when the young miller loses his illusions; that is, when he discovers that his lovely maid of the mill cares for another.[30] The incredibly beautiful and deeply satisfying final song of the cycle, "Des Baches Wiegenlied," is in E major and combines two types of escape: the fantasy of the brook as caring companion and death as the ultimate release from an unbearable grief.

The different sections of "Kriegers Ahnung" follow the minor-major dichotomy closely. The prelude and opening section, which share similar accompaniments, are in C minor (mm. 1–28). The text describes a dangerous and unpleasant present, a military encampment and the disturbed feelings of the protagonist. The second section begins in A-flat major and ends in D-flat major (mm. 29–41) as the warrior recalls blessed moments in the past: the many sweet dreams in the arms of his beloved. Thoughts of the present, however, intrude. Flames from the camp's fire gleam on stacked weapons; the key and mode change to F-sharp minor (mm. 44–48). The hero feels completely alone and weeps "tears of melancholy"; the song modulates from F-sharp minor through A minor to F minor (mm. 49–60). As he contemplates the many battles yet to come, the key, meter, and tempo change, but not the mode. The passage moves from C minor to A minor (mm. 61–72). Only when he anticipates death, at the text "Bald ruh' ich wohl und schlafe fest" (Soon I'll rest well and sleep deeply), does the mode change to (the relative) major, C (mm. 73–80). As his thoughts turn to the beloved and he bids her good night, "Herzliebste gute Nacht," first the key of A-flat major returns, and then, on repetition, another major key, this time F (mm. 81–88). The reappearance of words associated with fear and anxiety, and with thoughts of the many battles ahead, leads Schubert to repeat the music in C minor and A minor (mm. 89–99). Once more the premonition of a deep and final sleep returns and is set in C major (mm. 100–107). Again "Herzliebste gute nacht" is set in A-flat major. But the full implications of the protagonist's premonition of forthcoming death demand a more serious conclusion, and there is a return to the song's opening music for the final statements of "Herzliebste gute Nacht" (mm. 112–122).

The most striking alteration in the autograph of "Kriegers Ahnung" concerns the voice line. Schubert reshaped mm. 90–95, originally a repeat of earlier measures (64–67), to save the highest pitch, f' (m. 90), for the climax of the passage (m. 95). Perhaps one of the reasons for the change was the text. The new contour emphasizes the word "manche" of "manche Schlacht" (many battles), in one of which the warrior expects to die.

From the Literature

John Reed suggests that the "isolated accent chord groups [of the opening and close of the song] strike the imagination like a muffled drum beat."[31] Both Walther Vetter and Erdmute Schwarmath hear in this section a "Trauermarsche" (funeral march).[32] Marcel Beaufils goes further and sees in mm. 1–24 a citation from Beethoven's *Eroica*. Certainly the key, C minor, and mood resemble the funeral march of that work, although the meter is triple rather than duple and there is no particular melodic resemblance.[33] Vetter also sees a relationship between this section and the opening of the posthumously published Piano Sonata in C minor (D. 958), probably written shortly after the song.

Because the words "Gute nacht" begin the last stanza of "Des Baches Wiegenlied," the final song of *Die schöne Müllerin,* and the opening song of *Winterreise* is "Gute Nacht," Massin believes that "Kriegers Ahnung" "still seems to prolong the two previous cycles."[34] Others have stressed that this is the last of Schubert's songs to resemble an operatic scena;[35] however, only

E. G. Porter (*The Songs of Schubert*) has gone so far as to call "Kriegers Ahnung" a great but neglected work, "the most varied of the whole set, having
as it does two movements in $\frac{3}{4}$ time, two in $\frac{6}{8}$ and another in common time:
but there are no signs of discontinuity for the middle section in common
time has an accompaniment in triplets which . . . bridges the gulf between
$\frac{3}{4}$ and $\frac{6}{8}$ sections."[36]

In *Distant Cycles* Richard Kramer observes that "at the innermost recesses of the poem—[the third stanza]—the music recedes as well, to remote
regions a tritone from the tonic, and traces in serpentine motion a descent
back to its dominant."[37]

Frühlingssehnsucht[*]	**[Longing in Spring**
Säuselnde Lüfte	Rustling breezes
Wehend so mild,	Blowing so mild,
Blumiger Düfte	My breathing filled
Athmend erfüllt!	With flowery fragrance!
Wie haucht ihr mich wonnig	How blissfully you breathe
begrüssend an!	greetings upon me!
Wie habt ihr dem pochenden	What have you done to my
Herzen gethan?	throbbing heart?
Es möchte Euch folgen auf	It yearns to follow you on airy
luftiger Bahn!	paths!
Wohin?	Where to?
Bächlein, so munter	Brooklet, so lively
Rauschend zumal,	Above all rushing,
Wollen[†] hinunter	Desiring downward
Silbern in's Thal.	Silvery into the vale.
Die schwebende Welle, dort eilt	The floating waves, there
sie dahin!	hurry past!
Tief spiegeln sich Fluren und	Mirrored deep within are
Himmel darin.	meadows and sky.
Was ziehst Du mich, sehnend,	Why do you drag me, longing,
verlangender Sinn,	you demanding senses,
Hinab?	Down there?

[*]In Rellstab's printed *Gedichte*, "Frühlings-Sehnsucht."
[†]In ibid., "Wallen" (undulate). Schubert's "wollen" expresses more desire.

Grüssender Sonne
Spielendes Gold,
Hoffende Wonne
Bringest Du hold.
Wie labt mich Dein selig
    begrüssendes Bild!
Es lächelt am tiefblauen Himmel
    so mild
Und hat mir das Auge mit
    Thränen gefüllt!—
Warum?

Grünend umkränzet
Wälder und Höh'!
Schimmernd erglänzet
Blüthenschnee!
So dränget sich Alles zum
    bräutlichen Licht;
Es schwellen die Keime, die
    Knospe bricht;
Sie haben gefunden was ihnen
    gebricht:
Und Du?

Rastloses Sehnen!
Wünschendes Herz,
Immer nur Thränen,
Klage und Schmerz?
Auch ich bin mir schwellender
    Triebe bewusst!
Wer stillet mir endlich die
    drängende Lust?
Nur Du befreyst‡ den Lenz in
    der Brust,
Nur Du!

Welcoming sun
Playful gold,
Hopeful bliss
You bring graciously.
How your blessed, welcoming
    image refreshes me!
It smiles so gently in the deep
    blue sky
And has filled my eyes with
    tears!—
Why?

Adorned with green
Woods and hills!
Bursting forth shimmering
Snowy blossoms!
So everything presses toward the
    bridal light;
The shoots rise, the buds
    burst;
They have found what they
    lacked:
And you?

Restless longing!
Yearning heart,
Ever only tears,
Laments and sorrow?
I too am conscious of swelling
    impulses!
Who will at last still my pressing
    desires?
Only you can free the Spring in
    my breast,
Only you!]

‡Rellstab's *Gedichte* reads "befreist."

As is clear from the original lineation in the German version above, the structure of Rellstab's poetry is quite complex.[38] Every one of the five stanzas begins with four short lines, followed by three of considerably greater length and concluding either with a single word of two syllables or a pair of words of one syllable each. Cone has explained Schubert's treatment of the five stanzas in strophic form (see Chapter 3): why, within each strophe, the composer chooses to repeat certain lines and not others; how the text is related to the unusual tonal organization of the song (modulations to flat VII and iii within each strophe); how and why the last strophe is altered tonally, with a beginning in the tonic minor; how Schubert handles the poem's rhyme scheme for the first four lines (*abab*); and why the prevailing two- and four-measure rhythmic units do not leave us with a feeling of boredom.

Remarks on the Sketch

An eleven-measure fragment generally believed to belong to "Frühlingssehnsucht" is the shortest of the three extant sketches for *Schwanengesang*.[39] Although there is no title or text, it was identified by Eusebius Mandyczewski, chief editor of the old Complete Edition, who edited the song volumes and first printed the sketch more than one hundred years ago in the *Critical Commentary* to that series (vol. 20, p. 115). The fragment begins with five measures of ⅜ meter in the key of D major; the rhythms of the pitches as well as the meter match quite well with the four short opening lines of the poetry in dactylic dimeter.[40] These opening measures have nothing to do with the melody of "Frühlingssehnsucht" as we know it. (They are transcribed as Ex. 4.2a and are to be found in the discussion of "Ständchen," below.)

The next six measures, however, in common time and tonicizing briefly B minor, do resemble vaguely measures 42–45 in the later version of the song. Both metrically and rhythmically they match adequately the amphibrach tetrameter of the poem's lines 5–7, although not as neatly (syllabically) as did the music of the first part to lines 1–4. Compare Exx. 4.1a and 4.1b.

At the point that he abandoned the fragment, Schubert probably found insurmountable, at least for the moment, two problems. First was how to deal with the final line of the poem's first stanza, the short but important two-syllable question, "Wohin?" This "line" is absent from the sketch, marking the point at which Schubert stopped writing. Second was the question of what to do with the four remaining stanzas of the poem. As each stanza had an identical linear format, the most logical arrangement was to set the poem strophically, and this is what the composer finally did. But the constant shifting between two quite different musical meters would certainly

Ex. 4.1a. "Frülingssehnsucht" (sketch), mm. 6–11

Ex. 4.1b. "Frülingssehnsucht," mm. 42–49

have caused a serious problem for the pacing of the song. The single aspect
of the divergent meters retained in the final version was to contrast systematically a simple (duplet) subdivision of the beat in the voice with a compound (triplet) subdivision in the keyboard part. But the notated meter for
both is the same, $\frac{2}{4}$.

With the two remaining versions of "Frühlingssehnsucht" so different,
it is tempting to hypothesize an intermediate stage, perhaps a continuity
draft (that is, a version of the song with the complete voice part and at least
the melody of the intervening interludes) for the setting of the first and perhaps the last stanza of text. Be that as it may, given that none of the Rellstab
songs are in the same key, Schubert may have dropped the idea of beginning
the set with "Lebensmuth," a song in B-flat major, at the same time he
changed to that key for "Frühlingssehnsucht." Although there is practically
nothing of the opening measures of the sketch remaining in the final version, I think that a number of the ideas in that fragment reverberated in
Schubert's mind while he was composing the next song, "Ständchen." For a
fuller discussion see the next section.

There is no external evidence as to when Schubert decided to interpose
"Kriegers Ahnung" between "Liebesbotschaft" and "Frühlingssehnsucht,"
but it may well have been after he finished "Frühlingssehnsucht" and realized how much it had in common with "Liebesbotschaft." Both songs begin
with melodies that stress the third scale degree in the major mode, and their
fundamental melodic motion is stepwise. Because the meter of the poetry

for all of "Liebesbotschaft" and the first four lines of "Frühlingssehnsucht"
are dactylic, Schubert set them with almost identical and oft-repeated
rhythms. The differing tempos (Ziemlich langsam for "Liebesbotschaft" and
Geschwind for "Frühlingssehnsucht") account for the different note values,
but the aural result is much the same.

Furthermore, there are keyboard echoes in both songs during which the
accompanist plays pairs of notes in the left hand suggesting the harmony of
hunting horns (that is, with a perfect fifth often heard between a sixth and a
third). In m. 8 of "Liebesbotschaft" and mm. 21–22 of "Frühlingssehnsucht"
the pattern ascends (sixth–perfect fifth–third). In "Frühlingssehnsucht" the
horn fifths are to be found almost everywhere (for example, mm. 11–12, 17–21,
31–38, and 43–44).[41] It is quite possible that Schubert decided to interpolate
a song of a completely different character to make the similarities between
the two songs less obvious.[42] It seems significant that the similarities between
"Liebesbotschaft" and "Frühlingssehnsucht" did not exist in the sketch versions, that is, when they were positioned sequentially in the same manuscript.

From the Literature

While discussing "Frühlingssehnsucht," John Reed remarks, "If the Heine
songs seem to begin, emotionally speaking, at the point where *Winterreise*
ends, the tone and texture of the Rellstab songs frequently remind us of *Die
schöne Müllerin*. Most of all perhaps this one, where the strophic form is so
beautifully matched with the words . . . and where the move into minor for
the last verse recalls the heartache of 'Thränenregen.'"[43]

Ständchen	**[Serenade**
Leise flehen meine Lieder	Gently my songs implore
Durch die Nacht zu Dir;	You through the night;
In den stillen Hain hernieder,	Into the quiet grove below,
Liebchen, komm' zu mir!	Dearest, come to me!
Flüsternd schlanke Wipfel	Whispering, slender treetops
rauschen	rustle
In des Mondes Licht;	In the light of the moon;
Des Verräthers feindlich	Fear not the hostile
Lauschen	eavesdropping
Fürchte, Holde, nicht.	of betrayers, my lovely.

Hörst die Nachtigallen schlagen?	Do you hear the nightingales sounding?
Ach! sie flehen Dich,	Ah! They are imploring you,
Mit der Töne süssen Klagen	With the notes of sweet lament
Flehen sie für mich.	They are imploring you for me.
Sie verstehn des Busens Sehnen,	They know the bosom's longing,
Kennen Liebesschmerz,	Understand the pain of love,
Rühren mit den Silbertönen	Touch with their silvery tones
Jedes weiche Herz.	Each tender heart.
Lass auch Dir die Brust* bewegen,	Let them move your breast as well,
Liebchen, höre mich!	Dearest, listen to me!
Bebend harr' ich Dir entgegen!	Trembling, I await your coming!
Komm', beglücke mich!	Come, make me glad!]

Edward Cone's discussion of "Ständchen" (Chapter 3) takes as a point of departure its modified strophic construction (AAB). He then focuses on the many keyboard echoes and traces their development in the course of the song.

It may prove useful now to return to the idea advanced during the discussion of "Kriegers Ahnung," namely, that in his songs Schubert frequently tends to equate the minor mode with an often unpleasant reality, and the major mode with some form of illusory happiness, be it past, present, or future. In the first four Lieder of the Rellstab group, the relationship between the protagonist and his beloved is either positive (as in "Liebesbotschaft" and the A-flat-major section of "Kriegers Ahnung") or at least hopeful ("Frühlingssehnsucht" and "Ständchen"). But increasingly in the poems of these last two songs there are indications of insecurity. Recall the drawing downward into the depths of the stream in stanza 2 of "Frühlingssehnsucht" —perhaps an echo by Rellstab of Wilhelm Müller's poem "Des Baches Wiegenlied."[44] Did the negative implications of this thought justify Schubert's momentary turn to D minor while setting the repetition of the penultimate line of text in all five strophes? Or, perhaps, did they suggest to Schubert the A-flat-minor half-cadence for the ending text of the first four strophes? See also the inexplicable tears in stanza 3. The highest degree of

*Rellstab, *Gedichte:* "das Herz." Schochow, p. 74, does not indicate Schubert's substitution of "die Brust."

insecurity is evident both in poetry and song during the final strophe. Schubert sets the affective lines "Rastloses Sehnen!/Wünschendes Herz/Immer nur Tränen/Klage und Schmerz?" both in minor and major. Why? The very real longing, tears, and pain with which the verse begins are expressed in B-flat minor. The hope that they will be overcome by the positive response of the beloved ("Wünschendes Herz") is set in D-flat major. Never mind, for the moment, that this hope is shown to be illusory in the last three Rellstab songs. The intense desire for happiness, for "den Lenz in der Brust," is in part depicted by Schubert with the B-flat-major setting of mm. 132–135, the doubt by the repetition in D minor, mm. 136–139. The desire for happiness is, perhaps, reflected by the momentarily tonicized E-flat major (the "Nur du" of mm. 139–140), the doubt by the introduction of the pitch G *flat*, a minor third for that chord (lowered sixth degree in B-flat major) in m. 141 and again in m. 147, undercutting what otherwise would have been an overly cheerful ending in B-flat major. I suggest that this final strophe is one of the finest examples of Schubert's exquisite sensitivity to the emotional nuances of a poetic text in his last songs.

Schubert handles brilliantly a similar oscillation between insecurity (that is, reality, in minor) and hope (in major) during "Ständchen." The song begins in D minor, suggesting the very real longing of the serenader. The first musical period ends in a hopeful F major with the text "Liebchen, komm' zu mir." Similarly, the second period begins in minor, with a reality-oriented description of the rustling in the tall treetops by the light of the moon. The repetition of the symbolically positive—at least for lovers—moonlight turns again to F major, and the final lines of hopeful reassurance (that is, a plea to ignore the unpleasant onlookers) closes positively, even gloriously in D major. The interlude introduces the same lowered sixth degree borrowed from the minor mode that Schubert had used so successfully to imply doubt at the end of "Frühlingssehnsucht." During the second strophe the reference to the ostensibly realistic sounds of the nightingales begins again in D minor. Their imaginary pleading on behalf of the serenading lover is set in F major. The reference to the hero's very real "Busens Sehnen" and "Liebesschmerz" is again in D minor; the repetition of the nightingale's imaginary ability to know "Liebesschmerz" is a brilliant evocation of the bittersweet quality of love's desire. Hopefully, therefore in major, the sweet tones of the nightingales will touch the beloved's "weiche Herz."

During the final section the hopeful pleading ("Lass auch Dir die Brust bewegen") is sung in D major with touches of insecurity reflected in the lowered sixth degrees (B flats), heard as rhythmically weak neighboring notes in the accompanist's left hand (mm. 29–31). The hero then sings in B minor of

his real trembling ("Bebend") as he awaits his beloved, and once more (hopefully) urges her to "Komm', beglücke mich," in D major, to close the serenade. The chromatic descent through F natural (the critical lowered third
degree of minor) by the keyboard (m. 41), and the introduction again of the
lowered sixth (voice, m. 42; keyboard, mm. 42 and 45) suggest for the last
time the insecurity felt by the protagonist. What a difference from the assured D major of Don Giovanni's "Serenade" by Mozart, offered as a distant
model for the Schubert piece by John Reed.[45]

I wonder if the motive embodying the movement from dominant to
lowered sixth degree and back, suggested by Edward Cone as the underlying motive for "Kriegers Ahnung," is not heard subliminally by listeners to
the Rellstab songs as related, however distantly, to the similar motion in
"Frühlingssehnsucht" at the end of the first four strophes (A-flat minor,
5–flat 6–5) and only partially presented at the end of the fifth strophe (E flat
major, flat 6–5), as well as in the opening triplet of "Ständchen" (D minor,
5–flat 6–5)? Does this melodic fragment function as a kind of loosely unifying musical thread undercutting hope or, at the least, suggesting insecurity in the second, third, and fourth of the Rellstab songs? In this way isn't the
listener prepared, at least to some extent, for the suffering of the protagonist
in "Aufenthalt" and "In der Ferne"?

There may be yet another link between "Ständchen" and "Frühlingssehnsucht." In the introduction to Schubert, 'Schwanengesang': Facsimiles . . .
and Reprint (New Haven: Yale University Press, 2000), the suggestion is
made that the discarded ⅜ section of the sketch fragment for "Frühlingssehnsucht" may have influenced Schubert in composing "Ständchen," with
regard to the tonal center (D) and the rhythmic shape of the melody as well.
See Exx. 4.2a and 4.2b.

Ex. 4.2a. "Frülingssehnsucht" (sketch), mm. 1–5

Säuselnde Lüf - te   we-hend so mild.   blu-mi- ger Düf - te   atmender- füllt!

Ex. 4.2b. "Ständchen," mm. 5–8

Lei - se fle - hen mei - ne Lie - der   durch   die Nacht zu   dir,

From the Literature

There is remarkably little substantive writing in the Schubert literature about "Ständchen," unquestionably the best-loved and most frequently performed song in *Schwanengesang*. Typical are the remarks of E. G. Porter, who sees in the "Serenade" the "ecstatic joy and pain of love." He affirms, "The whole . . . has . . . a wonderful clarity combined with a genius for avoiding the obvious."[46]

Aufenthalt	[**Resting Place**
Rauschender Strom,	Raging river,
Brausender Wald,	Roaring forest,
Starrender Fels	Upright rocks
Mein Aufenthalt.	My resting place.
Wie sich die Welle	As breaker
An Welle reiht,	Follows on breaker,
Fliessen die Thränen	My tears flow
Mir ewig erneut.	Ever renewed.
Hoch in den Kronen	High in the treetops
Wogend sich's regt,	Surging, stirring,
So unaufhörlich	So unceasingly
Mein Herze schlägt.	Pounds my heart.
Und wie des Felsen	And, as of the rocks'
Uraltes Erz,	Primeval ore,
Ewig derselbe	Ever the same
Bleibet mein Schmerz.	Remains my grief.
Rauschender Strom,	Raging river,
Brausender Wald,	Roaring forest,
Starrender Fels	Upright rocks
Mein Aufenthalt.	My resting place.]

   In Chapter 3 Edward Cone explains the correlation between the poem's five stanzas, of which the first and last are identical, and the arch structure of the music, ABCB'A'. He remarks that further symmetry is provided by the near equivalence of the keyboard prelude and postlude.

   After "Ständchen," "Aufenthalt" is the most popular of the Rellstab songs;

it is also the most exciting song of the group of seven. As Richard Kramer suggests, following the increased closeness of "Frühlingssehnsucht" and "Ständchen," "in 'Aufenthalt' comes the catastrophe."[47] One of the reasons for the song's excitement is the consistent conflict between the duple subdivision of the voice as well as the pianist's left hand when performing the melody, and the constantly repeated triplet chords of the pianist's right hand. The result is a never-ending clash between two meters, $\frac{2}{4}$ and $\frac{6}{8}$. Richard Capell's advice to singers paints a vivid picture: "In performance it is important to preserve the squareness of the $\frac{2}{4}$ subjects against the unceasing triplets —to maintain one's foothold, so to say, against the beating of wind and rain."[48] The driving poetry also contributes to the excitement. Rellstab's short lines consist primarily of downbeat dactyls that recall the first four lines of each stanza in "Frühlingssehnsucht." Here, however, there is no shift to another meter or longer lines later in each stanza, as in the earlier poem.

Kramer writes at some length of the unexpected and sustained C-minor triad in the final strain of the song (mm. 124–127). He describes it as brutal, as "the most portentous of . . . all those signals that flash back and forth from one song to the next . . . a harmony without antecedent—with no apparent justification, no syntactic cover. . . . A non sequitur, its symbolic aspect brazenly displayed, [it] sounds forth in isolation as if to seek a cognate, a referent. The opening bars of 'Kriegers Ahnung' spring to mind."[49] This is exciting writing and a tempting explanation for the seemingly inexplicable sonority. But I wonder if the progression of which it is a part (I–flat VI–V) isn't the harmonic equivalent, and indeed an intensification, of the same melodic motive (5–flat 6–5) that Cone suggested as crucially important in "Kriegers Ahnung," and which may also be observed, if less prominently, in "Frühlingssehnsucht" and "Ständchen." In "Aufenthalt" the motion from scale degree flat 6 to 5 occurs melodically during the prelude (mm. 5–6), is embedded structurally in the melodic line at mm. 19–20, and appears more obviously in the bass melody at mm. 12–13 and 20–21 (see Ex. 4.3, with the important pitches marked by Xs). Melodic ideas with the same half-step descent are also important during the second and fourth sections (mm. 33–34, 44–45, 88–89, and 99–100).

Perhaps the most unusual feature of "Aufenthalt" is the degree to which it contrasts with all the earlier songs in the Rellstab group. This contrast mirrors the sequence of the poetry, the abrupt change from the (relatively) positive tone of the hopeful lover in "Frühlingssehnsucht" and "Ständchen" to the despair of "Aufenthalt." There are two parallel and related strains of thought in the poem: the first external (nature at its harshest), the other internal (the equally unrelenting pain afflicting the protagonist, including his

Ex. 4.3. "Aufenthalt," mm. 7–14

ever-flowing tears, unceasing pounding of the heart, and never-ending grief). And Schubert paints a remarkably vivid musical picture of this duality by writing what amounts to a duet between the voice and the left hand of the keyboard. The lower part, the bass, begins and ends the song with its longest and most sustained melody. In fact, throughout the song the bass provides (or doubles) much of the song's melodic interest as well as furnishes the harmonic direction, especially during the modulations of the interludes between sections. Reflecting one of the important ways in which duets develop, during the first section and its return later, the bass and voice engage in a contrapuntal dialogue in which the melodic ideas of the voice and bass overlap (see Ex. 4.3).

During the more homophonic second and fourth sections the bass emerges with an equivalent voice only during the final phrase (mm. 43–57 and 98–102). In the third section the two parts sing together, essentially doubling each other until the harmonic needs of the cadences momentarily separate them (mm. 62–63 and 74–76). The final section is much like the first, with contrapuntal interplay continuing into the unexpected C-minor triad discussed earlier. After the resolution of that chord to the dominant, the voice sings for its final phrase a shortened version of the bass melody of the prelude and postlude.

The importance of the duet between bass and voice brings to mind another setting by Schubert of a Rellstab poem, "Herbst," composed in April 1828, therefore in all probability not long before "Aufenthalt."[50] No doubt the similarity of the mood of the two poems, unrelenting darkness, led Schubert to adopt many of the musical features of "Herbst" for "Aufenthalt." The essence of the earlier poem, which is organized into three groups of two stanzas each, is that the blossoms of life have faded, the hopes of life have fallen away, and the roses of love have died. The parallelism of thoughts led Schubert to compose the song in strictly strophic fashion. But structure aside—the palindrome of "Aufenthalt" is more interesting—the many musical similarities are worthy of note. Both songs are in E minor, with the choice of mode reflecting a bitter reality. Given the strophic repetitions of the music and the four beats to the measure (that is, the $\frac{12}{8}$ meter of "Herbst" as opposed to the two beats to the bar of "Aufenthalt"), the two songs are of approximately equivalent duration. (To be sure, "Aufenthalt" is somewhat quicker, but it has a few more measures than "Herbst.") The right hand of each consists of repeated chords (repeated and broken in "Herbst"), which continue from the first note of the song to the last in a compound subdivision of the beat. Both songs begin and end softly. But it is the elevation of the keyboard left hand to duet status that provides the most striking similarity. A melody in the bass provides the prelude and postlude of "Herbst," and there is a contrapuntal alternation with overlapping of voice and bass through most of the song. In retrospect, "Aufenthalt" has a more interesting variety of duet textures (for example, the doubling of parts in the middle section), is more concise, and has more exciting melodic material; and its palindromic structure allows for greater variety then does the strophic form of "Herbst." Whereas "Herbst" is a very good song, "Aufenthalt" is superb. But I suspect that "Aufenthalt" would not have been as successful without Schubert's experience composing "Herbst."

In der Ferne
Wehe dem Fliehenden,
Welt hinaus ziehenden!—
Fremde durchmessenden,
Heimath vergessenden,
Mutterhaus hassenden,

[**Far Away**
Woe to those fleeing,
Setting out into the world!—
Traversing foreign places,
Forgetting their native land,
Hating their family home,

Freunde verlassenden,	Forsaking their friends,
Folget kein Segen, ach!	Alas, no blessing follows them
Auf ihren Wegen nach!	On their way!

Herze, das sehnende,	Heart, yearning,
Auge, das thränende,	Eyes, tearing,
Sehnsucht, nie endende,	Longing, never ending,
Heimwärts sich wendende!	Homeward turning!
Busen, der wallende,	Breast, seething,
Klage, verhallende,	Lament, fading,
Abendstern, blinkender,	Evening star, gleaming,
Hoffnungslos sinkender!	Hopelessly descending!

Lüfte, ihr säuselnden,	Breezes, whispering,
Wellen sanft kräuselnden,	Waves, gently ruffling,
Sonnenstrahl, eilender,	Sunbeams, hastening,
Nirgend verweilender:	Nowhere lingering:
Die mir mit Schmerze, ach!	Alas, to her who with grief
Dies treue Herze brach—	Broke this faithful heart—
Grüsst von dem Fliehenden	Greetings from the fleeing one
Welt hinaus ziehenden!	Setting out into the world!]

In Chapter 3 Edward Cone describes the modified strophic structure of "In der Ferne," four strophes of music for three stanzas of text (the last is repeated). He notes that each strophe moves further afield and that strophes 3 and 4 begin in major. Cone also identifies a recurring rhythmic figure in the music that matches the prevailing dactylic dimeter of the poetry.

Also noteworthy is Schubert's emphasis on the dominant, both as a scale degree and as a sonority in the prevailing key of B minor or B major. Joseph Kerman, for example, observes of "In der Ferne," "An introduction all on the dominant . . . is a great rarity in [songs by] Schubert."[51] One might add that the striking *fzp* triple-octave *F sharp*, the dominant, with which the prelude begins, is a dramatic stroke more reminiscent of the openings to overtures by Beethoven or Schubert himself than to openings of songs. Recall, for example, Beethoven's overtures to *Coriolanus*, *Leonore* No. 3, and *Egmont*,[52] as well as Schubert's early Overture for String Quintet in C minor (D. 8), or the overture to his opera *Claudine von Villa Bella* (D. 264).

During the prelude to "In der Ferne," Schubert effectively elaborates the dominant with movement to the lowered sixth degree and back (*F sharp–G–F sharp*). Cone noted that melodic ideas incorporating motion from 5 to flat 6 and back were of primary significance in "Kriegers Ahnung" (see Chapter 3), and this figure, or a portion of it (that is, flat 6–5) was also present to a lesser extent in "Frühlingssehnsucht," "Ständchen," and "Aufenthalt." Here it is not only critical for the prelude—which recurs twice more in the song—but is also present in the melodic line at the beginning of the first two strophes (m. 9, and with the lowered sixth highlighted by an ornament in m. 38).

Because of Schubert's emphasis on the dominant, there is an almost chant-like stress on that degree in the opening vocal phrases of the first strophe (mm. 8–12 and 13–16). In addition, there is a dominant pedal either in an upper voice or the bass, or both, for those same nine bars. It is almost as if a narrator or prophet were issuing a warning. In the second strophe the tone of the text becomes more personal and the voice part becomes more interesting; the melody is varied with ideas taken from the right hand of the keyboard in the first strophe. As a result, the voice stresses the fifth degree melodically somewhat less, but the dominant pedal remains. The vocal line at the beginning of the third strophe resembles that of the second strophe, but in major. For the moment, harsh reality gives way to "Breezes, whispering, / Waves, gently ruffling, / Sunbeams, hastening." However, the dominant pedal in upper part or bass is still important (mm. 66–73), and *F sharp* remains the fulcrum for the melody in mm. 66–69. As the poem focuses on the reason for the protagonist's painful departure, "to her who, with grief / Broke this faithful heart," the music returns to minor. The last strophe differs considerably from the previous three. Although repeating the complete text of stanza 3, musically it draws only from the second half of the strophe. As a result, there is no particular emphasis on the dominant. But a modulation to G-sharp minor (relative of B major) results momentarily in a melodic line incorporating motion from 5 to flat 6 and back (mm. 102–103, repetition in mm. 104–105). The threefold musical emphasis (the rhythmic patterns described by Cone, the melodic pattern of 5–flat 6–5, and the melodic and harmonic emphasis on the dominant) would seem to reflect the poem's single-minded subject, the agony of the departed protagonist.

Among a number of interesting corrections that Schubert made in the autograph of this song is the change from an octave *f sharp + f sharp'*, the dominant, to *g + g'*, the lowered sixth degree (m. 3 tied over to m. 4).[53] It would seem that Schubert introduced the figure 5–flat 6–5 into the prelude at a relatively late stage in the compositional process, that is, while preparing his autograph (perhaps for the printer).[54] The timing of the addition suggests that Schubert may have consciously introduced a cyclic element.

Another correction in the autograph opens a topic that has drawn more attention in the Schubert literature than it probably deserves. The subject

Ex. 4.4. "In der Ferne" (orig.), mm. 15–18

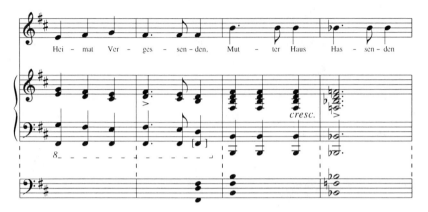

is the parallel fifths and octaves caused by the progression from a B-minor to a B–flat–major chord in mm. 17–18, and, with a different vocal line, the same chord succession in mm. 47–48. The progression bothered G. W. Fink in his review of the original edition of *Schwanengesang* in the *Allgemeine Musikalische Zeitung* in 1829.[55] Without access to the autograph, he and later commentators could not realize that Schubert had already made a signifi-cant change in that document at this point.[56] In the keyboard left hand at m. 16, Schubert originally had begun to write in the autograph three octave *F sharps,* as he did write before corrections in parallel m. 45. Had he left them, there would have been another set of parallel octaves (mm. 16–17) or direct fifths (mm. 45–46) to worry about (Ex. 4.4).

As the example indicates, originally there were potential parallel octaves between the *f sharps* of the voice part and keyboard bass as well as potential direct fifths in the keyboard part of mm. 16–17. To be sure, there was no change of harmony, rather a movement from a tonic chord in second in-version to one in root position, but the effect would have been harmonically weak, and Schubert made the change both here and in the analogous posi-tion in the second strophe (m. 45). The sensitivity to the harmonic weakness of parallel or direct perfect intervals displayed at this point makes the effect of mm. 17–18, the chromatic movement down by half step with both par-allel octaves (voice and bass) and fifths (keyboard), even more striking. It is clear that Schubert very much wanted that chromatic progression with the resultant parallelisms, as well as the modulation to a distant key (D minor), and the text explains it all. For someone like Schubert, who loved his fam-ily and friends very much, the text "Mutterhaus hassenden,/Freunde ver-lassenden" was shocking in the extreme, and the situation demanded music equally shocking. There are, however, two linear elements that give the passage a strong sense of continuity: the chromatically descending bass (*B* to *F sharp*, mm. 17–24) and the retention of the pitch *d* (mm. 17–20), which begins as mediant in B minor, remains as the third of the B-flat chord, then functions as the tonic of D minor, which in turn becomes D major.

From the Literature

For an extended discussion of the interest shown in Schubert's parallel progression, including that of Johannes Brahms, see the opening pages of Richard Kramer's chapter "In der Ferne" from his book *Distant Cycles.*

Reed feels that "'In der Ferne' is the most deeply felt of the Rellstab songs," and he compares it with "Der Doppelgänger" in this regard. He also sees in the "rhythmic irregularities of the middle section, the persistent juxtaposition of 3 against 4 . . . a sort of rhythmical disorientation analogous perhaps with the wanderer's distraught state of mind."[57] That both songs are in the same key, B, is another factor worthy of note.

After suggesting that the "underlying poetic idea could have come from the *Winterreise,*" Dietrich Fischer-Dieskau is bothered by the point of the poem: "Woe to the disappointed lover who leaves his homeland in a fit of temper." He feels that it trivializes the powerful relationship suggested in the song.[58]

Finally, E. G. Porter firmly believes that "Kriegers Ahnung" and "In der Ferne" are "two of the most neglected songs of this volume," and he says of "In der Ferne": "The harmonies are highly original, and the placing of four notes against three, and the three against two in the accompaniment give the great sense of restlessness that the poem requires."[59]

Abschied	**[Departure**
Ade, Du muntre, Du fröhliche Stadt, Ade!	Adieu, you lively, you frolicsome town, Adieu!
Schon scharret mein Rösslein mit lustigem Fuss;	With playful feet, already my horse paws the ground;
Jetzt nimm ich den* letzen, den scheidenden Gruss.	I offer now my last, my parting salute.

*Rellstab's *Dichtung* reads "meinen" in place of Schubert's "ich den," Schochow, 476. Schochow mistakenly attributes "noch den," a reading of the first edition, to Schubert. I see no reason to overrule Schubert, as does *Neue Schubert-Ausgabe,* series IV, vol. 14a, 133.

Du hast mich wohl niemals noch[†] traurig gesehen,	Indeed you have never seen me sorrowful,
So kann es auch jetzt nicht beim Abschied geschehn.	Nor shall it come to pass at parting.
Ade . . .	Adieu . . .

Ade, Ihr Bäume, Ihr Gärten so grün, Ade!	Adieu, you trees, you garden so green, Adieu!
Nun reit' ich am silbernen Strome entlang,	I ride now longside the silvery stream,
Weit schallend ertönet mein Abschiedsgesang;	My farewell song sounding far and wide;
Nie habt Ihr ein trauriges[‡] Lied gehört,	You have never heard a sorrowful song,
So wird Euch auch keines beim Scheiden beschert.	Nor will any be bestowed at parting.
Ade . . .	Adieu . . .

Ade, Ihr freundlichen Mägdlein[§] dort, Ade!	Adieu, you friendly maiden there, Adieu!
Was schaut Ihr aus blumenum- duftetem Haus	Why do you gaze from flow'r- perfumed house
Mit schelmischen, lockenden Blicken heraus?	With roguish, enticing glances?
Wie sonst, so grüss' ich und schaue mich um,	As before, I greet her and gaze about,
Doch nimmer[‖] wend'ich mein Rösslein um.	Yet never do I turn my horse around.
Ade . . .	Adieu . . .

Ade, lieber Sonne, so gehst Du zur Ruh', Ade!	Adieu, dear sun, so go you to rest, Adieu!
Nun schimmert der blinkenden Sterne Gold.	Now the twinkling star gleams golden.

[†]Rellstab's *Dichtung* reads "nimmermehr" in place of Schubert's "niemals noch," Scho- chow, 476.

[‡]Rellstab's *Dichtung* reads "klagendes" in place of Schubert's "trauriges," ibid.

[§]Rellstab's *Dichtung* reads "Mägdelein," ibid.

[‖]Rellstab's *Dichtung* reads "nimmermehr," ibid.

Wie bin ich Euch Sternlein am
  Himmel so hold;
Durchziehn# die Welt wir auch
  weit und breit,
Ihr gebt überall uns das treue
  Geleit.
Ade . . .

Ade, Du schimmerndes
  Fensterlein hell, Ade!
Du glänzest so traulich mit
  dämmerndem Schein
Und ladest so freundlich ins
  Hüttchen uns ein.
Vorüber, ach, ritt ich so manches
  mal
Und wär' es denn heute zum
  letzten mal?
Ade . . .

Ade, Ihr Sterne, verhüllet Euch
  grau! Ade!
Des Fensterlein** trübes,
  verschimmerndes Licht
Ersetzt Ihr unzähligen Sterne
  mir nicht;
Darf ich hier nicht weilen, muss
  hier vorbei,
Was hilft es,†† folgt Ihr mir
  noch so treu!
Ade, Ihr Sterne, verhüllet Euch
  grau! Ade!

As I do, you starlet in the heavens,
  so lovely;
We too pass through the world
  far and wide,
You provide us everywhere a
  faithful guard.
Adieu . . .

Adieu, you glimmering window
  bright, Adieu!
You gleam so cozy with
  dusky light
And into your cottage invite
  us so kindly.
I ride past, alas, so many
  times
And today, will it then be
  the last?
Adieu . . .

Adieu, you stars, veil yourselves
  gray! Adieu!
The dim glimmering light from
  the window
Does not displace for me your
  countless stars;
I dare not here tarry, I must here
  pass,
Of what help that you follow
  me so faithfully!
Adieu, you stars, veil yourselves
  gray! Adieu!]

Rellstab's *Dichtung* reads "Durchziehen," ibid., 477.
** Rellstab's *Dichtung* reads "Fensterleins," ibid.
†† Rellstab's *Dichtung* reads "hilft es *mir*," ibid.

According to Edward Cone (Chapter 3), the structure of the poem (six stanzas similarly formed) calls for some type of strophic arrangement. He takes the text as his point of departure and justifies Schubert's setting of stanzas 1, 3, and 5 in the key of E flat (tonic), the musical variation and key of A flat (subdominant) for stanzas 2 and 4, and the somewhat different treatment for the final strophe, which begins in the distant key of C-flat major. Cone also points to Schubert's consistent repetition of the text of line 5. Line 4 of the sixth strophe is also repeated, but not with identical music.

Considering the dark tone of "Aufenthalt" and "In der Ferne," the relatively lighthearted departure depicted in "Abschied" appears to reflect a conscious decision by Schubert to provide contrast; that is, to close his Rellstab group with a bright song, somewhat in the character of a rondo finale of a serious instrumental work. Whereas the key of E-flat major as tonic of a song in this set is new, the tonality relates to two previous Rellstab Lieder. It is the relative major of C minor, the key of "Kriegers Ahnung," and the subdominant of B-flat major, the tonic of "Frühlingssehnsucht." As Richard Kramer has pointed out, the C-flat-major section that begins the final strophe of "Abschied" is "prolonged, tonicized, and made more substantial than seems justifiable in the song itself, where C flat has otherwise no role to play. It evokes a nostalgia for those past musics in B major, no matter that Rellstab's lines here might bear only the faintest poetic relevance to the passages in 'Liebesbotschaft,' 'Ständchen,' and 'In der Ferne' awakened in this music."[60] In similar fashion, the A-flat sections of the song (the second and fourth strophes) may resonate, if faintly, with the passages in that key in "Kriegers Ahnung" (mm. 28ff. and 108ff.) and with the cadences in A flat (major and minor) present so strikingly in each of the strophes of "Frühlingssehnsucht" (mm. 38ff., 50ff., and *passim*).

The idea of presenting a cheerful song as a contrast to darker songs in close proximity may have been taken by Schubert from *Winterreise,* where "Die Post," a decidedly bright song in the same key (E-flat major), begins book 2 in the first edition as the thirteenth of twenty-four songs. It may not be purely coincidental that Haslinger was the original publisher of both *Winterreise* and *Schwanengesang.* And it was "Abschied," seventh of fourteen songs, that furnished the first song of book 2 in the original edition of the posthumously published cycle. There is little evidence in support of this notion, but was Schubert combining the Rellstab and Heine songs in the autograph with a view to publication by Haslinger, identified by Walther Dürr as the most careful publisher of the composer's at this stage of his life?[61] Schubert's choice of E flat for "Die Post" and "Abschied," two songs in which travel—in those days naturally by horse—is important, may signify something of a tradition in similar situations. The key of Beethoven's Piano Sonata Op. 81a, published at the time as "Les Adieux," is also E flat, and with the frequency of the word "Ade" (adieu) in the poem "Abschied," the key of the sonata may have been in back of Schubert's mind when he composed the song.[62]

The most significant of the changes in the autograph relate to the vocal line. In m. 24 Schubert improved the melodic line by raising the final note from *g'* to *c"*, and in m. 95 by lowering the tessitura considerably. He altered repeated *e flat"*s on the second beat to *b flat'*s and dropped the final *e flat"* an octave. As a result, an arpeggiated ascent to the same pitch in the next measure—the text is "weit und breit"—stands out wonderfully.

From the Literature

Marius Flothuis reports that "the German 'Ade' stands in folk poetry for 'adieu' and traditionally was sung on a rising fourth." He cites as his example "Schubert's song 'Abschied,' D. 957/7, which starts with the word 'Ade,' sung on a rising fourth."[63]

Brian Newbould remarks, "One should not look for a metronomically apt 'trot' in the relentless staccato jog of this song. As often, the accompaniment, and the simple and rather square snatches of tune, take hold of the mind, however ordinary the ingredients."[64]

The Heine Songs

The songs by Heine have long been recognized as representing a new, particularly successful stage in Schubert's Lied composition,[65] and a number of them ("Ihr Bild," "Die Stadt," and especially "Der Doppelgänger") have been written about extensively. In *The Composer's Voice*, Edward Cone suggests that a motive deriving from "Der Atlas" is to be found in several of the other songs of the group.[66] In Chapter 3 of this volume, he has extended the motivic relationship to "Die Stadt" and "Am Meer," and he points to a structural approach, tripartite form, shared by most of the Heine songs. In this regard it may be noted that in tripartite form (ABA) each capital letter refers to a section of some substance, normally the setting of one, or sometimes two, complete stanzas of poetry. The structure is not to be confused with ternary song (lyric) form (aaba), or ternary dance form (aababa), in which each lowercase letter refers to one or more phrases or periods of music within a section, normally the setting of a line of music or at most a couplet. It is probably not coincidental that Schubert used tripartite form in his larger instrumental compositions, especially for his slow movements, more frequently at the end of his life than in his earlier instrumental compositions. See, for example, the slow movements of the A-major and B-flat-major sonatas (D. 959 and D. 960), as well as that of the C-major Cello Quintet (D. 956).

A number of other features of the Heine songs deserve attention. By comparison with the poetry of Rellstab and Seidl, Heine's is remarkably concise. On average there are only three stanzas of text ("Der Atlas" has two, "Am Meer" has four, the others three); furthermore, each stanza consists of a single quatrain. Another aspect of Heine's poetry is that there are no returning stanzas, as in Rellstab's "Aufenthalt," or repeated lines of texts within a stanza, as in the Berlin poet's "Abschied." Apropos length, the longer the poem, the more likely Schubert, at this stage of his life, was to set it in a strophic or modified strophic manner. For example, the longest of the Heine poems, "Am Meer," is set in what Cone calls a "quasi-strophic" manner. It is particularly noteworthy that the fewer stanzas in a poem, the less guidance Schubert has for the structure of his setting. And, as mentioned earlier, the composer once wrote to Leopold von Sonnleithner that finding an appropriate structure for a vocal composition was no easy matter.

Normally a composer compensates for a short poem by repeating text: a stanza, a couplet, a line, a phrase, or even a word to fill out his musical design, and he frequently does so more than once. But in this group of songs Schubert matches Heine's conciseness, and four of the six settings do not repeat a single word of text ("Ihr Bild," "Die Stadt," "Am Meer," and "Der Doppelgänger"). In the Heine songs Schubert also tends to limit the number of syllables to which he sets two or more notes (melismas) more than he does in his Rellstab and Seidl settings. "Die Stadt" is set completely syllabically, and there are only three syllables of text in "Der Atlas" and "Ihr Bild" that are set melismatically.

Another interesting aspect of the Heine settings has to do with the keyboard writing. Far more than usual in his songs Schubert employs a device normally associated with orchestral strings for his piano accompaniment, and he does so for extended passages in three of the songs. In "Der Atlas" the prelude (and the identical postlude), the first section, and its return, together by far the largest portion of the piece, are accompanied by tremolo chords in the right hand; in "Die Stadt" the almost omnipresent octave Cs in the bass are a form of tremolo; and, finally, there are two significant passages of tremolo in "Am Meer" (mm. 12–18 and 33–39).

A remarkable feature of the songs in this group is Schubert's restraint, that is, his incredible control of the dynamic levels in the Heine set. Except for "Der Atlas," each vocal line begins pianissimo. As a result, each crescendo and each passage with a louder dynamic level has a strong impact. The cumulative effect of all these features is remarkably dramatic, despite the conciseness of individual songs. No wonder that Dietrich Fischer-Dieskau suggests that "Der Atlas" and "Der Doppelgänger," the first and last songs of the set, "held enormous importance for the development of dramatic singing, particularly as far as Wagner was concerned."[67]

A final aspect of these songs relates to Heine. Unlike Rellstab and Seidl, who in their poetry stress nature and who in their images choose natural phenomena as points of reference (the brook, the nightingale, and a pigeon as friends; the wind, the storm, and rocks as enemies), Heine's poems frequently turn toward the supernatural, at times even to the surreal. This is true of five of the six poems Schubert chose from *Die Heimkehr;* the single exception is "Das Fischermädchen."[68] "Der Atlas" is a mythological figure, one of the race of giants called Titans who must hold up the heavens. A painting, "Ihr Bild," seems to smile and shed tears in a dream-like setting. In "Die Stadt"—one of the eeriest, most evocative of the poems—the protagonist is enveloped in mist. The tears of the beloved prove poisonous in "Am Meer," and the protagonist's body wastes away after he imbibes them. And most fantastic of all, the horrified protagonist sees himself as "Der Doppelgänger."

Jack Westrup eloquently expresses his admiration for the Heine songs: "In all [of them] there is more than meets the eye, just as there is in Heine's poems. There is not complete unity of purpose: that would be impossible. But the evidence of suffering is as strong in the music as it is in the verse: the secrets are shared."[69] For further discussion of the Heine songs as a group, see Chapter 5, "The Sequence of the Heine Songs and Cyclicism in *Schwanengesang.*"

[**Der Atlas**]*	[(**Atlas**)
Ich unglücksel'ger Atlas! eine Welt,	Miserable Atlas that I am! A world,
Die ganze Welt der Schmerzen, muss ich tragen,	The whole world of sorrows, must I bear,
Ich trage Unerträgliches, und brechen	I bear the unbearable, and
Will mir das Herz im Leibe.	In my body, my heart wants to break.

*Schubert supplied the titles lacking in Heine's *Buch der Lieder* (Hamburg, 1827).

Du stolzes Herz, du hast es ja	You arrogant heart, this is what
gewollt!	you wanted!
Du wolltest glücklich sein,	You wanted to be happy,
unendlich glücklich,	immensely happy,
Oder unendlich elend, stolzes	Or immensely wretched,
Herz,	arrogant heart,
Und jetzo bist du elend.	And now you are wretched.]

Heine's unusually powerful, overtly expressive poetry evoked a comparable response in Schubert, who wrote a song unlike any other in *Schwanengesang*, or for that matter in any of his other song cycles. There is a symphonic gesture in "Der Atlas,"[70] although the brevity of the poem does not invite symphonic proportions. The protagonist, Atlas, brother of Prometheus, is of the race of Gods called Titans. Descended from the same ancestors as the Olympian deities, Uranus (heaven) and Ge (earth), the Titans fought their cousins for control of the universe and lost. As punishment, Zeus condemned Atlas to hold up the heavens on his head and shoulders; in John Reed's words, "He is the archetypal figure of the man who dares, and suffers."[71] It would be surprising if Schubert did not associate the "Schmerzenträger," the man carrying the sorrows of the world on his back, with Beethoven, and Hugo Riemann has pointed in convincing fashion to the similarities between the principal theme of the first movement of Beethoven's last piano sonata, the C minor, Op. III, and the opening of Schubert's song "Der Atlas."[72] As noted above, Edward Cone, and others after him,[73] see this theme as of particular importance, since it recurs, usually in altered form, elsewhere in the songs of the Heine group. See Exx. 4.5a and 4.5b.

As the examples reveal, the resemblances are extensive: both Beethoven's head motive (fig. x in Ex. 4.5a) and the continuation, the stepwise descent from the lowered sixth degree (fig. y), are important for Schubert. In addition, both Beethoven's and Schubert's figures labeled x are first presented in the bass and doubled at the octave. Although the keys are not identical—C minor for the sonata and G minor for the song—it seems to me significant that Beethoven's Maestoso introduction to the movement begins with a leap down to a number of octave *F sharps* in m. 1, and that they are harmonized with a dissonant sonority, a diminished-seventh chord, resolving to G in m. 2 (Ex. 4.6). Schubert also harmonizes his *F sharps* with a dissonant sonority, but this time an augmented triad, likewise resolving to G. Finally, the common time meter and the dotted rhythms permeating the Beethoven introduction find their analogue in both the first and last sections of the Schubert song.

Ex. 4.5a. Beethoven, Op. III, I, mm. 20–23

Ex. 4.5b. "Der Atlas," mm. 5–11

There seems to be considerable evidence, then, that Schubert was once again paying homage to his great and recently deceased contemporary. It was certainly not coincidental that Schubert scheduled his only private concert on 27 March 1828, the first anniversary of Beethoven's death. Performing at the concert were several players from the Beethoven circle, most notably the violinist Ignaz Schuppanzigh. At that event was first performed "Auf dem Strom," a song for voice, horn, and piano and probably the first poem by Rellstab to be set by Schubert.[74] If Anton Schindler's claim that Schubert received Rellstab's poems in manuscript from the Beethoven *Nachlass* is true,

Ex. 4.6. Beethoven, Op. III, I, mm. 1–5

the connection of the principal motive of "Der Atlas"—and, by motivic relationship, indeed of the entire Heine set—with Beethoven's music might
well explain Schubert's decision to follow his settings of the Rellstab poems
in the autograph manuscript with the Heine songs. It was as if Schubert
were consciously confirming the legitimacy of his succession to Beethoven's
position as Vienna's premier musician. It may be noted that during the nine-
teen or so months between Beethoven's death (27 March 1827) and Schubert's
(19 November 1828), the young composer repeatedly paid homage to his
great predecessor. Much evidence includes the choice to hold his private concert on the anniversary of Beethoven's death; the reference in his song "Auf
dem Strom" to the funeral march from Beethoven's *Eroica* Symphony;[75] his
setting of the other songs given to Beethoven by Rellstab; his last three piano
sonatas, with their numerous references to Beethoven's technique and structure;[76] his choice of a motive from Beethoven's last piano sonata, Op. III, to
provide the cyclic figure for the Heine songs; and the cyclic process itself, so
important for the late Beethoven string quartets and the older composer's
single song cycle, *An die ferne Geliebte*.

Schubert's new status after Beethoven's death freed him psychologically
for a remarkable burst of creative energy. Witness in his chamber music the
two piano trios (Op. 99 and Op. 100) and the C-major Cello Quintet, in the
piano music the three last sonatas and the stunning Four-Hand Fantasy in
F minor, in orchestral music the extraordinarily progressive sketches for a
large-scale symphony in D, and among the songs, *Schwanengesang*.

Ex. 4.7. "Der Atlas" (orig.), mm. 5–8

For a discussion of Schubert's use of tripartite structure as a possible unifying element in the Heine songs, see Cone's analysis of "Der Atlas" in Chapter 3.

Significant Autograph Corrections

Corrections in mm. 4–7 indicate that Schubert originally had designed his vocal part to resemble more closely Beethoven's head motive, fig. *x* (that is, with no deviation from the pitches *g, b flat,* and *f sharp*). Compare Ex. 4.7 with the final version.

To provide more space between the close in B minor, with its text "und brechen / Will mir das Herz im Leibe," and the new contrasting section in B major beginning "Du stolzes Herz," Schubert inserted m. 22, a bar of rest for the voice. Similarly, he added another bar of rest (m. 27, anacrusis to m. 28 formerly in m. 26) between the lines of text "du hast es ja gewollt" and "Du wolltest glücklich sein." Both insertions result in an additional statement in major of fig. *x* by the keyboard. The result for this portion of the song is more spaciousness, a greater sense of temporal distance between the painful agony of the present (in G minor and B minor) and the past, when Atlas "wanted to be infinitely happy" (in B major).

From the Literature

Gernot Gruber observes that "'Der Atlas' is probably the only poem in Heine's youthful lyrics in which the subject is not mainly love and love's pain."[77]

Massin indicates the progressively rising vocal climax in each of the three sections: *f sharp"* in the first part, *g"* in the second, and *a flat"* for the final section.[78]

J. H. Thomas notes Schubert's compression in the return of the opening section; "the recap contains a dramatic climax of enormous intensity . . . [and] the climax . . . defines the physical strain and superhuman effort which is Atlas's eternal fate."[79]

Helga Utz suggests that "Der Atlas" is freer than the other Heine songs of period structure; notes the presence of text-related affects; and observes that the musical expression is "supported by musical topoi (grief associated chromaticism at 'Ich trage Unerträgliches'; long notes on 'unendlich' etc.)."[80]

According to Newbould, Schubert "selects his key with care and precision. . . . The G minor of 'Der Atlas' permits gravity without opacity. . . . The choice of B major and a rollicking accompaniment for the lines which refer back to the protagonist's bold bid for happiness . . . is a powerful irony."[81]

[Ihr Bild]
Ich stand in dunkeln Träumen,
Und starrt'* ihr Bildniss† an,
Und das geliebte Antlitz
Heimlich zu leben begann.

Um ihre Lippen zog sich
Ein Lächeln wunderbar,
Und wie von Wehmuthsthränen
Erglänzte ihr Augenpaar.

Auch meine Thränen flossen
Mir von den Wangen herab—
Und ach, ich kann es nicht glauben,
Dass ich dich verloren hab'!

[(Her Portrait)
I stood in dark dreams,
And stared at her portrait,
And that beloved countenance
Mysteriously came to life.

To her lips was summoned
A miraculous smile,
And as if from tears of sadness
Her eyes glistened.

My tears also flowed
Down from my cheeks—
And alas, I cannot believe
That I have lost you!]

Heine's poem is extraordinary. Externally nothing happens. A man stands immobile and unhappy ("in dunkeln Träumen"). What follows is entirely in his imagination, yet he reacts intensely. The setting is quiet, mysterious, even eerie.

With unusually simple means Schubert caught the essence of the poem, and his setting elicited an *Urlinie,* a reduction of the essential contrapuntal-harmonic motion, by Heinrich Schenker and also an essay of considerable interest.[82] Schenker suggests, for example, that the two-bar introduction, the octave *b flat* and its repeat, represents the protagonist staring at the portrait. Joseph Kerman acknowledges that "The two chords [sic] are remarkable, evocative" and that "Schenker was on to something [but] . . . did not get to the bottom of it."[83] If there is a bottom, I wonder if it doesn't relate

---

*In Heine, "Starrte." See discussion below.
†This older spelling of "Bildnis" is used by both Heine and Schubert.

somehow to the function of all song preludes or introductions, namely, to establish a tempo and provide the singer with a clue to the first pitch. Schenker rhetorically asks "why the Master sounded the same note [actually an octave] *twice*" and then presents his idea of staring. Another possible answer might be that Schubert wanted to set the tempo—slow—and that the pitch involved, *b flat,* was to be the first pitch to be sung by the vocalist. But perhaps we should take it a step further. Why is there no harmony, merely a unison with the keyboard for mm. 3–6? Two thoughts occur. For Western composers of the early nineteenth century, four-part harmony was the norm. An unharmonized sequence of pitches (or melody) signaled something out of the ordinary. Surely the fantastic quality of Heine's poem would call for an unusual introduction; one that would suggest, or at least allow to emerge in the music, the extraordinary vision in the poetry. Furthermore, unharmonized melodies, both in song and in opera, are often employed to suggest loneliness or isolation. For example, during the opening act of Verdi's *Don Carlos,* the protagonist is lost in Fontainebleau forest, very much alone. The opening of that scene is played by a solo clarinet, unaccompanied. Beginning Act IV of the same score is one of the greatest scenes for bass in the operatic repertory. A despondent King Philip is alone in his study. Much of the introduction of that scene is given over to a solo cello, again unaccompanied. There seems to be a comparable isolation and sense of despondency for the protagonist of "Ihr Bild," and the opening six measures of the song in unison establish that sense for the listener.[84]

Further, the repeated, in effect stationary, *b-flat* octaves of the tiny prelude provide what Walther Dürr has suggested, I think quite brilliantly, to be one of the primary functions of keyboard parts in Schubert's Lieder: to provide what is in effect stage directions for the song's dramatic setting. In this case they are minimal stage directions, namely, the absence of movement, the deliberate restriction of melodic and rhythmic motion, the perfect musical analogue to the protagonist's first words "I stood." And, of course, he remains standing, immobile, before the portrait for the remainder of the song. In these terms we can understand Schubert's choice of a slow tempo, a very soft dynamic level (pianissimo), and quiet melodic motion (that is, primarily motion by step, with a fair number of repeated notes; when there are leaps, they are small, never more than a fourth). There is also an emphasis on the pitch *b flat,* especially as a point of departure, but also often as the melodic cadence, for most of the musical phrases in the song. In the first of the three sections the opening phrase (mm. 3–4) contains four *b flats;* the setting of the third line, the second phrase, begins with three *b flats* (m. 9);

and the cadence of the third phrase, vocally the end of the section, returns once again to *b flat* (m. 12). Striking in this regard is the fact that, despite the change of key from B flat (minor then major) to G-flat major to begin part 2, the melodic emphasis remains on the pitch *b flat* for the entire section. Observe the four *b flats* in mm. 14–15 with the melodic cadence on that pitch in m. 18. Note the similar beginning and close of the next pair of phrases, those closing the section (mm. 19–22). The brief retransition continues to focus on *b flat,* as does the return of the music of the first part. Restricting the melodic motion as much as Schubert does in this song suggests well the physical immobility as well as the unchanging emotional state of the protagonist.[85]

By following the changes in mode of the song, a close correlation with the dramatic sequence of events may be observed. In part 1 a troubled young man (that is, with "dark dreams") stands before a portrait: unpleasant reality set in minor. He imagines the face gradually coming to life: beginning of the illusion and a turn from minor to the tonic major with a free echo in the keyboard also in the tonic major. During part 2 the illusion becomes more intense; there is now a smile on the lips, and tears of melancholy glimmer in the eyes: still major but in the more distant key of G flat, a musical analogy for the intensification of the illusion in the poetry. Part 3 contains a return to the protagonist and his present unhappiness. He, too, sheds tears: minor. He can't believe (a form of delusion) that he has lost his beloved: major. But this time the free echo in the piano establishes the reality of the situation once and for all, and it does so in minor to conclude the song. Notice that Schubert reenforces the keyboard's view of the situation by introducing the single forte passage in the piece.

It is interesting that Schubert makes a single modification in Heine's poetry. He changes "starrte" of the poem's second line to "starrt" in m. 5 of the song. This allows a rhythmic correspondence in his setting of lines 1 and 2. The monosyllabic verb form "stand" now has a parallel monosyllabic "starrt." Of the minor corrections Schubert made in the autograph of "Ihr Bild," it is noteworthy that two sonorities in the keyboard part were reduced. In m. 23 the accompanying chord originally included *g flat,* and in m. 35 the final vertical configuration included an additional *c'* and *e flat.* In both instances the reduced sonority of the final version would seem to be more in keeping with the keyboard scoring and the texture of the song as a whole. Certainly the almost impressionistic, dream-like quality of the poetry benefits from the reduced sonorities, as it does from the unharmonized opening.

From the Literature

Charles Brauner sees irony in Schubert's ending to "Ihr Bild," and his discussion of the setting of stanza 3 of the poem is perceptive:

> The text of the final couplet is a surprise (just as the awakening of the
> portrait had been in the first strophe): despite the dark dreams and tears
> we do not expect all to be lost, though in fact all has been lost through-
> out the scene. In this light, the "affirmation" on these lines becomes
> ironic. We are reminded of the previous affirmation and are now shown
> how illusory it was. This juxtaposition of the musical affirmation with
> the statement of loss gives the setting a quality of paradox also present
> in the poem, and seems much more effective than a literal expression of
> the last couplet would have been. The irony is made explicit only in the
> postlude, a repetition of that of the first strophe, but now unexpectedly
> in minor.[86]

In a psychologically oriented analysis, Dieter Schnebel discusses the static
quality of the melody, much as I have above. He discusses the ternary structure, but in terms of the grouping of the prevailing two- and four-bar units:

$$2\,4\,2\,4\,2 \;/\; 4\,4 \;/\; 2\,4\,2\,4\,2$$
$$[= \text{A} \qquad \text{B} \quad \text{A}]$$

He particularly stresses the expansion and contraction of the *Klang-
gräume* (sounding space) from the unison outward and back as related to the
movement into the deepest layers of psychic life, a movement from the external to the internal reality, which can no longer be expressed in language—only in music—and where the dreamer's loss is most deeply felt.[87]

In her article "Kreutzer's *Wanderlieder*: The Other *Winterreise*," Luise Eitel
Peake draws attention to Kreutzer's song "Scheiden und meiden," which
contains a passage remarkably similar to mm. 9–12 of "Ihr Bild."[88] Schubert
knew Kreutzer's music, and indeed is reputed to have defended him from
denigration by his own supporters;[89] in all probability, he was not conscious
of citing Kreutzer's melody so closely. Compare Exs. 4.8a and 4.8b.[90]

[Das Fischermädchen]
Du schönes Fischermädchen,
Treibe den Kahn ans Land;
Komm zu mir und setze dich
    nieder,
Wir kosen Hand in Hand.

[(The Fishermaiden)
You lovely fishermaiden,
Row your boat to the land;
Come and sit beside
    me,
We'll cuddle hand in hand.

Ex. 4.8a. Conradin Kreutzer, "Scheiden und meiden," mm. 1–4

Ex. 4.8b. "Ihr Bild," mm. 9–12

Leg an mein Herz dein Köpfchen,	Lay your head on my bosom,
Und fürchte dich nicht zu sehr;	And you needn't be so afraid;
Vertraust du dich doch	You entrust yourself quite
sorglos	fearlessly
Täglich den wilden Meer.	Each day to the turbulent sea.
Mein Herz gleicht ganz dem	My heart is just like the
Meere,	ocean,
Hat Sturm und Ebb' und Fluth,	Has storms and ebb and flow,
Und manche shöne Perle	And many pearls of beauty
In seiner Tiefe ruht.	Rest in its depths below.]

The poem Schubert set to music and named "Das Fischermädchen" differs considerably from the other Heine poems he selected. The protagonist doesn't suffer; he is playful. He is not the rejected lover; he is the pursuer. Instead of a song of agony, this is a seductive love song. To some observers the question is: How sincere is this love song? According to Jack Westrup there is a "cynical tone [to] Heine's apparently innocent verse."[91] In Reed's view, "a simple uncomplicated love of a fisher girl is beyond the reach of a disenchanted poet."[92] To be sure, even in this poem Heine is a complex person. His usual twist of meaning at the end, his famous "sting in the tail," is not all that clear here. After his relatively straightforward opening verses, with their invitations: "Come and sit beside me. . . . We'll cuddle. . . . Lay your head on my bosom," the last stanza changes direction and provides a richer image of a poet with a heart resembling a raging sea, a heart with treasures.

Is the young, presumably timid, perhaps frightened girl of a class distinctly lower than that of her complex would-be lover reassured by the fact that his heart also has "storm and ebb and flow"? How sincere is the poet? Most important, how did Schubert read the poem? Westrup hears in the music "a hint of mockery that matches the . . . verse."[93] Reed says no: Schubert's song "is more interested in the carefree life of the fisher girl than in the reflections of the poet." The structure of the song—see Cone's analysis in Chapter 3—suggests that Reed is right. Stanza 3 of the poem is quite different than stanza 1, yet Schubert's music is the same. He doesn't react to the new poetic content. There is a unity of mood maintained throughout the song, despite the modulation to the relatively distant key of the lowered submediant for the second stanza of text. Reed further remarks that "'Das Fischermädchen' is a charming barcarolle, without the emotional intensity or the psychological depth of the other Heine songs," although he also feels that "in its own way it is as successful as the others."[94] But what exactly is its own way?

In a survey of Schubert's solo songs from the point of view of their folk orientation—their *Volkston*—Ludwig Scheibler singled out "Das Fischermädchen" as the most folk-like of all Schubert's songs of 1828.[95] He sees the song as standing between the tripartite form (ABA) and varied strophic. One of his main requirements for a Lied in Volkston is that it be some form of strophic structure. The other requirements are that the melodies, harmonies, modulatory plan, and rhythms be relatively simple. I tend to agree, however, with Helga Utz who insists that even though "in no way can 'Das Fischermädchen' be considered contrary to the period principle," it displays "a certain metric lability" whereby the listener's expectations of a "preexisting scheme of periods" are "getäuscht" (deceived).[96] At this stage in his career, Schubert's immense compositional skills with regard to rhythm are indeed brilliantly displayed in this song. Three procedures that tend to frustrate the inherent regularity of the four- and eight-bar rhythmic units are especially noteworthy. The first and perhaps most important is elision or overlap. As the eight-bar prelude concludes, the voice overlaps the keyboard cadence (m. 8), directing our attention to a new beginning. Schubert does precisely the same thing at the beginnings and endings of each of the interludes (mm. 23, 29, 44, and 50) and at the beginning of the postlude as well (m. 65). But even within the eight-bar prelude Schubert plays with our rhythmic expectations. Instead of the usual antecedent and consequent phrases of four bars each, he lengthens the initial phrase to five, with an extra measure of A-flat (tonic) chord at the beginning. This additional bar never appears again. See mm. 23, 44, and 65. Furthermore, the cadential bar (m. 5) is extended by three additional measures (6–8). In fact, there is a single eight-bar unit in place of the two fours we had been led to expect by the simple barcarolle rhythm. Extension, either internally or at the cadence, then is the second rhythmic device for greater flexibility. The third, keyboard echo, has been discussed in detail by Cone in Chapter 3, although not with regard to this song. Here it is present in mm. 12–13, 33–34, and 54–55. Returning to the prelude, I should like to suggest that Schubert may well have intended the listener to relate the first harmonic change (that is, to a B-flat–minor chord with the fifth, f', on top in m. 3) to the final sonority of the previous song, "Ihr Bild," which ended with a B-flat-minor triad and the same f' on top. In both instances the triad is played by the piano. Perhaps to reinforce this relationship, Schubert's first tonicizations away from the tonic A-flat major are to B-flat minor (mm. 14–15 and 18–19).

It is tempting to think that Schubert chose to set this poem, and to set it in the manner he did, in order to provide a lighter moment between the two darker songs preceding it ("Der Atlas" and "Ihr Bild") and the equally dark triad to follow ("Die Stadt," "Am Meer," and "Der Doppelgänger"). This reverses the procedure in the Rellstab songs, where Schubert inserted a darker song, "Kriegers Ahnung," between the lighter, more cheerful "Liebes-botschaft" and "Frühlingssehnsucht." Might not "Das Fischermädchen" be viewed as functioning much in the way a minuet or scherzo does in a Late Classic symphony or string quartet? It certainly seems to provide a momentary point of relaxation following the tension created by a powerful first song—in this case "Der Atlas," which is actually based on themes from an impressive first movement by Beethoven (Op. 111)—and an emotionally charged slow song, "Ihr Bild." Following "Das Fischermädchen" the analogy no longer holds. The last three Heine songs are hardly comparable to an instrumental finale. A final observation: one of the lighter touches, by comparison with, for example, "Der Atlas," is the manner in which Schubert does *not* increase the tension in "Das Fischermädchen" with regard to the vocal climax of each section. In this song the vocal high points of the three sections remain the same, *g flat"*.

Among the changes Schubert made in his autograph of "Das Fischer-mädchen" are added pitches in the piano part for the sake of resonance, and some small but telling improvements in the melodic line. In mm. 27–28 he also altered the harmony and melody slightly to provide a smoother transition from the key of the first section, A-flat major, to that of the middle section, C flat.

From the Literature

E. G. Porter, for whom "Das Fischermädchen" is a completely successful song, describes well the harmonic function of the interludes. After generally praising the "masterly simplicity [which] abounds in these last songs," he points to the "slight variation in the second stanza of 'Das Fischermädchen' which is a minor third higher than the first or third," and he suggests that "the manner in which the key is introduced and left is most beautiful. The first ritornello [interlude] is like the prelude except for the subtle insertion of an F flat [mm. 27–28] which turns the harmonies to C flat: then in the bar before the third stanza [m. 49] the F flat is followed in the next chord by F natural to bring about the simple but magic return to A flat. The many delicate nuances in this song raise it far above all the other Schubert barcarolles."[97]

Another admirer of the song, Arnold Whitall, writes: "'Das Fischermädchen' . . . achieves greatness not just through the freshness of the melody and the attractive lilt of its rhythms, but through the way in which the ambiguities of Heine's text promote subtle irregularities of phrase structure and unexpected enrichments of harmony."[98]

[Die Stadt]
Am fernen Horizonte
Erscheint, wie ein Nebelbild,
Die Stadt mit ihren Thürmen
In Abenddämmrung gehüllt.

Ein feuchter Windzug kräuselt
Die graue Wasserbahn;
Mit traurigem Takte rudert
Der Schiffer in meinem Kahn.

Die Sonne hebt sich noch einmal
Leuchtend vom Boden empor,
Und zeigt mir jene Stelle,
Wo ich das Liebste verlor.

[(**The Town**)
Upon the far horizon
Appears, as if a misty image,
The town with its towers
Veiled in evening twilight.

A moist gust of wind ruffles
The gray watery path;
With sorrowful strokes, rows
The sailor in my skiff.

Once again the sun rises
Radiantly upward from the earth,
And shows me that place,
Where I lost my beloved.]

If the first three Heine songs incorporate a number of decided contrasts, the last three, "Die Stadt," "Am Meer," and "Der Doppelgänger," each relatively short, form a tightly organized group with a great deal in common from the poetic and musical points of view. In contrast to "Das Fis-

chermädchen," in which there is a systematic repetition of text at the end
of each strophe (the final couplet is repeated, and then the last line is repeated again) in order to fill out the musical design, Schubert doesn't repeat
a single word in the last three Heine Lieder. In this regard, and in the subject
matter—the misery of the protagonist—these poems resemble "Ihr Bild."
Another feature, and a musically important one, uniting the three songs is
Schubert's advanced harmonic thinking, his exceptional use of chromatic
chords: the diminished seventh in "Die Stadt," the augmented sixth in "Am
Meer," and both augmented sixths and Neapolitan chord in "Der Doppelgänger." Not one of these sonorities is treated in traditional (common practice) fashion, and the fact that the bass of each is the octave $C + C'$ provides,
perhaps, one of the most powerful bonds between these works. Further, the
dyad *e flat* = *d sharp* + *f sharp* is present in the diminished-seventh chord
dominating "Die Stadt"; is also heard in the startling augmented-sixth chord
opening and closing "Am Meer"; and provides the third and fifth of the
B-major triad that concludes "Der Doppelgänger." The shared use of specific pitches would seem to suggest that Schubert deliberately intended the
three songs as a single musical unit.

The most important corrections in the autograph differentiate the voice
part of the returning section 3 (A') from the similar music but quite dissim-
ilar poetic text of section 1 (A). In the process Schubert strengthened considerably the climax of the song at the crucial line of text "Wo ich das Liebste verlor" (Where I lost my beloved).

From the Literature

As Gernot Gruber observed, "In the song 'Die Stadt' the major-minor contrast is missing."[99] He might have also added the reason; namely, that there
is a total absence of any illusions, dreams, or references to past happiness.
From beginning to end the song reflects the gray, "traurig" (melancholy)
mood of the misty sea. Even in stanza 3, when the setting sun finally illu-
minates the scene, the clearer view of the town only deepens the protagonist's despair by reminding him of his loss. Gruber also remarks how unusual it is for the composer of a composition in tripartite form to lay the
principal stress on the B section, here inextricably linked with the prelude
and postlude.

The song has repeatedly been called impressionistic and described as far
in advance of its time.[100] Massin sees a relationship between the pedal point
in "Die Stadt" and that of "Im Dorfe" of *Winterreise*. In both "the city" and
"the village" there is a decidedly hostile environment for the protagonist.[101]

Dürr approaches the music from the poetry: "The uniform mood of the poem conceals an inner dialectic: on one side the singer in his boat, which the boatman moves along 'with mournful stroke'; on the other 'the town with its towers' to which the singer is attracted, where one time his loved one was, but which now seems as unreal as a misty image."[102] As remarked earlier, elsewhere he suggests we think of the keyboard accompaniment to "Die Stadt" and other songs as if it were a set of stage directions setting the mood for the drama of the poetry and the music. The reason for the impressionistic feeling is undoubtedly the importance of the unprepared and unresolved diminished-seventh chord that dominates the song (prelude, both interludes, middle section, and postlude). Even the voice part of the second strophe is fundamentally little more than a slightly ornamented and descending diminished-seventh chord, as a number of commentators have observed.[103] The essential pitches for the middle section (mm. 18–25) are:

c"–e flat"–c'–a'–c"–a'–f sharp'–a'–f sharp'–e flat'–c'

There are a number of reductive diagrams of the song, which has been discussed more than any of the Heine songs except "Der Doppelgänger."[104] Surprisingly, Heinrich Schenker provides a reductive diagram only for mm. 7–14. As this is just the first section of the tripartite structure, he avoids coming to grips with the unresolved diminished-seventh chord of the prelude, middle section, and postlude, which is indisputably the crucial harmonic element of the song.[105] By far the most interesting diagram is in Robert Morgan's essay "Dissonant Prolongation: Theoretical and Compositional Precedents."[106] During his analysis, he convincingly suggests that the resolution of the diminished-seventh chord at the end of "Die Stadt" takes place in the next song, "Am Meer." Here is the relevant portion of his example (Ex. 4.9):

Ex. 4.9. Robert Morgan, harmonic progression from "Die Stadt" to "Am Meer"

Lawrence Kramer notes that "Die Stadt" "closes with the solo piano once more tossing up its haze of arpeggios, a move that reverses the speaker's effort to expose an obsession and explain it away in the same breath. Instead of being glossed over, the feeling of psychological disturbance intensifies as the song ends in vocal silence amid the tonal uncertainty of its gray water-music."[107]

Focusing on Schubert's originality, Alfred Einstein makes the important point that there are no models of any kind for "Die Stadt" or "Der Doppel-gänger."[108]

[Am Meer]	[(By the Sea)
Das Meer erglänzte weit hinaus	The sea sparkled far and wide
Im letzten Abendscheine;	In the last glow of evening;
Wir sassen am einsamen	We sat by the lonely
Fischerhaus,	fisherhouse,
Wir sassen stumm und alleine.	We sat silently and alone.
Der Nebel stieg, das Wasser	The mist rose, the water
schwoll,	swelled,
Die Möwe flog hin und wieder;	The seagulls flew back and forth;
Aus deinen Augen liebevoll	From your eyes filled with love
Fielen die Thränen nieder.	The tears dropped down.
Ich sah sie fallen auf deine Hand,	I saw them fall upon your hand,
Und bin aufs Knie gesunken;	And sank to my knee;
Ich hab' von deiner weissen Hand	From your white hand, I
Die Thränen fortgetrunken.	Drank away the tears.
Seit jener Stunde verzehrt sich	From that hour my body wastes
mein Leib,	away,
Die Seele stirbt vor Sehnen;—	My soul dies of desire;—
Mich hat das unglücksel'ge Weib	The wretched woman has
Vergiftet mit ihren Thränen.	Poisoned me with her tears.]

If Schubert avoided the major mode completely while setting Heine's despairing poem "Die Stadt," he returns to modal contrast in "Am Meer." But the polarity with regard to the implicit drama of reality and illusion does not work quite so neatly here as elsewhere. The superficially idyllic scene depicted in stanza 1 is set in C major. At the beginning of stanza 2, when nature shows herself to be somewhat less benign (mist rising, water swelling), Schubert turns to C minor, the same key as the "Nebelbild" (misty image) in stanza 1 of "Die Stadt." Here, however, he modulates immediately. The second couplet of stanza 2 in "Am Meer" is ambiguous. Tears are falling from the woman's "eyes filled with love." Are they tears of happiness? Of misery? Is she recalling some event of the past? In any case, the major mode returns. But with just a bit of doubt displayed, Schubert introduces into the accompaniment tones borrowed from the minor scale: *b flats* (lowered seventh degree, the normal seventh in minor) in m. 21 and passing minor thirds (*e flats*) in mm. 22 and 23.

With Heine's exaggerated response to the tears (the protagonist on his knee, drinking the tears) in stanza 3, Schubert returns to major and the music for stanza 1. This might be interpreted as an attempt to re-create the idyllic situation of the poem's beginning. But at this point I think Schubert opted in favor of a logical musical design; that is, he wrote music for stanza 4 almost exactly like that of stanza 2, with different cadences. (See Cone's original way of looking at Schubert's approach to form in the song in Chapter 3.) But Heine's almost viciously anti-romantic "sting in the tail" presents problems for the final couplet. Schubert's setting of lines 1 and 2 of the stanza in minor works well enough, but the return to major at "The wretched woman has poisoned me with her tears" seems to me problematic. Perhaps Gernot Gruber is right when he suggests that Schubert depends on his prelude and postlude to show on what "schwankendes Grund" (shaky ground) the sweetness of the music in the two A sections (stanzas 1 and 3) rests.[109] It would appear that here, as in "Die Stadt," the burden of depicting reality is entrusted to the prelude and postlude, in "Am Meer" the unprepared, accented, and quite dissonant augmented-sixth chords.[110]

A correction in the autograph shows that originally the augmented-sixth chord in m. 1 was written with *e flat* rather than *d sharp,* a spelling revealing the relation to the diminished-seventh chord in "Die Stadt" and suggesting that Robert Morgan is correct in seeing the resolution of that dissonant sonority (spelled *c* + *e flat* + *f sharp* + *a natural*) in the opening progression of "Am Meer." Schubert may have changed the spelling to have a single accidental on *d sharp* rather than two successive accidentals on *e* (*e flat* and *e natural*). In addition, the normally upward-resolving *d sharp* better suggests C major than does *e flat.*

From the Literature

Dietrich Fischer-Dieskau believes that "the [ornamental] turn on "Tränen" (tears) has that sort of irony which some critics claim to be absent from the Heine songs."[111]

Brian Newbould relates the tremolo passages in "Am Meer" with other late pieces by Schubert (for example, the G-major Quartet) and sees it as "a means of promoting sonority at a slow tempo, action without 'real' speed, excitement in an 'accompaniment' which can be combined with long full-toned notes in . . . instruments (or voice)."[112]

[Der Doppelgänger]	[(The Phantom Double)
Still ist die nacht, es ruhen die Gassen,	Still is the night, the streets are at rest,
In diesem Hause wohnte mein Schatz;	In this house dwelt my loved one;
Sie hat schon längst die Stadt verlassen,	She has long since left the town,
Doch steht noch das Haus auf demselben Platz.	Yet the house still stands on the same place.
Da steht auch ein Mensch und starrt in die Höhe.	There too stands a man and stares on high.
Und ringt die Hände, vor schmerzensgewalt;	And wrings hs hands, for the power of grief;
Mir graust es, wenn ich sein Antlitz sehe,—	I shudder when I see his face,—
Der Mond zeigt mir meine eigne Gestalt.	The moon shows me my own countenance.
Du Doppelgänger!* du bleicher Geselle!	You phantom double! You pale fellow!
Was äffst du nach mein Liebesleid,	Why do you mock the pain of my love,
Das mich gequält auf dieser Stelle,	That tormented me on this spot,
So manche Nacht, in alter Zeit?	So many nights, in times past?]

One of Schubert's most remarkable songs, if not the most remarkable,[113] "Der Doppelgänger" is unique among his Lieder with regard to its structure: it is almost entirely a set of harmonic variations (see Cone's analysis in Chapter 3). Of the extensive literature to which the song has given birth, perhaps the most significant item is a study by Werner Thomas, "'Der Doppelgänger' von Franz Schubert," which has become something of an icon for

* "Doppeltgänger" in Heine's *Buch der Lieder*.

German musicologists.[114] Thomas believes that Schubert's last Heine song should be examined not only for its anticipations of the future, those aspects that influenced such later composers as Johannes Brahms, Hugo Wolf, and Richard Wagner, but also for its debt to the past. Thomas divides his contribution into four sections. First he discusses the keyboard part, then the voice line; this is followed by an analysis that both combines and contrasts the two; and, finally, he offers his conclusions. Of the four sections, I find Thomas' reflections on the voice part especially interesting. He stresses the declamatory nature of the melody for all but the setting of Heine's final couplet; points to the importance of the pitch f $sharp'$; and suggests that Schubert's treatment of the melody was less influenced by operatic recitative than by the accentus, presumably of chant. I wonder if the slightly more formal recitative of eighteenth-century oratorios (such as those by Handel) might not represent a third influence. He further attributes much of Schubert's melodic freedom in the song to the influence of Heine's poem, which he believes to be closer to prose than to poetry, despite the rhymes and overall verse scaffolding. Unfortunately he gives no indication of precisely how the poem more closely approaches prose. More convincing is his discussion of rhythmic aspects of the voice line, which differ markedly from the invariably downbeat quality and triple meter of the keyboard part. He points to the almost consistently upbeat melodic line and to a tendency for the vocal part at times to imply duple meter. For example, he offers a diagram in which the opening three lines of the voice part (from the second beat of m. 5 through the second beat of m. 10) might be thought of as eight measures of $\frac{2}{4}$ meter while the piano sonorities move in triple meter. Both his diagram and the accompanying discussion indicate the high degree of contrapuntal independence of the voice from the highly structured keyboard part. Not until the cadence points of mm. 11 and 23 do the rhythms converge.

I find less convincing the description of the harmony as essentially "functionless" except for the cadences. Thomas attributes this to the many sonorities that consist of perfect intervals. Furthermore, with his eye on the *C naturals* in the bass at mm. 32–33, 41–42, and 59, and the resulting melodic descent from *D* to *C natural* to *B'*, Thomas also insists on the importance of what he calls "the ethos of the phrygian [mode] . . . the tonality of affliction" for the song.[115] I suspect that some analysts may question this. Certainly with regard to the chromatic sonorities built on the *C naturals*, augmented-sixth chords, and the sonority constructed on the lowered second degree (the Neapolitan chord), Schubert had more contemporary views in mind (see the discussion of chromatic chords in the next chapter).

Although Thomas recognizes Schubert's keyboard ostinato as related to the basso continuo technique characteristic of the Baroque era, he reaches much further back in music history to explain the sonorous quality of that ostinato. Focusing on the octaves, fourths, and fifths, he invokes as their "Urahnen" (original ancestors) the earliest era of polyphony, organum, and does so at some length. I find, however, the sonorities to which he refers more in the nature of incomplete triads, with distinct functional implications. See, for example, the incomplete triads with major thirds in mm. 2 and 3. Notice also that when the vocal line begins, many of the incomplete triads are completed (for example, in mm. 7, 9, and 10), a procedure quite opposed to the organum principle. To be sure, in the early nineteenth century, an age oriented toward increased rather than decreased resonance, the incomplete triads of "Der Doppelgänger" would have been startling. But wasn't Schubert reacting imaginatively to the text? Wasn't he representing the shadow-like phantom double with those spare, less substantial sonorities? When the vocal line begins, isn't it sung by the protagonist? Examining the song from this perspective (that is, the keyboard as Doppelgänger and the sung portions as the protagonist), the extreme musical dichotomy for most of the song makes sense. And when the protagonist engages the phantom double, addresses him in stanza 3, it also makes good sense for both the ostinato and the rhythmic disparity between voice and keyboard to vanish. Note that the incomplete sonorities are still heard to the initial words of the stanza, "Du Doppelgänger! du bleicher Geselle!" (You phantom double! You pale fellow!), but disappear as the protagonist focuses on his own "Liebesleid" (pain of love).

This is not to say that the past is not important for Schubert, but I doubt that it is the very distant past he had in mind. The final line of the poem reads "So manche Nacht in alter Zeit?" (So many nights, in times past?). Did the words "alter Zeit" lead Schubert to consider using a musical form and musical procedures from the past? And if so, which musical past did he invoke? It is well known that on 14 December 1826 Beethoven received Samuel Arnold's forty-volume edition of Handel's music as a gift from an admirer in England. This was the first collected edition devoted to any composer and was heavily weighted toward the oratorios. While examining the scores, the ailing composer is quoted as saying, "Handel is the greatest, the ablest composer who ever lived. I can still learn from him."[116] Less well known is the fact that Schubert also received a copy of that edition near the end of his life. Otto Erich Deutsch believes it may have been a loan from Tobias Haslinger, publisher of *Winterreise, Schwanengesang,* and other late compositions of Schubert; and the copy may even have been Beethoven's.[117] Two reliable sources report that the young composer visited the Fröhlich family a few months before his death and "told them he had got the scores of Handel's oratorios. He added: Now for the first time I see what I lack; but I will study hard with Sechter so that I can make good the omission."[118]

The point to be made from this biographical excursion is that for Schubert the "furthest musical past" was in all probability the early eighteenth century. His admiration for Handel may explain both Schubert's choice of a repeating, bass-controlled harmonic pattern, to organize the last of the Heine songs, and the harmonic orientation of the postlude: a plagal cadence and the archaic Picardy third (that is, a major chord ending a composition otherwise in minor). Frank Schneider, in his article "Franz Schuberts Heine-Liedern," makes an additional, related point. While discussing the pair of chromatically descending half steps of the ostinato, he remarks, "The four note motive is an archaic figure in liturgical music [functioning] as the Baroque musical symbol of lamentation and weeping."[119] As do W. Thomas and others, Schneider points to the same figure (transposed) in the Agnus Dei of Schubert's E-flat Mass, a work whose composition overlapped with that of "Der Doppelgänger."

Among the corrections in the autograph, two deserve mention. In mm. 13–15, originally the right hand of the accompaniment begins another four-bar ostinato statement. But Schubert crosses it through and writes a slightly altered echo of the previous vocal cadence (mm. 11–12). This may have been a simple lapse on Schubert's part as he copied from an earlier draft of the song no longer extant. But whether planned earlier or corrected later, the result is a degree of rhythmic freedom from the ostinato's strict patterning, which is of considerable importance later in the song (mm. 23–24 and especially mm. 42ff.)

At the song's climax, the protagonist recognizes "meine eigne Gestalt" (my own countenance). Originally the vocal part in mm. 39–41 had the same pitches as mm. 31–33 (that is, a drop from high *f sharps"* to middle-register *f sharps'*). In Chapter 3, Cone indicated that in the settings of both stanzas 1 and 2 the music of the second couplet essentially repeated that of the first. This was precisely the situation in the autograph before the changes made here. The ascent to *g"* in the final version—now the highest pitch in the song—provides a climax far superior to the original. It seems clear that had Schubert remained with the earlier vocal line, the augmented-sixth chord in mm. 41–42 would have resembled that of mm. 32–33 (that is, a French rather than a German augmented-sixth chord).

Finally, in the voice part of m. 48, the upbeat to the next bar was originally *c sharp'* rather than *c double sharp'*.

The Seidl Song

Die Taubenpost

Ich hab' eine Brieftaub in meinem
   Sold,
Die ist gar ergeben und treu,
Sie nimmt mir nie das Ziel zu kurz,
Und fliegt auch nie vorbei.

Ich sende sie
   vieltausendmal
Auf Kundschaft täglich hinaus,
Vorbei an manchem lieben Ort,
Bis zu der Liebsten Haus.

Dort schaut sie zum Fenster
   heimlich hinein,
Belauscht ihren Blick und Schritt,
Gibt meine Grüsse scherzend ab
Und nimmt die ihren mit.

Kein Briefchen brauch' ich zu
   schreiben mehr,
Die Thräne selbst geb' ich ihr;
O sie verträgt sie sicher nicht,
Gar eifrig dient sie mir.

Bei Tag, bei Nacht, im Wachen
   im* Traum,
Ihr gilt das alles gleich:
Wenn sie nur wandern, wandern
   kann,
Dann ist sie überreich!

[The Pigeon Post

I've a carrier pigeon in my
   employ,
Who is quite devoted and true,
She never fails to reach her goal,
And also never flies past.

I send her forth many thousand
   times
Daily to gather reports,
On past many a well-loved place,
Right to my dearest's house.

There at the window she peers in
   secretively,
Spies on her glance and step,
Delivers my greetings playfully
And takes hers back to me.

No more need I write
   letters,
I even give her my tears;
Oh certainly she never miscarries,
She serves me quite zealously.

By day, by night, awake, in
   dreams,
It's all the same to her:
As long as she can wander, just
   wander,
Then she is more than rich!

---

*Seidl's *Gesammelte Schriften* (1877) reads "und." As is clear from the date of the poem's (first?) publication, in all probability Schubert composed the song from a manuscript of the poem.

Sie wird nicht müd', sie wird nicht matt,	She doesn't weary, doesn't tire,
Der Weg ist stets ihr neu;	Her path is constantly new;
Sie braucht nicht Lockung, braucht nicht Lohn,	She needs no enticement, needs no reward,
Die Taub' ist so mir treu!	The dove is so faithful to me!
Drum heg' ich sie auch so treu an der Brust,	That's why she's so truly preserved at my breast,
Versichert des schönsten Gewinns;	Assured of the fairest reward;
Sie heisst—die Sehnsucht! Kennt ihr sie?—	She's called—longing! Do you know her?—
Die Botin treuen Sinns.	The messenger of faithfulness.]

Some comments by Dietrich Fischer-Dieskau may provide an introduction to a discussion of Schubert's last Lied:

> In the final song of [*Schwanengesang*], "Die Taubenpost" . . . , one senses the spiritual pivot of Schubert's musical testimony:
>
> > Sie heisst-die Sehnsucht!
> > Kennt ihr sie? Die Botin treuen Sinns.
> > (She is called Longing! Do you know her?
> > The messenger of faithfulness.)
>
> Although it belongs in content and meaning neither to the Heine nor the Rellstab group, "Die Taubenpost" . . . is nevertheless first-class Schubert. . . . We feel that [he] has returned to the style of the *Schöne Müllerin* songs . . . a return of that longing to which Schubert was never afraid to give voice, even when it pained him. . . . There is no sense of finality here; hope, and the anticipation of experiences yet to come, speak to us out of this music.[120]

Other positive and illuminating remarks are made by Edward Cone (Chapter 3) and Steven Lubin (Chapter 7) in this volume. My comments will focus on the many differences between the sketch (continuity draft) and the final version.

The Continuity Draft

The sketch of "Die Taubenpost," reproduced in facsimile in Schubert, *'Schwa-nengesang': Facsimiles . . . and Reprint* (New Haven: Yale University Press, 2000), is a continuity draft. This means that there are a complete vocal part and at least the melody of the instrumental interludes written on two staves (for voice and bass), rather than the three staves (voice and keyboard) of the more developed format of "Liebesbotschaft." In the sketch for "Liebes-botschaft," the almost complete coincidence of the voice part with the final version of the song, the three staves, and the full brace left blank for the pre-lude at the beginning of the song suggest a later stage in the compositional process, called earlier in the chapter a "skeleton score." Furthermore, there is just enough of the keyboard part included in the "Liebesbotschaft" sketch to indicate that Schubert had the texture and rhythmic shape of the accom-paniment in mind at the time he wrote out this version of the song, even if many details remained to be worked out. This is not true of the two-stave draft of "Die Taubenpost." Although there is a complete version of the voice part on the top stave, there are only twenty-two bars of bass on the lower one. The only other instrumental indications are entered on the top stave while the voice is silent: the right-hand portions of four interludes, the last of which was omitted from the final version of the song. There is no pre-lude or postlude, and no indication of the type of accompaniment Schubert had in mind for the song.

Unlike the exceptionally clean sketch for "Liebesbotschaft," and even less like the sketch fragment for "Frühlingssehnsucht," the draft for "Die Tauben-post" provides a fine opportunity to observe Schubert at work. There are dramatic changes in the oft-repeated opening vocal melody, and alterations of substance in the interludes; and the tonal shape of the last section, the cli-max of the song, also differs substantially from that of the final version. This last section Cone labels C in his ABAC formal design (see Chapter 3). In the draft the opening idea of the vocal line begins with a repetition of the tonic, g', then leaps to the dominant, d'', in place of the melodic succession of me-diant to dominant, b' to d'', of the song as known today (mm. 6, 10, 52, and 56).[121] Once the final version is in our ear, the opening stress on the tonic seems heavy, even stolid when compared with the lighter mediant, poised as it were between the weightier tonic and dominant (see Ex. 4.10).

In m. 24 of the draft there is a high g'' set to the clumsy, interpolated ex-clamation "Ja," and it is deleted; when the same note reappears in m. 69, for-tunately there is a syllable for it at the beginning of the verse *"Die* Taub' ist so mir Treu!" In both instances the line in question is a repeat of the final

Ex. 4.10. "Die Taubenpost" (draft), mm. 1–8

Ich   hab ei – ne Brief-taub' in   mei – nem Sold,   die   ist   gar er – ge – ben und treu;   sie

nimmt   mir nie   das   Ziel   zu   kurz,   und   fliegt   auch nie   vor –   bey

verse of a stanza (2 and 6), and as such they demonstrate well the practice of repeating text to accommodate a musical design, here to provide a convincing closure to section A.

Beginning section B (stanzas 3 and 4 of the text), Schubert improved the melody of the draft corresponding to mm. 30–34 of the final composition. Once more the draft began with the tonic but was altered in the final version to the mediant. Moreover, in m. 32 the first pitch was originally *e natural"*, improved to *c sharp"* for the definitive version.

Schubert revised the final section of the draft significantly during the restatement of the critical text "Sie heisst—die Sehnsucht! Kennt ihr sie?" In order to reflect once again the surprise inherent in the text, he replaces a repetition of the area of the supertonic (A major and minor), with which he had set that text the first time, with a new, unexpected, and even more distant tonal region, the lowered sixth degree (E-flat major). And, in the process, he increases the purely musical interest of the passage as well. This is extraordinarily sensitive and skillful compositional self-criticism on Schubert's part. Compare mm. 89–95 of the draft and final versions in Exx. 4.11a and 4.11b.

In the completed song the lower tessitura of the new voice part allows a gradual rise through *f natural"* (m. 96) to *g"* (mm. 99–100), where Schubert made his last revisions of the melody.

The absence of the rhythmically attractive syncopated accompaniment is, perhaps, the most striking feature of the draft. When one adds the dotted pattern on the second part of the measure and the newly lightened melodic line mentioned previously, there is an airborne effect that is highly appropriate to the imagery of the poem. Nor is there any sign in the earlier version of the piano's descending sixteenth-note figure, suggesting, perhaps, the pigeon's descent "bis zu der Liebsten Haus" (m. 23, and with different text, mm. 45 and 99).

Ex. 4.11a. "Die Taubenpost" (draft), mm. 87–95

[Drum heg ich sie auch so treu an der Brust, ver- si - chert des schönsten Ge- winns;

sie heißt: die Sehn-sucht kennt ihr sie?]

Ex. 4.11b. "Die Taubenpost," mm. 87–95

Drum heg ich sie auch so treu an der Brust, ver- si - chert des schön-sten Ge - winns;

sie heißt: die Sehn-sucht kennt ihr sie?

Schubert also made noteworthy changes in the keyboard interludes of the draft. Once more the original effect was heavy: predominantly blocks of chords in a middle register set mainly with repetitive dactylic rhythms. For the final version two of them were completely rewritten (mm. 13–14 and 59–60), with syncopations and dotted patterns combined. Meanwhile, Schubert also simplified slightly the harmony. He did away with the overly affective augmented-sixth chord in m. 14, as well as in m. 60 where it is implied even without a written bass. In the interlude between stanzas 4 and 5 (mm. 48–51), the prosaic dactyls were eliminated in favor of the lighter patterns, and Schubert completely omitted the final interlude (in the draft following m. 71). The single remaining interlude that resembles the original (mm. 26–29) has one dactylic pattern less in m. 26, and those remaining are lightened by the substitution of single notes in place of chords (mm. 28 and 29).

In closing, it may be observed that the the penultimate bar in the draft repeats m. 85. This is not a bad ending. Yet, with a minimum of change, Schubert created a better one. See Cone's discussion in Chapter 3 and Ex. 3.11.

From the Literature

In August 1937 Alfred Orel published a valuable study of the "Taubenpost" sketch in the periodical *Die Musik*. Recognizing that not everyone admires

the song, he compared it in this regard to "Das Fischermädchen" and argued for the fine details and musical logic of both songs. Near the beginning
of the article he introduced a thought that may resonate, at least to some
extent, with the idea of Edward Cone that Schubert may actually have intended "Die Taubenpost" to conclude the group of songs now comprising
Schwanengesang. Orel, who knew quite well the history of the transactions
between Schubert's brother Ferdinand and the publisher Haslinger after the
composer's death, says: "Ob Schubert die 14 Lieder des Schwanengesangs als
"Zyklus" aufgefasst wissen wollte, ob er sich die "Taubenpost" als Abschluss
dachte oder noch Lieder anfügen wollte, weiss man nicht."[122] (Whether
Schubert wanted the fourteen songs of *Schwanengesang* conceived of as a
"cycle," whether he thought of "Taubenpost" as the close or wanted to add
still additional songs, one doesn't know.)

NOTES

Epigraph: Cited in Brendel, *Musical Thoughts,* p. 74. See Chapter 1 for a discussion
of Liszt's arrangement of the complete *Schwanengesang* for piano solo and its importance for the early performance history of the songs.

1. The German text is based on *Franz Schubert: Die Texte seiner einstimmig komponierten
Lieder und ihre Dichter,* edited by Maximilian and Lilly Schochow but with Schubert's emen-
dations in the body of the poem. As far as can be determined, these are the texts Schubert set
as they were first published. It should be kept in mind, however, that Schubert probably
worked from a now-lost manuscript of "Die Taubenpost," and in all likelihood from no-longer-
extant manuscripts of the poems by Rellstab as well. The English translations throughout the
chapter are my own unless otherwise specified.

2. Undated letter, perhaps written in January 1823, Deutsch, *Schubert Reader,* 264.

3. Beethoven made this remark on the manuscript of his Cello Sonata Op. 102, No. 2.
Cited in Steblin, *Key Characteristics,* 307.

4. Dürr, "Ausweichungen," 80. In support, he cites Kraus, *Beiträge,* esp. 204–209, which
lists her ideas on Schubert's associations for twenty-three keys. B minor is missing. Dürr also
cites Auhagen, *Studien zur Tonartencharakteristik,* which provides a critique of Kraus's
Beiträge. See also Steblin, *Key Characteristics,* and Dittrich, "Die Lieder."

5. Reed, *Schubert Song Companion,* 484.

6. Steblin, *Key Characteristics,* has a useful appendix that lists the specific descriptions of
keys by a large number of theorists and composers. For G major a good percentage of them
suggest some form of "rustic" setting. For example, C. F. D. Schubart (c. 1784) describes it as
"everything rustic, idyllic and Lyrical . . . faithful love" (274); J. H. Knecht (c. 1792) calls it
"pleasant and rustic" (275); and G. J. Vogler (1812) deems it "always the favorite [key] for Pas-
torales" (275).

7. Examples of songs in G major in which water is important include "Wohin" and
"Danksagung an den Bach" from *Die schöne Müllerin.* Those in G that refer to birds include
"An die Nachtigall" (D. 487) and "Lebensmelodie" (D. 395), where there is a conversation be-
tween a swan, an eagle, and pigeons.

8. "Nahezu ausnahmslos Natur- und Liebesempfindungen." Kraus, *Beiträge,* 204–209.

9. R. Kramer, *Distant Cycles*, 165.

10. Reed, *Schubert Song Companion*, 492.

11. Dürr, "Entwurf-Ausarbeitung-Revision," 229.

12. Massin, *Franz Schubert*, 1267.

13. Chochlow, in "Zur Frage," suggests that Schubert clarifies the structure of a vocal composition with text repetitions and that he does so more frequently in quick songs (353–355).

14. See the manuscript at the library of the Gesellschaft der Musikfreunde, Vienna, in which "Lebensmuth" is followed by sketches for "Liebesbotschaft" and "Frühlingssehnsucht."

15. Georgiadis, *Schubert: Musik und Lyrik*, vol. 1, 351–356.

16. Hallmark, "Schubert's 'Auf dem Strom,'" 25–46.

17. Recall the delicious musical pun in *Le nozze di Figaro*, first section of the Act II Finale. After modulating to the dominant, Mozart writes the returning tonic chord, signifying the key of E flat, just as the Count sings "Quà la chiave" (Give me the key).

18. Massin, in *Franz Schubert*, 1258, suggests that the play of bass echoes returns in later songs. For a useful discussion of echoes in the Rellstab songs, see Cone's remarks in Chapter 3.

19. Noted by Georgiadis, *Schubert*, vol. 1, 355.

20. See, for example, R. Kramer, who calls his chapter on the Rellstab songs in *Distant Cycles* "'In der Ferne': Schubert's Rellstab."

21. See the introduction to my edition of *Rigoletto*, vol. 17 of *The Works of Giuseppe Verdi* (Chicago: University of Chicago Press; Milan: Ricordi, 1983), xxii. The Italian musician and theorist Francesco Galeazzi has written of preparing a score in this fashion as "in scheltro" (in skeleton) in his *Elementi teorico-pratici di musica . . .* (Rome, 1791, 1796). I am indebted to Gregory Harwood for bringing Galeazzi's term to my attention.

22. Georgiades, *Schubert*, vol. 1, 351 and 355–356.

23. Georgiades knows that Rellstab's lineation is eight short lines per stanza, but he prefers the longer textual units for his analysis. Ibid., 352.

24. Einstein, *Schubert*, 309.

25. Salzer, *Structural Hearing*, vol. 2, nos. 476a and 476b. In the background reduction (476b) there is a misplacement of the boxed number 2 indicating the beginning of the poem's second stanza. It should have been placed under the first C-major triad, not the first of the E-minor chords.

26. J. H. Thomas, "Schubert's Modified Strophic Songs," 95.

27. Tovey, "Franz Schubert," 132.

28. During his discussion of *Winterreise*, Einstein (*Schubert*, 304) suggested that "the major mode has the principal function of symbolizing the happiness of the past, while the minor represents the darkness of the present." H. Lowen Marshall developed this idea further in his article on the same cycle, "Symbolism in Schubert's *Winterreise*." While analyzing "Gute Nacht," for example, he remarks, "At the beginning of the fourth stanza, when he thinks tenderly of his loved one, there is a poignant shift to the parallel major. Indeed throughout the cycle, major is used to symbolize past happiness while minor symbolizes the cold, hard facts of the present and reality." H. H. Eggebrecht, in "Prinzipien des Schubert-Liedes," 96, also states that in Schubert's songs major and minor are often juxtaposed with one another as the illusory world of beautiful, bright dreams and the real world of banal, wretched, naked reality." (translation is from Kinderman, "Schubert's Tragic Perspective," 65).

29. In "Schubert and the Biedermeier" David Gramit discusses the subject of death as "a final escape . . . a peaceful release from the troubling world"; and specifically with reference to *Die schöne Müllerin* he remarks on "the calming refuge the cycle's protagonist finally achieves in death" (370 and 373).

30. The five songs are No. 14, "Der Jäger," No. 15, "Eifersucht und Stolz," No. 16, "Der liebe Farbe," No. 18, "Trockne Blumen," and No. 19, "Der Müller und der Bach." The song interrupting the sequence, No. 17, "Die böse Farbe," has important passages in minor and ends in that mode. By contrast, *Winterreise*, which is completely devoted to the reactions of a rejected lover, has fully sixteen of its twenty-four songs in minor. The texts of most of the songs in major suggest some form of escape from the protagonist's painful reality.

31. Reed, *Schubert Song Companion*, 362. Lotte Lehmann, in *Eighteen Song Cycles*, 67, hears the opening as depicting "with heavy but rather subdued chords the loneliness of the battlefield at night."

32. Vetter, *Der klassiker Schubert*, vol. 2, 247; Schwarmath, *Musikalischer Bau*, 78.

33. Beaufils, *Le lied romantique allemande*, 99. Cited in Massin, *Franz Schubert*, 1258 n. 1. For much closer citations by Schubert from Beethoven's movement during the last year of the younger composer's life, see Hallmark, "Schubert's 'Auf dem Strom,'" 41–42, and Chusid, "Schubert's Chamber Music: Before and after Beethoven." The last citation is a reference to the Trio of the Scherzo in the C-major String Quintet (D. 956).

34. Massin, *Schubert*, 1258 n. 2.

35. See, for example, Capell, *Schubert's Songs*, 249; and Fischer-Dieskau, *Schubert . . . Songs*, 278. Einstein describes it as "the final echo of the cantata-like type of song which found its first expression in the Ossian songs" (*Schubert*, 309).

36. Porter, *Songs of Schubert*, 103. It is perplexing that Porter, while describing the contents, seems to have missed completely the point of the song, the warrior's premonition of death. Ibid., 98.

37. R. Kramer, *Distant Cycles*, 116.

38. It is unfortunate that almost all citations of the German text for this song combine lines 1–4 of each strophe into two long lines, thus masking much of the poem's structural complexity and interest. See, for example, Wigmore, *Schubert . . . Song Texts*, 312–313.

39. Reproduced in facsimile in Schubert, *'Schwanengesang': Facsimiles . . . and Reprint*.

40. Dietrich Fischer-Dieskau is surely in error when he refers to the sketch as "a quite different version of the poem ['Liebesbotschaft'] in $\frac{9}{8}$ meter and $\frac{4}{4}$ time" (*Schubert . . . Songs*, 277). The poem "Liebesbotschaft" has alternate lines (2, 4, 6, etc.) that begin with a weak syllable. These call for a musical setting with an anacrusis; yet there is none in the fragment's five measures in $\frac{9}{8}$ meter.

41. Fischer-Dieskau, in *Schubert . . . Songs*, 278, observes, "The mood [of 'Frühlingssehnsucht'] and the use of the left-hand in the piano suggest a close relationship to 'Liebesbotschaft.'"

42. In *Neue Schubert-Ausgabe*, series IV, vol. 14a, xxiii, Walther Dürr suggested that "Kriegers Ahnung" "was inserted presumably for variety, to create contrast." He did not, however, refer to the similarities between "Liebesbotschaft" and "Frühlingssehnsucht."

43. Reed, *Schubert Song Companion*, 363.

44. As a young man Rellstab was a frequent visitor at the literary and artistic salon of Elisabeth Stägemann in Berlin, where Müller participated in the creating of the Liederspiel *Rose, des Müllerin*, which led in turn to his famous cycle of poetry *Die schöne Müllerin*. See Susan Youen's valuable study "Behind the Scenes: *Die schöne Müllerin* before Schubert," 5, 10–11, 21, 22, and *passim*.

45. Reed, *Schubert Song Companion*, 363.

46. Porter, *Songs of Schubert*, 136–137.

47. R. Kramer, *Distant Cycles*, 118.

48. Capell, *Schubert's Songs*, 251.

49. R. Kramer, *Distant Cycles*, 114–115.

50. Without citing evidence, Massin suggests that at one time Schubert intended "Herbst" to be included among the Rellstab songs that became part of *Schwanengesang* (*Schubert*, 1260).

51. Kerman, "A Romantic Detail," 57.

52. Schubert specifically mentions two of these overtures, *Coriolanus* and *Egmont*, in a letter to a Herr Peitl. Deutsch, *Schubert Reader*, 265.

53. For a more detailed discussion of these and other corrections, see the introduction to Schubert, *'Schwanengesang': Facsimiles . . . and Reprint*.

54. I suspect there was at least a sketch, if not a continuity draft, for "In der Ferne" at one time, as there were sketches of some sort for "Liebesbotschaft," "Frühlingssehnsucht," "Ständchen," and "Die Taubenpost." This hypothetical draft would have had the version represented by Ex. 4.4 for each of the recurrences as well. Interestingly enough, Schubert wrote *f sharps* in place of *g*'s in m. 59, during the third statement of the introductory material. Both notes of the octave were written as *f sharp*, then corrected and tied to perfectly written *g*'s in the following bar. Was there a residual memory of the original version?

55. *Allgemeine Musikalische Zeitung* (Leipzig), no. 40, 7 October 1829, cols. 659–662. A reprint of the original review may be found in Waidelich, *Dokumente 1817–1830*, 653–661.

56. See, for example, the extensive discussion by Richard Kramer of the subject in his chapter "'In der Ferne:' Schubert's Rellstab," in *Distant Cycles*, 102–108.

57. Reed, *Schubert Song Companion*, 364.

58. Fischer-Dieskau, *Schubert . . . Songs*, 279.

59. Porter, *Songs of Schubert*, 103, 104.

60. R. Kramer, *Distant Cycles*, 113. It may be noted that there are indeed B-major sections in "Liebesbotschaft" (mm. 40ff.) and "In der Ferne" (strophes 3 and 4), but there is only a short passage in B minor in "Ständchen" (mm. 33b–36). B, as dominant chord, dominant pedal, and dominant key, is also of considerable importance in "Aufenthalt" (esp. mm. 25–47 and 80–110).

61. See Dürr, "Vorwort," *Neue Schubert-Ausgabe*, series IV, vol. 4a, xv.

62. A number of writers on music in the early nineteenth century identify the outdoors with brass instruments in E flat. E. T. A. Hoffmann writes in "Kreislers musikalisch-poetischer Klub" (c. 1814): "E flat major (forte). Go after him! Go after him! Green is his coat, like the dark wood. His yearning words are the sweet sound of horns . . . Do you hear the sound of horns . . . ? . . . Let us go to meet him." Cited in Steblin, *Key Characteristics*, 246.

63. Flothuis, "Schubert Revises Schubert," 81.

64. Newbould, *Schubert*, 311.

65. Walther Vetter is particularly eloquent on the subject: "The Heine Lieder deserve a special place in the history of art. Individually each [song] bears the mark of the highest originality. A completely new style of song is born which anticipates a portion of the development of an entire century [and] in the instant of its birth [that development] is . . . completed!" *Der Klassiker Schubert*, vol. 2, 220. The single dissenting voice is that of Jack Stein in his *Poem and Music in the German Lied*. He singles out Schubert's settings of Heine's poetry for special excoriation, although his point of view, that poetry must remain preeminent, disallows *any* song setting that transforms or aspires to equality with its poetry. Not surprisingly, his views have little credence with musicians.

66. Cone, *The Composer's Voice*, 40.

67. Fischer-Dieskau, *Schubert . . . Songs*, 281.

68. The titles were given by Schubert to his songs, and even Heine scholars use them when referring to these six poems.

69. Westrup, "Some Settings of Heine," 194.

70. The point has been made by Capell, who says, "The song begins like a symphony,

so charged and tragic is the musical thought" (*Schubert's Songs*, 252). Fischer-Dieskau also remarks, "The symphonic atmosphere of "Der Atlas," staggering along and groaning under its [his?] burden . . ." (*Schubert . . . Songs*, 280).

71. Reed, *Schubert Song Companion*, 260.

72. Riemann, *Ludwig van Beethovens . . . Klaviersonaten*, vol. 3, 453.

73. Reed, in *Schubert Song Companion*, 260, also remarks that the subject "framed by hammer blows in the bass—G, B flat, F sharp, G—strikes with the inexorable finality of fate itself. Those four notes are nearly akin to the germ-cell of 'Der Doppelgänger' also and, with the first interval changed from a minor to a major third, form the harmonic basis of the middle section of 'Der Atlas.' It is easy to see that the opening bars of 'Ihr Bild' provide us with a kind of melodic version of the theme. It pervades the Heine songs like a musical image of the force of destiny." Earlier in his discussion of the song he suggests that in "Der Atlas" "the idea of alienation takes on a symphonic grandeur." See also Reintjes (*Aspects of Cyclical Structure*, 96), who traces the "Atlas" motive in "Ihr Bild," "Am Meer," and "Der Doppelgänger."

74. Hallmark has suggested that this composition was also a tribute to Beethoven. See his article "Schubert's 'Auf dem Strom,'" especially 40–46.

75. Ibid., 40–42.

76. See, for example, Cone, "Schubert's Unfinished Business."

77. Gruber, "Romantische Ironie," 325.

78. Massin, *Schubert*, 1264.

79. J. H. Thomas, "Schubert's Modified Strophic Songs," 87.

80. Utz, *Untersuchungen zur Syntax*, 78.

81. Newbould, *Schubert*, 311.

82. Schenker, *Der Tonwille*, 46.

83. Kerman, "A Romantic Detail," 49.

84. While discussing "Ihr Bild," Reed makes the same point: "Bare unison phrases . . . always with Schubert [suggest] an image of loneliness and desperation" (*Schubert Song Companion*, 261). Many years earlier, Paul Mies wrote an article titled "Die Bedeutung des Unisono im Schubertschen Liede," in which he suggested that in slow tempos Schubert tends to associate the unison or octave setting with eerie situations ("unheimlichen Stellen") and the minor mode. The occurrence of such passages in "Ihr Bild" provides the musically outstanding example for Mies of the expression of "the pessimistic, desperate mood." See especially 103–108, and for "Ihr Bild," 106.

85. William Kinderman makes the point concisely: "In a sense, the basic idea of ["Ihr Bild"] is the reinterpretation of the single note, B flat, which acts as a focal point for the voice throughout." Later he suggests, "The sound of the cryptic B flat is carried through the entire song, and the changing harmonic interpretation of this note embodies the change in feeling, or state of being, suggested in the Heine poem." "Schubert's Tragic Perspective," 71, 74–75.

86. Brauner, "Irony in the Heine Lieder," 278.

87. Schnebel, "Klangräume—Zeiträume."

88. Peake, "Kreuzer's *Wanderlieder*," 93–94.

89. Deutsch, *Schubert: Memoirs by His Friends*, 27 and 135. The story is related twice by Josef von Spaun, considered by Deutsch the most reliable of all Schubert's friends with regard to anecdotes about the composer.

90. Ex. 4.11a cited from Peake. Ibid., 94.

91. Westrup, "Some Settings of Heine," 193.

92. Reed, *Schubert Song Companion*, 261.

93. Westrup, "Some Settings of Heine," 193.

94. Reed, *Schubert Song Companion*, 261–262.

95. Scheibler, "Franz Schuberts einstimmige Lieder im Volkston," 1094. Seaton also recognizes the "Volkstil" (folk style) of "Das Fischermädchen." See his "Interpreting Schubert's Heine Songs," 95.

96. Utz, *Untersuchung zur Syntax*, 64.

97. Porter, *Schubert's Song Technique*, 80–81.

98. Whitall, *Romantic Music*, 27.

99. Gruber, "Romantische Ironie," 326.

100. See, for example, Alec Robertson ("The Song," 171), who remarks, "'Die Stadt' opens the door into the post-Wagnerian era of impressionism"; Einstein (*Schubert*, 310), who says, "'Die Stadt' . . . the town dimly visible through the mist . . . is the prototype of the impressionist song"; Westrup ("Some Settings of Heine," 194), for whom the song "provides an impressionistic background to the misty scene"; and, finally, Reed (*Schubert Song Companion*, 262), who begins his short discussion of the song by saying, "The impressionistic brilliance of 'Die Stadt' seems to mark the beginning of a new phase in Schubert's development as a pictorial composer."

101. Massin, *Franz Schubert*, 1266.

102. Dürr, "Schubert's Songs and Their Poetry," 21.

103. For example, Reintjes, *Aspects*, 109.

104. See, for example, David Schwarz, "Ascent and Arpeggiation in "Die Stadt," "Der Doppelgänger," and "Der Atlas," 40–41. As the reduction of "Die Stadt" has a key signature of three flats, all three *a*'s should have natural signs.

105. Schenker, *Free Composition*, supplement, fig. 103, 4.

106. Morgan, "Dissonant Prolongation," esp. 58–60.

107. L. Kramer, "The Schubert Lied," 208.

108. Einstein, *Schubert*, 310.

109. Gruber, "Romantische Ironie," 328.

110. More than thirty-five years ago I discussed Schubert's powerful and frequently unorthodox way of handling dissonance, especially augmented-sixth chords, in my dissertation, "The Chamber Music of Schubert," 94–95, 142, 223–224 and *passim*. Perhaps Schubert's most brilliant use of this chord as coloristic (that is, in a progression without bass movement and with the augmented sixth both approached and left by the same chord) rather than as a traditionally functional chord (that is, passing from some form of subdominant or supertonic chord by chromatic alteration to the dominant or tonic in second inversion) is to be found in the A–flat–minor Ländler, No. 8 of the wonderful set of 12 Ländler D. 790 (Op. 171), first edited by Johannes Brahms.

111. Fischer-Dieskau, *Schubert . . . Songs*, 281.

112. Newbould, *Schubert*, 313.

113. Franz Krautwurst, and he is certainly not alone, calls "Der Doppelgänger" "vielleicht die Krone aller Schubertlieder" (perhaps the crown of all Schubert songs). "Franz Schubert," *Die Musik in Geschichte und Gegenwart*, vol. 12, col. 160.

114. First published as a periodical article in 1954, it has been reprinted in Thomas' *Schubert Studien*. My comments refer to the more recent book.

115. Ibid., 120–121. He transfers this idea to the melodic motion at the cadences (a'–g'–f *sharp'*) in mm. 11–12 and the keyboard echo of that cadence in mm. 13–14, pointing as a model to the Lutheran chorale "Aus tiefer Not schrei ich zu dir." Ibid., 123. I find little interest in modality by Schubert, and this example strikes me as particularly unlikely for the Catholic composer.

116. See Elliot Forbes, ed., *Thayer's Life of Beethoven,* 1024 and 1035.

117. Deutsch, *Schubert Reader,* 819. Deutsch, in *Schubert: Memoirs by His Friends,* 123, reports that this copy ultimately came into Meyerbeer's possession.

118. Leopold von Sonnleithner, in ibid., 114. Essentially the same story is repeated by Gerhard von Breuning, in ibid., 255.

119. Schneider, "Schuberts Heine-Liedern," 1061.

120. Fischer-Dieskau, *Schubert . . . Songs,* 282–283.

121. All measure numbers refer to the final version of the song.

122. Orel, "Die Skizze zu . . . Schuberts letzem Lied," 766.

PART III

Performance

CHAPTER 5

The Sequence of the Heine Songs and Cyclicism in *Schwanengesang*

MARTIN CHUSID

In an article dating from 1972, "Welches war die ursprüngliche Reihenfolge in Schuberts Heine-Liedern" (What was the original sequence of Schubert's Heine songs), Harry Goldschmidt suggested that these six songs be rearranged to follow their order in the poet's collection *Die Heimkehr* (The homecoming), the largest and most important section in Heine's most popular volume of poetry, *Buch der Lieder*.[1] According to this theory, this sequence was altered by Schubert at the publisher's request. Table 5.1 shows the ordering of the Heine songs in Schubert's manuscript (and all publications of the music to date), the suggested reordering with Heine's numbering of the poems in *Die Heimkehr,* and the keys in both situations.

At the heart of the new tonal sequence is the chromatic fall from C to B natural to B flat. Goldschmidt also suggested that the first publisher of the songs lowered the key of "Der Atlas" from A minor to G minor. If this were true and we followed Goldschmidt's suggestion to return to Schubert's "intended" key, there would be a further chromatic descent to *A,* thereby filling in all possible half steps from the C major of "Am Meer" to the A-flat major of "Das Fischermädchen." It is clear that Goldschmidt had never seen the autograph manuscript. Without accepting Goldschmidt's suggestion that the key of "Der Atlas" should be A minor, in 1985 Richard Kramer published an article, "Schubert's Heine," supporting the theory with additional, mainly musical, arguments.[2] Neither Goldschmidt nor Kramer seems to have been aware that in 1967 Maurice J. E. Brown had already written:

TABLE 5.1.

Order according to Schubert ms. and later publications		Order according to Die Heimkehr	
Title	Key	Title	Key
"Der Atlas"	G minor	"Das Fischermädchen" (No. 8)	A♭ major
"Ihr Bild"	B♭ minor	"Am Meer" (No. 14)	C major
"Das Fischermädchen"	A♭ major	"Die Stadt" (No. 16)	C minor
"Die Stadt"	C minor	"Der Doppelgänger" (No. 20)	B minor
"Am Meer"	C major	"Ihr Bild" (No. 23)	B♭ minor
"Der Doppelgänger"	B minor	"Der Atlas" (No. 24)	G minor

It is doubtful if the order in which [the Heine songs] appear in *Schwanengesang* is according to Schubert's wish, for it differs considerably from the order in *Die Heimkehr*. Heine's lyrics are partly autobiographical and the sequence, although not narrative, is coherent. The altered order in *Schwanengesang* destroys this coherence and gives us an unconnected group of songs in which "Fischermädchen," for example, seems out of place. It should actually be the first song and as such would introduce us to the woman whom the poet loved and lost. After "Fischermädchen" the next two songs, "Die Stadt" and "Am Meer," are settings of poems with the sea as a very important factor in the conveying of the heavily charged emotions. The most casual glance shows that they were published in the wrong order, an arrangement which has obscured the fact that they actually form a pair of songs.

Later Brown provided the songs in the order of the poems in *Die Heimkehr*, with the remark "Arranged thus, they do form a miniature song cycle."[3]

This theory, which has aroused both interest and controversy, rests on several premises that deserve scrutiny. First, there is an implication that narrative cycles of poetry or music occur with some degree of regularity and that they are somehow preferable to other types of grouping. Second, it is assumed that Heine's cycle *Die Heimkehr* has, or at least implies, a narrative base.[4] And finally, it is implied that relations by half step between the principal keys of three or more successive songs (or dances, or movements of larger instrumental works) occur with sufficient frequency in Schubert's music to warrant altering his own arrangement of the Heine songs in the autograph.[5]

In a useful survey titled *The Lyric Cycle in German Literature,* Helen Mustard suggested that poets have approached the construction of cycles in one of two ways. Either previously written poems were "arranged" into groups, or poems were "conceived from the very beginning as a group form." The second type she designates as "composed" cycles. Among the "composed" groups are "narrative" cycles. These, as their name implies, consist of "groups whose members form a sequence based on more or less concrete, successive events."[6] An excellent example is Wilhelm Müller's *Die schöne Müllerin*. However, she remarks, narrative cycles are less common than one might imagine. When examining the lyrics from the first fifteen years of the nineteenth century by the Romantic poets Friedrich Novalis, the brothers August Wilhelm and Friedrich Schlegel, and Ludwig Tieck, Mustard found only three narrative cycles: F. Schlegel's *Bekenntnisse* and Tieck's *Des Jünglings Liebe* and *Reisegedichte*. Even here she suggests that the narrative implications of *Bekenntnisse* "are very indefinite," and that *Reisegedichte* is "not a narrative in the usual meaning of the word, but only in the sense in which a diary is a narrative, an aimless, unselective account of unorganized experience." Almost all the cycles of this period proved to be "loose clusters of poems around a central theme usually broad in scope." Of F. Schlegel's *Abendröthe* and most of Tieck's cycles, she claims, "It is the mood, the emotional atmosphere as much as the thematic core which binds the poems together."[7]

During the period of particular concern to us, 1815–1830, Mustard reports a flowering of narrative poetic cycles and focuses on the lyrics of Ludwig Uhland, Wilhelm Müller, and Heinrich Heine. But, she says, many of these are simply groups of nature poems on a thin narrative thread—for example, Uhland's *Wanderlieder,* a work of particular importance for Müller. Although the author from Dessau arranged all his poems into cycles for publication, Mustard believes that with the notable exception of *Die schöne Müllerin,* his cycles, even *Die Winterreise,* "are loosely connected sequences . . . arranged as cycles, not composed . . . and betray their origin in frequent gaps and interruptions of continuity." Heine is "another poet whose entire lyric production tends to be cyclic. From his first collection [*Gedichte*] of 1821 to the *Romanzero* of 1851 the group arrangement predominates."[8] Considering that almost all of them are of the looser "arranged" variety and that Schubert drew his six texts from the most extensive, the eighty-eight poems of *Die Heimkehr,* we might well ask to what extent Brown, Goldschmidt, Kramer, and others are erecting their own narrative rather than Heine's. Perhaps literary specialists may be of assistance here.

Although they do not agree on the details, analysts of *Die Heimkehr* tend to see the cycle as dividing into subcycles, and all identify a group of sea poems, Nos. 7–14, a set including the poems Schubert named "Das Fischermädchen" (No. 8) and "Am Meer" (No. 14). Jeffrey Sammons, for example, describes them as "a group of North Sea poems."[9] Mustard sees them as re-

lating to "the sea where the poet has taken refuge from his sorrow," following the opening poems (Nos. 1–6), which "contain reminiscences of the
poet's first love." In this reading "Das Fischermädchen," far from initiating
a tragic love affair, depicts a momentary dallying on the part of the poet in
reaction to a more serious, and unhappy, romantic experience. The text of
the poem (see Chapter 4) supports this analysis and strongly suggests that
Schubert understood not only the meaning of the individual poems but also
their significance in terms of the cycle *Die Heimkehr* as a whole. His placement of "Der Atlas" and "Ihr Bild" at the beginning of the cycle is a good
substitute for the unhappy prior experience. In regard to Schubert's choices,
it seems noteworthy that literary scholars tend to see the most significant
subcycle of *Die Heimkehr* as beginning with No. 16 (Schubert's "Die Stadt").
According to Mustard it depicts "the poet's return to the city where his
sweetheart lived."[10] In *Heinrich Heine: Poetry in Context, a Study of 'Buch der
Lieder,'* Michael Perraudin expresses this idea more forcefully. He claims that
the subcycle Nos. 16–20, which includes both "Die Stadt" (No. 16) and "Der
Doppelgänger" (No. 20), represents "the narrative of a homecoming to the
urban site of past pains, [which] constitutes the 'inner' *Heimkehr*, and . . . the
prime justification of the full cycle's title." He further claims that the sequence of Nos. 16, 17, 18, and 20 has "experiential basis. It was written almost certainly in the second half of 1823, either in Hamburg, where Heine
spent part of that summer, or thereafter at his parents' home in Lüneburg.
The poems, like the title of the cycle, refer to the poet's return, for the first
time since 1819, to the city which saw the amorous, social and professional
humiliations of his late adolescence."[11]

By this stage in his career, Schubert's well-developed poetic acumen
caused him to select four of the six poems he set from the two most clearly
identifiable subgroups of *Die Heimkehr*, the sea poems and the actual return;
to place "Die Stadt," the return by sea, between the two poems from the sea
group, thereby linking the two separate groups; and then to provide a shattering climax to his short cycle of songs by closing with "Der Doppelgänger."
In his study *Heine: The Tragic Satirist*, S. S. Prawer unequivocally identifies
"Der Doppelgänger" as "the key-poem of *Buch der Lieder*."[12] Far from representing what Kramer takes to be a careless reading of the verses, "a failure
of nerve" or "malicious tinkering,"[13] Schubert's selection and placement of
Heine's poetry is as brilliant as is his music. Heine, incidentally, never com-
plained about Schubert's "reordering" of his *Heimkehr* poems; nor did he
ever accuse the composer of "botching the job" in setting his poetry to
music, as did Rellstab about the first seven songs of *Schwanengesang*.[14]

Evidence suggesting the validity of the sequence of the Heine songs in Schubert's autograph may also be found in the music. Edward Cone has traced the opening melodic idea of "Der Atlas" in each of the other five Heine songs (see Chapter 3), and many years ago, Hugo Riemann indicated the source of that theme, namely, the principal subject in the first movement of Beethoven's final piano sonata, the C minor (Op. 111).[15]

As for the order of "Die Stadt" and "Am Meer," Robert Morgan has suggested that the dissonant diminished-seventh chord on C of "Die Stadt," which is left hanging at the end of that song, actually resolves at the beginning of the next song, "Am Meer" (see Chapter 4). Richard Kramer, without reporting Morgan's theory of resolution—perhaps because it conflicted with the new ordering under which "Am Meer" precedes "Die Stadt"—argues elliptically against Morgan's view. He points out that in "tonal theory after Rameau . . . the diminished triad has no authority, for it has no root. The 7 of the diminished seventh is generally understood as a local appoggiatura (in the sense of 9–8) to the root of a plain dominant seventh, the actual root determined by the context."[16] To be sure, Schubert often resorted to this traditional manner of writing the diminished-seventh chord, that is, treating it functionally as a kind of substitute for the dominant; and this is in accordance with Classic (eighteenth-century) practice and Rameau's harmonic theory. But it is precisely Schubert's generation, and this includes Carl Maria von Weber, Ludwig Spohr, Mendelssohn, Chopin, and Schumann, that began to treat the diminished seventh, and other chromatic sonorities such as the augmented-sixth chord, in a new and non-functional fashion, in a coloristic manner. They became interested in these sonorities for their own sake, without reference to normal root progression. One of the most famous of all diminished-seventh chords used in this way appears in the opening progression of Schubert's C-major String Quintet (D. 956), in all probability written at the same time as, or only shortly after, *Schwanengesang*.[17] The unusual feature of the diminished-seventh chord in "Die Stadt" is that during the song neither of the two dissonant intervals, the diminished fifth (*C* + *G flat*, spelled *F sharp*) and the diminished seventh (*C* + *B double flat,* spelled *A natural*) is resolved. Morgan's suggestion not only provides a resolution for these intervals, but it also suggests a preparation for the dissonant augmented-sixth chord beginning "Am Meer." Both the voicing and the resolution of that chord deserve comment.

Increasingly since the early Baroque, composers freed themselves from the obligation of preparing dissonances. But until Schubert's day the augmented-sixth chord tended to be an exception. It usually remained either an

altered form of the supertonic (the so-called French variety) or an altered
subdominant (the Italian and German types). The dissonant interval resulted from the chromatic lowering of the sixth degree of the scale and the
raising, also by half step, of the fourth scale degree. The lowest tone was
normally the altered sixth degree, the highest most often the raised fourth.
The resolution was consistently to the dominant in root position or its substitute, the unstable tonic in second inversion, which subsequently resolved
to the dominant. Looking at the augmented sixth of "Am Meer," however,
we find the augmented-sixth interval inverted to become a diminished third
and the resolution bypassing the dominant completely. Instead, the chord of
resolution is a stable tonic triad in root position. Nor does the augmented
sixth suggest a supertonic or subdominant function. What is significant
about this chord is its emotional effect as a highly charged dissonant configuration or, put another way, its coloristic quality.[18] An equally unusual treatment of augmented-sixth chords takes place in the next song, "Der Doppelgänger." At mm. 31 and 32, we hear an augmented sixth that is neither a
subdominant nor a supertonic chord; instead it is an inverted dominant
with lowered fifth (*C natural* + *E natural* + *F sharp* + *A sharp*), which again resolves to a tonic (B-minor) triad in root position. A similar situation occurs
at the climax of the song (mm. 41 and 42), as the protagonist recognizes his
"eigne Ge*stalt*." The single difference is that the root of the dominant chord
is delayed until the third beat of m. 42. Along the same lines, during the
postlude of the same song (m. 59), Schubert writes a triad on the lowered
second degree. The position of this triad is that of a cadential Neapolitan
chord. However, in this instance there are two unusual features: the root of
the chord is in the bass (again it is *C natural*) instead of the usual first inversion, and once more the following chord is a tonic in root position instead of
the dominant that normally follows a Neapolitan sixth chord. In all three instances, the two augmented-sixth chords and the Neapolitan in root position, Schubert calls special attention to the chromatic pitch in the bass, *C
natural*. Why? I think the answer is that he is more closely relating his final
song of the cycle, "Der Doppelgänger," with the two preceding songs. Not
only is "Die Stadt" in C minor and "Am Meer" in C major, but both of these
Lieder have highly important chromatic chords built on *C natural*. Other
pitches of importance shared by the three songs will be discussed later.

There is another aspect of the suggested reordering of the Heine songs
to be considered. If Goldschmidt's ideas are entirely followed (that is, if we
accept that "Der Atlas" belongs in A minor), a chromatic sequence of keys
results for all but the first song: "Am Meer" and "Die Stadt" in C, "Der Doppelgänger" in B, "Ihr Bild" in B flat, and "Der Atlas" in A. How often does Schu-

bert relate four successive songs, dances, or movements of his composite compositions in this fashion? The answer is: never. If we drop Goldschmidt's A minor for "Der Atlas" and ask the same question, the answer is: just once. In Op. 95 the keys of the first three songs ascend by half steps.[19] If this is not a common approach, how, then, does Schubert relate keys in his grouped pieces? Except for his composite instrumental works, where a single tonal center may be expected to dominate (in sonatas, symphonies, and so on), he actually prefers to avoid any systematic succession. As in *Schwanengesang,* he likes a mixture of tonal relationships: by third, as in "Frühlingssehnsucht" (B flat) to "Ständchen" (D), by whole step, as in "Ständchen" to "Aufenthalt" (E), by fourth or its inversion the fifth, as in "Liebesbotschaft" (G) to "Kriegers Ahnung" (C), or he may just change mode, as in "Die Stadt" (C minor) to "Am Meer" (C major). One of the less common relationships is by half step, as in "Am Meer" to "Der Doppelgänger." Another less common procedure is to remain in the same key, as in *Die schöne Müllerin,* where "Des Müllers Blumen" and "Tränenregen" are both in A major. Not that Schubert's key choices are haphazard; far from it. His sense for the dramatic implications of tonal distance is extraordinary, and especially in his song cycles the choice of a related or distant key for the next song is a reflection of the closeness or distance of the subject matter. Or, as Anthony Newcomb remarked with regard to *Winterreise,* "The function of tonality within Schubert's cycle is especially to draw together some songs and separate others."[20] For example, in the Rellstab songs, "Aufenthalt" in E minor following "Ständchen" in D minor/major reflects the considerable distance between a rejected lover and a previously hopeful serenader. The more or less logical deterioration to the deep depression of the protagonist in the next song, "In der Ferne," is matched tonally by a move to the closely related key of B minor/major, the dominant of E minor. But the change in emotional tone from depressed to somewhat cheerful in the poetry of "Abschied," the next song, calls for more tonal distance and is reflected by the considerable tonal leap from B minor/major across the key circle to E-flat major. This key, in turn, recalls the relatively bright poetry of the earlier song "Frühlingssehnsucht," set by Schubert in the related key B-flat major, dominant of E flat. As narrative, the relative cheer of "Abschied" does not smoothly follow the dark "In der Ferne." But musically it provides a satisfying finale for the Rellstab group.

Because the manuscripts of the poetry were returned to the poet by Schindler and have since been lost, we do not know in what order Schubert received the Rellstab poems from Beethoven's *Nachlass*—if indeed he did receive them that way. In any case, the sequence of the seven Rellstab songs in *Schwanengesang* is remarkably close to their positioning in the volume

TABLE 5.2.

No. in Schwanengesang	Title and key	Page nos. in *Gedichte* of 1827 *
	["Lebensmuth" (B-flat major)]	16–17
4	"Ständchen" (D minor/major)	101–102
1	"Liebesbotschaft" (G major)	103–104
2	"Kriegers Ahnung" (C minor)	105
	["Herbst" (E minor)]	106–107
3	"Frühlingssehnsucht" (B-flat major)	114–115
6	"In der Ferne" (B minor/major)	118–119
	["Auf dem Strom" (E major)]	120–121
5	"Aufenthalt" (E minor)	124
7	"Abschied" (E-flat major)	134–135

* Page numbers derived from Schochow, *Texte*, 468–477.

Gedichte von Ludwig Rellstab (Berlin, 1827). As Table 5.2 indicates, the only changes are that the order of "Aufenthalt" and "In der Ferne" is reversed and "Ständchen" is printed earliest of the seven.[21]

Otto Erich Deutsch once suggested, "It is quite possible that both . . . stories [that is, Schindler's that he lent Schubert the songs from Beethoven's *Nachlass* and Rellstab's that Schubert set them at Beethoven's request] are wrong and that Schubert found the Rellstab poems he set in the latter's collection of 1827."[22] Wherever he found them, Schubert wrote splendid songs on Rellstab's poetry, and as we know—see *Schubert's 'Schwanengesang': Facsimiles . . . and Reprint* (New Haven: Yale University Press, 2000)—he continued writing the Heine songs into the same manuscript. Furthermore, they continue to be linked frequently in performances and in recorded sound today, and it may prove useful to consider why what appear to be two separate cycles seem to work well together. Certainly there have been innumerable recitals and sound reproductions of all fourteen songs in Schubert's compositional sequence.[23] For one thing, the poetry of each tends to stress the subject of the rejected lover. Furthermore, since the two groups of poems were written at the same time, they share features of Schubert's late style of song writing. For example, the voice and piano parts are essentially equivalent in importance, and the keyboard writing is remarkably imaginative and varied. Whereas the Rellstab songs are somewhat longer, there is no single Lied in either group that overpowers the others, and there is a good proportional balance within each group and between the two. But perhaps the single feature that most promotes compatibility is tonal. The

TABLE 5.3. Primary Tonal Centers Shared by the Rellstab and Heine Songs

Tonality	Rellstab	Heine
G	"Liebesbotschaft" (No. 1, major)	"Der Atlas" (No. 1, minor)
B	"In der Ferne" (No. 6, minor/major)	"Der Doppelgänger" (No. 6, minor)
C	"Kriegers Ahnung" (No. 2, minor)	"Die Stadt" (No. 4, minor) and "Am Meer" (No. 5, major)
B flat	"Frühlingssehnsucht" (No. 3, major)	"Ihr Bild" (No. 2, minor/major)

TABLE 5.4. Subordinate Regions Relating to B (C flat)

Rellstab songs, keys, measure nos.	Heine songs, keys, measure nos.
"Liebesbotschaft" (B major: 40–49)	"Der Atlas" (B major: 22–30)
"Liebesbotschaft" (E minor: 12–16, 58–63)	"Der Atlas" (E minor: 31–35)
"Kriegers Ahnung" (F-sharp minor: 44–49)	"Ihr Bild" (G-flat major: 16–22)
"Ständchen" (B minor: 33b–36)	"Das Fischermädchen" (C-flat major: 28–46)
"Aufenthalt" (B minor: 40–51, 95–106)	
"Abschied" (C-flat major: 132–44)	

two groups share many keys both as primary and subsidiary tonal centers. As a result, I think that both performers and listeners accept what are essentially two separate subcycles as a single larger unit. Two tables (5.3 and 5.4) show the tonal relationships.

The most important of the subordinate tonal areas in both subcycles tend to relate to keys centering on B (C flat). As Table 5.4 indicates, six songs make use of B or C flat itself as a contrasting region, and two each stress its dominant (F sharp or G flat) and subdominant (E) for secondary keys. There is also one song ("Aufenthalt") whose primary key is E minor with its most important tonal contrast provided by B minor.

Furthermore, although keys relating to B or C flat are not contrasting regions per se in "Die Stadt" and "Am Meer," the pitches *F sharp* and *D sharp (E flat)* are of great importance in those songs and help prepare the ears of the listener for the tonal center on *B,* its melodically stressed dominant, *f sharp,* and the tonicized area of D-sharp minor in "Der Doppelgänger." Together with the emphasis on the pitch *C* in those three songs, the additional connections derived from the sharing of *F sharp* and *D sharp* result in a sense of bonding into a further subset with "Der Doppelgänger," providing a powerful climax both for the last three Heine songs and the group as a whole.

Opposition to the Brown-Goldschmidt-Kramer reordering of the Heine songs has been registered by a number of musical scholars. Kurt von Fischer, in his essay "Some Thoughts on Key Order in Schubert's Song Cycles," argues from the basis of Schubert's autograph, where "the songs are unmistakably in the familiar order," suggesting further that "primarily this break with the ordering found in Heine answers Schubert's musical conception." He finds "an analogy . . . in *Winterreise,* where . . . realistic notions alternate with dream visions and delusions." He goes on, "This cycle [the Heine songs] begins with a wild eruption: 'Der Atlas.' Then comes 'Ihr Bild'; it is structured as a rigid dream-vision. 'Das Fischermädchen' contains reminiscences. By means of an unstable meter Schubert makes the song into a fragile, barcarole-like piece. In 'Die Stadt' the ironically cheerful mood of the preceding piece clouds over. . . . 'Am Meer' establishes a connection with 'Das Fischermädchen' by being another recollection, one now grown painful. The cycle concludes with the delusions of 'Der Doppelgänger.'"[24] He then argues, perhaps a bit too briefly, for Schubert's tonal logic.[25]

Douglass Seaton argues at considerably greater length on behalf of Schubert's order in his article "Interpreting Schubert's Heine Songs." At one point he writes, "We may take issue with Kramer's proposed tonal plan at its core by pointing out that it may not be particularly valid to ask how Schubert's music can be made to follow Schenkerian tonal outlines (even if we are willing to accept Schenkerian fragments, as Kramer is)." Instead he suggests, "We might discover some poetically motivated key-structure in Schubert's order for the cycle." Further, Seaton observes that "the Schubert-Heine songs, like many of Schubert's other late works, clearly stress 3rd-relations as the tonal determinants of large-scale structural contrast. Relatively common 3rd-relations in the cycle are those of B flat minor–G flat major in 'Ihr Bild' and A flat major–C flat major in 'Das Fischermädchen.'" He then associates the drama with the use of third relations:

> The most striking modulation, that to the raised 3rd in minor-key songs, occurs in Schubert's first and last songs, at the moment when the poetry expresses the greatest self-alienation. . . . The Atlas of Schubert's first song describes himself in G minor, but he speaks to his heart in B major. The two keys are as distant as possible (in terms of the cycle of 5ths), providing a convincing symbol for alienation. This tonal polarity establishes a tension that is resolved into B in Schubert's last song, "Der Doppelgänger." There again . . . self-alienation is suggested by another parallel shift to the key of the raised 3rd, this time from B minor to D sharp minor, when the unhappy one addresses his "Doppelgänger." . . . Moreover, "Der Doppelgänger" concludes on B *major,* making the connection to "Der Atlas" even more explicit.

Concluding, Seaton stresses the cyclic aspects of the Heine songs: "But instead of asking how the order of the poems can be made to form a narrative, we should enquire what sort of relationship exists among the texts in the order in which Schubert placed them. . . . We must resist the temptation to test the songs against our own readings of the poems or our preferred methods of musical analysis."[26]

Returning to the composer himself, I wonder if Schubert's decision to include songs contrasting strongly in mood with their neighbors—such as "Kriegers Ahnung" and "Abschied" of the Rellstab songs or "Das Fischermädchen" in the Heine set—as well as his choice of combining two shorter cycles in his manuscript rather than composing a single, larger one, may have been influenced by a review of the first part of *Winterreise,* which appeared in the *Allgemeine Musik-Zeitung* of Munich on 28 July 1828, shortly before Schubert arranged in final order his collection of thirteen songs by Rellstab and Heine. Deutsch suggests as the possible author of the review Franz Stoepel, who had previously reviewed favorably other compositions by Schubert in the same journal. The critic "does not on the whole approve of song cycles." He believes that "true song should unfold itself in single flowers." After describing the first part of *Winterreise* as "a song cycle . . . with love and tears for its main subject," he complains that the "whole suffers from a certain monotony, and . . . the composer in particular has spread it all rather too much."[27] The timing of the review and the date on the autograph of "August 1828" supports the idea of a possible impact on *Schwanengesang.*

It is curious that as yet no one has objected to the order of Schubert's Rellstab songs in the way that the Heine set has been questioned. The composer does not follow precisely the sequence of the Berlin poet's lyrics as they are published in the *Gedichte* of 1827, one of the three possible sources for the poetry, and Rellstab himself once suggested a cyclic, though not narrative, intent for the poems he gave Beethoven. In a letter believed to have been written to the great composer, he wrote: "I send you herewith some songs which I have had copied fairly for you; some others, written in the same vein, will directly follow. They have perhaps this novelty about them, that they form in themselves a connected series, and have reference to happiness, unity, separation, death, and hope on the other side of the grave, without pointing to any definite incidents. I should wish that these poems might succeed so far in winning your approval as to move you to set them to music."[28]

Citing Rellstab's letter, but not the fact that the ordering of the songs in the *Gedichte* is not the same, Richard Kramer argues persuasively in favor of Schubert's arrangement. In "Liebesbotschaft" he sees "a song to set a cycle in

motion," and of "Abschied" he suggests, "There is a sheer physical exuberance
. . . that dispels the pathological brooding that precedes it." Later he describes
each song's position in what he describes as "a characteristic scenario":

"Liebesbotschaft."	The distant beloved. Messenger as surrogate.
"Kriegers Ahnung."	Distance of time and place reinforced.
"Frühlingssehnsucht."	Eroticism intensified.
"Ständchen."	The lovers are very close now.

In "Aufenthalt" comes the catastrophe . . . the title itself bespeaks
a sense of time stopped, the journey broken.

A denouement of sorts is played out in "In der Ferne" and "Abschied" and, at the same time, a receding to some remote point equivalent to the measure of distance established in "Liebesbotschaft," but ir-
reversible in its temporal aspect.[29]

But even without Kramer's scenario—and he makes no attempt to ra-
tionalize the relatively lighthearted "Abschied" after the dark and painful
"Aufenthalt" and "In der Ferne"—the Rellstab songs work well as a unit. The
key sequence makes excellent sense on Schubert's terms. That is, songs that
are close textually are close tonally; those that suggest new emotional directions are set in more distantly related keys. Furthermore, as noted above
and in Kramer, there are harmonic and tonal relationships between the songs.
In Chapter 4, "Texts and Commentary," I also suggested that the melodic
(and at times harmonic) motion from the dominant to the lowered sixth
scale degree and back helps link most of the Rellstab Lieder.

Although the topic is almost never discussed, successive songs in a group
normally provide an important measure of contrast as well as unity in order
to maintain the interest of the listener. In addition to the contrasting of lyric
and dramatic Lieder in *Schwanengesang* mentioned in Chapter 4 (for example, the insertion of the dramatic "Kriegers Ahnung" between the lyric
"Liebesbotschaft" and "Frühlingssehnsucht"), Schubert quite consistently
alternates meters for the thirteen songs of the original manuscript of the
Rellstab and Heine songs (see Table 5.5).

It may be noted that in the reordering of the Heine songs by Brown-
Goldschmidt-Kramer and others the alternation of meters present in the
autograph sequence is lost. Haslinger's addition of "Die Taubenpost" continues the original alternation of meters: Alla breve (C).

With regard to "Die Taubenpost," I tend to agree with Edward Cone
(Chapter 3) and Steven Lubin (Chapter 7) that the song provides a successful
conclusion to the double set of Rellstab and Heine Lieder. Somewhat in the
nature of an epilogue, the effect of "Die Taubenpost" after the emotionally

TABLE 5.5.

Song	Meter	Additional remarks
"Liebesbotschaft"	Duple ($\frac{2}{4}$)	
"Kriegers Ahnung"	Triple ($\frac{3}{4}$)	At beginning and end; other meters between.
"Frühlingssehnsucht"	Duple ($\frac{2}{4}$)	In voice; compound subdivision in keyboard.
"Ständchen"	Triple ($\frac{3}{4}$)	
"Aufenthalt"	Duple ($\frac{2}{4}$)	In voice; compound subdivision in keyboard.
"In der Ferne"	Triple ($\frac{3}{4}$)	A number of passages of accompaniment in compound or combination of compound and simple subdivision.
"Abschied"	Quadruple ($\frac{4}{4}$)	
"Der Atlas"	Triple ($\frac{3}{4}$)	In voice; compound subdivision in piano of section B.
"Ihr Bild"	Alla breve (C)	
"Das Fischermädchen"	Duple compound ($\frac{6}{8}$)	
"Die Stadt"	Triple ($\frac{3}{4}$)	
"Am Meer"	Alla breve (C)	
"Der Doppelgänger"	Triple ($\frac{3}{4}$)	

shattering triad of "Die Stadt," "Am Meer," and "Der Doppelgänger" is much like that of the lighter "Abschied" following the dramatically darker pair of songs "Aufenthalt" and "In der Ferne." Although Schubert may not have intended it, there are many similarities between "Die Taubenpost" and the opening song of the cycle, "Liebesbotschaft": cheerful mood, tempo (*Ziemlich langsam*), meter (duple), and key (G major), as well as the aspect of longing, but not an unhappy one, in the texts of the two poems. This results in a sense of rounding for *Schwanengesang* that at least in part is a tribute to the musical as well as the commercial perspicacity of the publisher Tobias Haslinger.[30]

NOTES

1. Goldschmidt, ". . . Reihenfolge."

2. The article was reprinted in Kramer's book *Distant Cycles*.

3. Brown, from a British Broadcasting Company Music Guide, *Schubert's Songs*, first published in 1967. Citation from the American edition, 59–61.

4. In a review of Kramer's *Distant Cycles*, Louise Litterick aptly remarks, "Schubert selected six poems from among eighty-eight or, to put it another way, from among a spread of seventeen poems (Nos. 8 through 24), with other poems intervening between all but one pair

(Nos. 23 and 24, 'Ihr Bild' and 'Der Atlas'). Whatever autobiographical or thematic coherence Heine may have intended for this large nonnarrative collection, a selection of a handful of mostly noncontiguous poems from it would in itself seem to countermand whatever coherence the collection might have had" ("Recycling Schubert," 83). She concludes this passage with the statement "Although the idea that an autograph manuscript could mislead in such a significant way has great appeal in a time of reinventing the discipline of musicology, the theory of an inherent 'Heine sequence' for Schubert to violate appears unfounded" (ibid., 84).

5. Saul Novak kindly shared with me his thoughts for another arrangement of the Heine songs, primarily based on musical considerations. He suggests that the most logical musical arrangement would be "Die Stadt," "Der Doppelgänger," "Ihr Bild," "Das Fischermädchen," "Der Atlas," and finally "Am Meer." This sequence posits a central tonality for the cycle of C, and the succession of keys would be C minor–B minor–B-flat minor–A-flat major–G minor–C major. Personal communications by mail and telephone, November 1996.

6. Mustard, *Lyric Cycle*, 5.

7. Ibid., 57, 60. For a study of Schubert's attempt to set Schlegel's cycle, see Kramer's essay "Schlegel's *Abendröthe* and the Failure of Cycle," in *Distant Cycles*, 195–218.

8. Mustard, *Lyric Cycle*, 81, 90–91.

9. Sammons, *Elusive Poet*, 57.

10. Mustard, *Lyric Cycle*, 102.

11. Perraudin, *Poetry in Context*, 72–74.

12. Prawer, *Buch der Lieder*, 2.

13. Kramer, *Distant Cycles*, 128 and 130.

14. See Chapter 1 for Heine's remarks and Chapter 2 for Rellstab's.

15. Riemann, *Beethovens . . . Klaviersonaten*. See the discussion of "Der Atlas" in Chapter 4 of this volume.

16. Kramer, *Distant Cycles*, 130 n. 9.

17. Walter Piston, in *Harmony*, labeled this sonority sharp II^7 when it resolved to the tonic chord and sharp VI^7 when followed by the dominant. Weber's *Invitation to the Dance* also makes extensive use of this kind of diminished seventh. I first began to distinguish between functional and coloristic harmonies of the early nineteenth century during a seminar on the history of dissonance treatment with Manfred Bukofzer at Berkeley in the early 1950s. I also referred to this concept in my dissertation "The Chamber Music of Schubert" (Berkeley, 1961). Joseph Kerman then made imaginative use of my idea in his well-known study "A Romantic Detail."

18. I have always been struck by the similarity in emotional power of the very same chord as the first sonority in the Prelude to *Rigoletto* (first performance in Venice, March 1851). There also the augmented sixth is inverted and there is a resolution to a C chord in root position, except that it is a C-minor triad. Schubert's songs were popular in Paris during the 1830s and 1840s, and Heine, writing from the French capital at the time, specifically points to *Schwanengesang* (see Chapters 1 and 2). In the summer of 1847, Verdi began living in Paris with a teacher of singing and his future wife, the soprano Giuseppina Strepponi. Did he become familiar with "Am Meer" at this time?

19. "Die Unterscheidung" (D. 866) is in G major; "Bei dir allein" is in A-flat major; and "Die Männer sind Méchant!" is in A minor.

20. Newcomb, "Structure and Expression," 174 n. 31.

21. I wonder when someone will call for performances of the Rellstab songs in the order of the first printed edition, which was very much under the poet's control. In a letter the poet wrote (possibly to Beethoven), he indicated that his poems "form in themselves a connected series." Complete letter cited in Kreissle von Hellborn, *Life of Schubert*, vol. 2, 134.

22. Deutsch, *Schubert Reader,* 843.

23. See, for example, Richard LeSueur's discography in this volume (Chapter 8).

24. Citations from von Fischer, *Essays in Musicology,* 122–132.

25. The argument is as follows: "No. 1 in G minor ('Der Atlas') is bound to No. 2 ('Ihr Bild') through the common tone *b [flat]:* here revolt congeals into 'dunkeln Träumen.' No. 3 in A flat major ('Das Fischermädchen') is separated from the preceding song, since it is an illusory happy recollection of it: 'Das Fischermädchen,' however, is brought into close relationship with No. 4 ("Die Stadt," in C minor) through two common tones, *c* and *e flat.* Moreover, the first chord suspension in "Am Meer" appropriates three tones from the seventh-chord that continues to sound to the very end of 'Die Stadt.' The three sea-songs thus form a group, [to] which the B minor of 'Der Doppelgänger' then marks a sharp contrast." Ibid., 130–132.

26. Seaton, "Interpreting Schubert's Heine Songs," 97–99.

27. Deutsch, *Schubert Reader,* 677–678, 795.

28. Hellborn, *Life of Schubert,* vol. 2, 134. Hellborn adds the following comment: "Herr Alexander W. Thayer, the musical biographer, thinks it certain that this letter was addressed to Beethoven." More of the letter is cited in Chapter 2.

29. R. Kramer, *Distant Cycles,* 113, 118–119.

30. Walther Dürr, chief editor of the *Neue Schubert-Ausgabe* and also editor of all the song volumes, has spent much of his life examining the primary sources, prints and manuscripts, for Schubert's music. He remarks, "Among Schubert's publishers of this time [the composer's last years] Tobias Haslinger stands out; in addition to *Winterreise* . . . he published Opp. 80–83 (as he had published Op. 79 previously). On principle, his prints are distinguished by special care, a care not only for the pitches, but also for the dynamic and articulation markings and even for the punctuation of the [poetic] text." *Neue Schubert-Ausgabe,* series IV, vol. 4a, xv.

CHAPTER 6

On Singing *Schwanengesang*

WALTHER DÜRR AND MARTIN CHUSID

I have noticed that, no matter how attractively my songs were performed, the singer almost never quite sang them correctly. When I in-
vestigated, I found that all those who failed to do so had first played the
notes as a melodious instrumental piece and only later coupled the
words to them. This is the exact reverse of the way that I composed
them! My melodies take shape automatically in every case from repeated reading of the poem without my having to search for them.
And the only thing else that I do is this: I repeat them with slight
changes, and do not write them down until I feel that the grammatical,
logical, emotional and musical accents are so closely interwoven that
the melody speaks properly and sings pleasantly, and not just for one
stanza, but for all of them. If the singer is to feel this when he performs
them, he must first read the words in their entirety and keep reading
them until he feels that he can read them with the correct expression.
Only then should he sing them.

So wrote Johann Friedrich Reichardt (1752–1814), who composed, among
other works, 1,500 songs, which "cover a range of styles unsurpassed until
Schubert, whom he influenced importantly."[1] A similar statement was made
by Carl Friedrich Zelter (1758–1832), a contemporary of Reichardt's in Berlin.
A composer of more than 200 published songs, he taught Mendelssohn,
Meyerbeer, Otto Nicolai, and Carl Loewe, and was much admired by Goethe
for his settings of the latter's poetry. Zelter revealed, "When I decide to compose a poem, I try first of all to penetrate to the meaning and realize the situation depicted as vividly as possible. I read it aloud until I have it by heart,

and then while I keep reciting it the melody comes of its own accord."[2] Finally, Christian Gottlob Neefe (1748–1798), who taught Beethoven piano, organ, thoroughbass, and composition in Bonn, suggested in the preface to his setting of the Odes of Klopstock that "the singer should above all study attentively each poem previously, before he sings it."[3]

It may not come as a surprise that anecdotes by Schubert's friends indicate that he, too, concentrated on the poem before setting it to music. Josef von Spaun, one of the composer's closest friends and considered one of the most reliable, wrote of the setting of Goethe's ballad "Erlkönig" in the autumn of 1815: "I went with [the poet Johann] Mayrhofer to see Schubert who was then living with his father. . . . We found [him] all aglow, reading the "Erlkönig" aloud from a book. He paced up and down several times with the volume; suddenly he sat down and in no time at all (just as quickly as one can write) there was the glorious ballad finished on paper. It was performed that same evening at the [Vienna City] Seminary."[4]

A comparable episode, recounted by Leopold von Sonnleithner, another close friend and reliable witness, concerned the composition of the Serenade for Contralto and Chorus, "Zögernd leise": "Schubert took the poem [by Franz Grillparzer], went into the alcove by the window, read it through carefully a few times and then said with a smile: 'I've got it already, it's done, and it's going to be quite good.' After a day or two he brought the composition and it had really turned out quite good."[5]

In 1860 Sonnleithner also wrote about the performance of Schubert's songs within the framework of a lengthy essay, "The Art of Singing." In a separate chapter he explains the manner of delivery of Johann Michael Vogl, the singer most closely tied to Schubert and one who was famous in his own time.[6] Sonnleithner points to the originality of the Schubertian vocal lines, which on the one hand derive from the poetry—in the sense described above —but on the other transform the poetry afresh in such a manner that a purely naturalistic presentation is intolerable:

> One of the chief merits of Schubert's songs lies in the altogether noble, charming and expressive melody; with him this is always the most important thing and, interesting as the writing of his accompaniment usually is, it nevertheless plays a merely supporting role and frequently only forms the background, the general atmosphere, or a particular movement, e.g., that of the saddle-horse, the spinning wheel, the oar, the mill wheels, the surge of the sea, etc. . . . One can play these melodies (like those of Mozart) on the hurdy-gurdy or on the *Stockflöte* [cane flute] and they still remain charming; their musical beauty is in

no way dependent on a declamatory style of performance.—Schubert, therefore, demanded above all that his songs should not so much be declaimed as sung flowingly, that the proper vocal timbre should be given to every note, to the complete exclusion of the unmusical speaking voice, and that by this means the musical idea should be displayed in its purity.

In this context, rejection of a declamatory style by no means indicates that the singer should pay no attention to the text being sung. It is the foundation of Schubertian song. However, the singer should proceed in a manner similar to that of the composer himself. He should read the poetic text as such many times, until it seems to sing spontaneously. But then he should allow the melodic line obtained in this fashion, the Schubertian melody, [to] speak for itself without burdening it with additional accents and ornaments not already provided in the music. (When dogs growl, as in the last song of *Winterreise,* he need not again especially emphasize the "r" sound, since it is not the dogs singing the melody, but the Wanderer, who meets the Organ Grinder and observes the dogs encircling him.)

"This does not mean in the very least," writes Sonnleithner again, "that Schubert wanted to hear his songs ground out merely mechanically . . . but the singer should on no account give himself airs, should not try to be more poetic and inventive than the composer, who has clearly indicated, by means of notes and signs, just exactly what he wants and how he wishes it to be sung."

Reading the Poem

To understand the poetry, as Reichardt, Zelter, Neefe, and presumably Schubert meant the singer to do, requires reading on several levels. Most important, and sometimes most difficult, is the necessity to penetrate the text of the poem for its meaning. While reading for comprehension, it is useful to visualize as imaginatively as possible the setting of the text, as if it were the stage of a drama. As an example, we may take "Kriegers Ahnung" (Warrior's premonition), the second of the Rellstab songs in *Schwanengesang.* (The complete poem, with English translation, appears in Chapter 4.) The "premonition" in the title is of death, as is suggested by the words "Bald ruh' ich wohl und schlafe fest" (Soon I'll rest well and sleep deeply). The repetition of the line near the end of the song provides additional emphasis. As a release from a dangerous existence—"Es ruft noch manche Schlacht" (Many a battle yet calls)—death here has a benign component. The premonition of death is combined and indeed contrasted with the warrior's longing for, reminiscence of, and farewell to his beloved. The setting is a military camp at night. Near a fire, whose flames are flickering and intermittently shining on stacked weapons (stanza 3), are the watchful warrior and his sleeping comrades. Schubert's first section (which is identical to the last), a kind of triple-meter funeral march, contributes to the foreboding of death.

Whereas individual poems may have a variety of meanings, Schubert tends to treat a relatively small number of general subjects; and, as in "Kriegers Ahnung," more than one of these may appear in an individual song. By far the most common of these for Schubert is longing (*Sehnsucht*), as is apparent in the first stanza of "Kriegers Ahnung": "das Herz . . . von Sehnsucht mir so heiss" (My heart . . . I burn with such ardent desire). Longing also emerges as the subject, the meaning, of the song "Die Taubenpost," which Ferdinand Schubert has added to Schubert's manuscript of the Rellstab and Heine songs. And longing plays a crucial role in a number of the other songs of the cycle, as well as in *Die schöne Müllerin* and *Winterreise.*

Another subject of importance for Schubert is nature, the countryside, which in the composer's native land, Austria, is very beautiful. The composer perceives it more often than not as friendly, or at least benign, as in "Liebesbotschaft" and "Frühlingssehnsucht" of *Schwanengesang,* and, despite the unhappy ending, throughout *Die schöne Müllerin.* Yet nature is not always benign in Schubert's Lieder, as is clear from "Aufenthalt" and most of the songs in *Winterreise.*

Death, which in the composer's day more often than in our own came unexpectedly to the young and to those in the prime of life, provides another significant, if less frequently encountered, subject area in the poetry Schubert set. Many of the poems associated with death in Schubert's day seem to be intended to reconcile humans with the prospect of an early demise. A prime example is "Death and the Maiden," but we saw another instance in "Kriegers Ahnung," and the final section of *Die schöne Müllerin* also falls into this category. In *Winterreise* at times death seems to be preferable to the constant suffering of the wanderer. (Witness the song "Das Wirtshaus.")

Although there are others, the last of the subject areas to be discussed here is music. Poems about music usually inspired Schubert, as it did for one of the most beautiful of the songs in *Schwanengesang,* the "Serenade" ("Ständchen"). Here, in addition to the musical form of the serenade itself, we find references in the poetry to nightingales with their "Töne süssen Klagen" (notes of sweet lament); and later the same musical birds understand the "Sehnen" (longings) in the breast and stir each tender heart with their "Silbertönen" (silvery tones).

In addition to its meaning, another aspect of the poetry worthy of consideration is the structure: the division of the poem into stanzas, each usually consisting of four, six, or eight lines (verses). The stanza is then often subdivided grammatically or by meaning into pairs of lines, or couplets. The manner in which the poetry was originally printed, that is, with proper stanzaic and linear arrangement on the page, is extremely important for the composer, who normally shapes his song in a way reflecting closely the structure of the poem. Unfortunately, the original arrangement of the poetry is not easily determined from texts printed in musical scores of the songs, and often editors who assemble the poetry from those scores make errors in the lengths of the lines, sometimes even in the division into stanzas. In this regard, the edition of Schubert's complete solo song texts by Maximilian and Lilly Schochow, which is based on the earliest printings of the poetry, is exemplary.[7] If this is not available, at least for the poetry of *Schwanengesang* it may prove useful to consult Chapter 4 of this volume, which includes the poetic text of each song in the poet's original lineation and stanzaic format together with a literal translation into English.

It is also useful, even crucial, to consider the meter of the individual lines of the poetry, in effect its rhythmic organization. Unlike French or Italian poetic meter, which is determined by the number of syllables per line, German and English verse is dependent on the frequency of accents in a line. Each accented syllable will normally be accompanied (either preceded or followed) by one or more unstressed syllables. The number of stressed syllables per line then determines the meter: four stresses result in tetrameter, five in pentameter, and so on. Of special significance for the composer setting German verse is whether the line begins with an accented syllable (crucis or downbeat) or with an unaccented syllable (anacrucis or upbeat). Of equal if not more importance is whether the line ends with an accented syllable (a strong line ending) or not (a weak line ending). This will have much to do with the type of cadence for the musical phrase setting the poetry. For example, the first pair of lines, the initial couplet, of "Die Taubenpost" reads:

> Ich hab' eine Brieftaub in meinem Sold,
> Die ist gar ergeben und treu.
>
> [I've a carrier pigeon in my employ
> Who is quite devoted and true.]

The meter is alternating; the first line has four stressed syllables, the second only three. Both lines, however, begin with an unaccented syllable (an

Ex. 6.1. "Die Taubenpost," mm. 6–13

Ex. 6.2. "Die Taubenpost" (draft), mm. 1–8

upbeat) and end with an accent (strong ending). It is not surprising, there-fore, that Schubert should set these verses as in Ex. 6.1.

If we examine the way Schubert set these lines in the continuity draft, we find that although the initial pitches are quite different in the two ver-sions, the rhythmic shape is identical (Ex. 6.2). Schubert's rhythmic deci-sions in setting these verses appear, then, to have been determined by the meter and rhythm of the poetry. This suggests that attention paid to the meter and syllabic accentuation of the poetry *before* the performer or ana-lyst approaches the music may well lead to a more insightful, more intelli-gible performance.

Performing Strophic Songs

There are two related aspects worth discussing in the development of the German Lied in the late eighteenth and nineteenth centuries. The first is the influence of folk music. Under the patronage of the musically oriented King of Prussia, Frederick the Great (1712–1786), the aptly named Berlin Lied School was initiated and flourished. We have already met the two most im-portant composers of this school, Reichardt and Zelter. In 1752 Christian Gottfried Krause (1719–1770), the self-appointed founder of the school, de-scribed his concept of the Lied in a volume entitled *Von der musikalischen Poesie* (About poetry set to music). Among his main points were "that the Lied should be folklike (*Volkstümlich*), easily singable even by the nonpro-fessional, [and that it] should express the mood and meaning of the text."[8]

Thirty years later J. A. P. Schulz (1747–1800) published a collection of songs called *Lieder im Volkston* (Songs in the folk style). In the preface he argued, "Only by a striking similarity between the musical and poetic tone of the song, by a melody whose progress never deviates from the text, a melody which molds itself to the declamation and meter of the words as a dress shapes itself to the body . . . does the song present an unforced, artless, familiar appearance, in a word, that of the folk song."[9] This was the late eighteenth century, the Age of Rousseau, an era during which the expression "back to nature" resonated powerfully.

The second point to be made is that poets and musicians of the time conceived of their poetry much as the founders of Italian Baroque opera conceived of Greek drama: the words were sung. Many German poets, and this included the greatest among them, not only expected their poems to be set to music but in many cases felt that the words alone were insufficient. They frequently called their poetry *Lieder,* and this habit continued to the time of Heinrich Heine, who called his early and most successful collection of poetry *Buch der Lieder.* (This volume includes all six poems set by Schubert.) Furthermore, Heine was delighted when he learned that his poetry had been set by Klein and Schubert.[10] But long before Heine, writers referred to their poems as Lieder; to distinguish these from settings with music, they sometimes called the latter *Lieder mit melodien* (songs with melodies). For example, during his student period in Leipzig Goethe gave an early collection of "Lieder mit melodien" to Frederike Oeser.[11]

When sending his poems for setting by the composer Johann Abraham Peter Schulz (1747–1800), the poet Johann Heinrich Voss was constantly concerned that the musician find them "singable," that is, suitable for setting to music.[12] Several times Voss wrote to Schulz that "a poem without melody (*Lied ohne Weise*) is only half what it should be," and some years later he begged Schulz to provide one of his poems with "its completion, the melody."[13] In similar fashion Goethe once wrote to Schiller that both poets had much to be thankful for Zelter's settings of their poems, because "through him their poems [again *Lieder*] and ballads are awakened from the dead."[14]

Most of the songs by composers of the Berlin school, as well as many written elsewhere, are composed in strophic form. This means that each stanza, sometimes a pair of stanzas together, is set to the same music. With this musical repetition, however, there is a potential problem. Will the same music suit the new text? Here is where the skill of the performer comes into play, as Goethe once indicated forcefully. Visiting the aged poet, the singer Eduard Genast performed Reichardt's setting of Goethe's "Jägers Abendlied." He said of his experience:

Toward the end of the song [Goethe] leaped up and cried, "You sing the song badly!" He paced up and down in the room for a while humming the song to himself. Then he stepped up to me . . . and said "The first stanza and the third must be delivered pithily (*markig*), with a kind of savagery, the second and the fourth more gently, for in them there is a different feeling. See, this way (with strong emphasis) "Da rammm! Da ramm! Da ramm! Da ramm!" At the same time he beat the tempo with both arms and sang the "Da ramm" on a deep note. I knew then what he wanted and at his request sang the song again. He was satisfied and said, "That's better. In time you will learn how such strophic songs should be sung."[15]

That Goethe's reaction reflected the thinking of composers of his time is suggested by a comment of Neefe: "A composer need not suggest all the places where the minute rules for the benefit of the expression are to be used. He must also leave something for the individual feeling of the performer."[16]

In all performances of strophic or modified strophic song—Schubert's preferred form in the last years of his life—the key to success again rests in studying the text carefully. With regard to *Schwanengesang,* the remarks by Goethe and Neefe are especially pertinent for the strophic songs "Frühlingssehnsucht," "In der Ferne," and "Am Meer," as well as for the modified strophic "Ständchen" and "Das Fischermädchen." But in *Schwanengesang* they are also appropriate for the returning sections in songs with other formal schemes: "Liebesbotschaft," "Abschied," "Ihr Bild," "Die Stadt," and "Die Taubenpost."[17]

Schubert's Notation of Ornaments

Since time immemorial, composers have conceived the notation of their works in two categories: the essential and the nonessential. "Essential" was everything that a work comprised, the determinations of note length (rhythms) and note height (pitches), of intervals and sonorities. "Nonessential," in contrast, was everything pertaining to performance (tempo and dynamics, articulation, and free ornamentation). The composers in earlier times simply wrote what was essential in their works, but then in the course of time, and especially since the beginning of the seventeenth century, more and more they included elements belonging to the realm of performance. The concept of the "essential" was constantly stretched to include aspects of notation previously left to performers, so that in the eighteenth and early nineteenth centuries even performance ornaments could become "essential."

As late as 1843 Gustav Schilling described this precisely.[18] First he presents the "so-called genuine [that is, essential] ornaments," such as those the composer himself frequently adds because our musical notation has generally accepted specific symbols or other indications for that purpose (for example, turns, mordents, tremolos, vibrato, arpeggios, and trills) and "optional" (*willkürlich*)—that is, "nonessential"—ornaments, which in turn could be "general" or "specific." To the general category belong any agreeable "quantitatively increased notes or tones, as precisely described, which the player or singer deems fitting to shape the phrase or passage with more liveliness, more expression, even though semiotics does not have any specific name or accepted symbol for it." Specific nonessential ornaments, in contrast, are variants of expression "such as accelerando and ritardando, crescendo and decrescendo, mezza voce and portamento, ligato [*sic*] and staccato etc.," but also any sort of "agreeable roulades, runs and other similar fioratura . . . which in technical terminology we include together under the name coloratura."

What has been described here as a general rule is also valid for Schubert's Lieder; we know from isolated songs adapted for actual performance by a specific singer (in copies of songs, above all in the "Songbooks" of Schubert's friend Johann Michael Vogl, or from supplementary insertions in printed editions),[19] that at the beginning of the nineteenth century it was understood that the ornaments described by Schilling were only partially notated by the composer; that above all it was the responsibility of the singer to adapt the notated form of the song to his individual voice, but also to the character of a performance (to the place and the occasion). In the later nineteenth century such adaptations were declared to be inadmissible;[20] in the course of the century, the composer's concept of the work came to include control over the realm of ornamentation.

Schubert himself, however, perceived this matter of control differently. Not only do his own changes in songs, whenever he wrote them out for a particular singer, bear witness to this fact (compare, for instance, the setting of "Rastlose Liebe," D. 138, written out for his friend the singer Karl von Schönstein, with the version intended for publication),[21] but it is also validated by his emphatic approval of Vogl's performance style as expressed in a letter of 12 September 1825, to his brother Ferdinand, in which he reports of concerts that he and Vogl gave jointly in Salzburg: "The manner in which Vogl sings and the way I accompany, as though we were one at such a moment, is something quite new and unheard-of for these people."[22] To be sure, for *Schwanengesang* we possess only one song "varied" in this fashion, the "Serenade" ("Ständchen"), transmitted in two not-completely-identical copies (one in a manuscript from the Witteczek-Spaun collection in the archives of the Gesellschaft der Musikfreunde in Vienna, and the other in a Lieder album that is presently preserved in the Austrian National Library).[23] The two sources, of which the second is more richly adorned than the first, might in the end be traced back to Vogl; both were probably found in the archive of the music publishing firm Diabelli and Company.

Essential Ornaments

Among the "essential" ornaments that Schubert himself added to the voice part—and this applies unreservedly to his last major song manuscript, *Schwanengesang*—we find primarily appoggiaturas and grace notes. Sometimes there is also an isolated articulation-slur. This presumably signifies something like a portamento and is to be differentiated from the usual slurs, which specify only the precise text underlay. Or there may be an accent when this is especially important. See, for example, the ends of the strophes in "Frühlingssehnsucht" or in mm. 21 and 42 of "Am Meer." As a rule, dynamic markings and such indications as "accelerando" and "ritardando" are lacking. The reason is that Schubert regarded singers, even if they were amateurs, as soloists who, in accordance with older traditions, decided for themselves with regard to their ornaments. Dynamic, even articulation, signs are, however, often hidden in the keyboard part of the composition. See, for example, "Kriegers Ahnung" (m. 57). Following a crescendo hairpin, an accent on the third beat marks the delayed accent on the peak tone ("Wehmut"). This is required primarily by the voice for declamatory emphasis. The keyboard writing also allows this at corresponding places. In the same song, for instance, something similar holds for the decrescendo hairpins in mm. 32 and 38, which for Schubert likewise have the character of an accent and stress the words "Busen" and "meinem." Another example is provided by the slurs in the left hand of the keyboard at the beginning of "Frühlingssehnsucht," which signify that mm. 13–16 are to be sung as a pair of two-bar units, not as a single phrase. At this point the upper "voice part" of the left hand moves in parallel motion with the vocal line. Almost always, and this means everywhere that the compositional structure permits, it is appropriate to transfer the general performance indications from the keyboard to the voice part.

As mentioned earlier, among the "essential" ornaments notated in the voice part, the appoggiaturas and grace notes predominate. It is characteristic of Schubert's notational style that—independently of its performance—he basically writes appoggiaturas at half value: an eighth-note appoggiatura before a quarter note, a sixteenth-note appoggiatura before an eighth note. Occasionally he deviates from this usage, but only with short appoggiaturas before long notes. Then he sometimes also writes a sixteenth-note ornament before a half note. For the meaning of an appoggiatura, then, Schubert's style of writing provides no help. In this situation we are directed to the performance practice of Schubert's day as evidenced in the general music instruction of his time.[24] Yet we may also find its validity confirmed in the second and third versions of the songs written out by Schubert himself. There, often the appoggiaturas are notated as symbols in one version, yet in another the identical musical context is written in modern notation. Similar variants are to be found in the copies of songs prepared for singers by members of the Schubert circle.[25]

Accordingly, the great majority of Schubert's ornaments that are notated before the beat (that is, *Vorschläge*) are to be understood as appoggiaturas: the ornamental tone (*Vorschlagsnote*) displaces the main tone. For example, in m. 8 of "Die Stadt" the two quarter notes, *a flat–g*, are to be sung on the final syllables of "Horiz*onte*." This is always true when a verse (line) or phrase has a weak ending (*Klingend*), that is, with the accent on the penultimate syllable. In *Schwanengesang* such appoggiaturas are mostly written out by Schubert. See, for example, m. 29 of "Die Stadt" ("einmal").

In the middle of a phrase, however, long appoggiaturas are performed in the usual manner: the ornamented note takes half the value of the principal note and is linked with the latter in the sense of a short melisma. In contrast, preceding groups of shorter notes, the ornamental tones before the beat are short (that is, they function as grace notes). See, for instance, m. 59 in "Liebesbotschaft," the ornamental pitch *c″* before *b′*. Or they are also short (grace notes) before groups of three notes, but only when these are metric units, that is, when the groups of three belong together as a musical figure. See, for example, in m. 93 of "In der Ferne," the eighth-note grace note *f″sharp* before *e″*; here the melodic analogy with m. 90, which lacks an ornamental tone, would be lost if the ornamental note were performed long. Short ornamental tones (grace notes) are basically sung "on the beat"; most are lightly stressed; and they are also heard distinctly—not just as snaps (*Schnalzer*).

For double ornaments, in which the second note is a step higher than the first (*Schleifer*), however, this approach is not valid. Schubert notates such ornaments sometimes in precise rhythmic fashion as principal (normal-sized) notes, sometimes as ornaments in decorative (smaller) notes. When he writes them out precisely, however, he does so before the bar line, and they are notated distinctly as an upbeat. When written as decorative notes, they

Ex. 6.3. "Ständchen"

are found in the usual manner at the beginning of the measure, after the bar
line.[26] Similarly, the double ornaments found in "Ständchen" (mm. 19, 21, 25,
and 37), despite the rhythmically short notes preceding and the large
melodic leaps, are to be performed "before the beat." This is also true in m.
31 of "Die Taubenpost." With reference to "Ständchen," see Ex. 6.3.

The same is true of ornaments that occur between two principal (normal-
sized) notes. They subtract from the value of the preceding note. Occasionally Schubert's placement of a slur indicates that the principal note following the ornament is again to be sung "on the beat." As a rule, in *Schwanengesang* Schubert has written out such ornaments. See, for example, mm.
6 and 25 in "Am Meer," as well as the turn in m. 43. To a certain extent there
is a similar manner of performance for the turn in m. 21 of "Der Doppelgänger."

Nonessential Ornaments

One should not expect a singer of today to vary a piece by Schubert by
freely adding ornaments in order to suit his personal style of singing, at least
not in that far-reaching sense described by Schilling. Indeed, the manner and
extent of such variation are closely related to the type and character of a
piece. When singing, writes Friedrich Rochlitz in an article for the Leipzig
Allgemeine musikalische Zeitung, "in a room [accompanied by] piano, one performs in order to provide an idea of one's self, and of one's style; essentially
one performs without embellishment." That means, at most, adding a trill
at cadences, small linking slides at leaps; and, naturally, above all varying dynamics and tempo in strophic songs according to the text. In contrast, in
Lieder that are closest to stage singing and are performed publicly, it would
be a mistake, according to Rochlitz, to want to present them in a "dry and
bare" manner.[27]

The songs of *Schwanengesang* stand on the border between such songs
as are intended for "the chamber" and those in which the singer enters "into
the realm of the scenic."[28] Such songs as "Liebesbotschaft," "Frühlingssehnsucht," and all the Heine songs are rather of an intimate character; in con-

trast, "Kriegers Ahnung," but also "Aufenthalt" and even "Die Taubenpost,"
show elements of stage singing. "Ständchen," finally, is a special case. According to the style of writing and character, it is without doubt an "intimate" song. Yet because of its function as a serenade, it aims for effect. With
his artistic skill the singer will make an impression. It is no accident that we
have ornamented copies of this very song as performance documents, and
that they show what could generally be expected of a vocalist singing Lieder
in Schubert's day. To be sure, this is not true in the areas of dynamics and
tempo. Here the arranger of the version that served as source for the copies
has remained faithful to the indications of the first edition of *Schwanengesang*. Indeed, an additional variant by Vogl, this time of the strophically conceived ballad "Der Fischer," D. 225, provides another work similarly poised
on the borderline between an "intimate" song "for a chamber" and one conceived for the stage.[29] This variant shows us a singer whose freedom with regard to the written musical text far surpasses what we might expect from
the rules mentioned in Sonnleithner's preface. This is true in the effort to
vary the performance of the individual strophes (following the text). For example, near the end of the last strophe, the singer inserts a tension-enhancing
rallentando followed by fermatas, then a diminuendo (which with Schubert
and Vogl are both slower and softer) and two further fermatas ("halb sank
er hin—und ward nicht mehr—und ward nicht mehr gesehn") (He half
sank down—and was never again—and was never again seen).

Although Schilling's directions for performing "nonessential ornaments"
play no role in the adornment of "Ständchen," the smaller free embellishments suitable for an "intimate" Lied are relatively abundant. There is also
a surprising observation: Schilling expressly warns the singer against repeating the same ornament often, because it may too easily result in a
mannered performance.[30] However, in "Ständchen" the singer adds additional material, as Schubert did not write out the second strophe. The composer wrote only repeat signs. Nevertheless, in his ornamentation the singer
varies the two strophes only once. The "feindliche Lauschen" (hostile be-
trayer) in m. 24 of the first strophe is left unadorned. The "silvery tones"
(second strophe), in contrast, is characterized by means of a small ornament (Ex. 6.4).

Moreover, the two strophes are so much alike in their emotional content that a variation of the ornaments hardly seems possible. Individually,
each makes clear how the singer should react to the text. In m. 13 "komm zu
mir" (come to me) becomes a "lockende" (enticing) call with a small slide;
in m. 18 the trees "rauschen" (rustle); "des Mondes Licht" (the light of the

Ex. 6.4. "Ständchen"

Ex. 6.5. "Ständchen"

Ex. 6.6. "Ständchen"

moon) shines in mm. 19 and 21; and, finally, the "Holde" (darling) in m. 25 becomes the true light of the night (Ex. 6.5).

It would seem that only once does the embellishment not follow the text. At the word "beglücke" (make [me] happy) in m. 43, the vocalist stresses the insignificant final syllable of the song's penultimate word, which in German is practically mute. In this regard he follows an old tradition of singing reaching back to the sixteenth century, according to which the penultimate note in a vocal line (the penultimate syllable at the cadence) is accentuated by means of a longer decoration and thereby helps prepare the close of the entire piece. In this instance, it is a matter of scarcely more than a turn with an accented neighboring note—again corresponding to the intimate character of the song (Ex. 6.6).

Once more it may be emphasized that with regard to Vogl's embellishments, both here and elsewhere, it is a matter of adjusting a song specifically for the singer Vogl. At most it can serve today's vocalist as an example, helping in his own adaptation. Whoever has a lighter voice than the baritone Vogl will interweave even richer ornamentation. If a singer prefers a more exact declamation, he should select from among the ornaments suggested by Schilling those more suitable. The warning issued previously against "the constant repetition of the same ornament" is even more valid for all of them together. Without question the mindless acceptance and ap-

plication of the ornaments from a model will lead to a stilted performance
—and to the solidifying of a performance convention that should actually
be free; and they raise the "unessential ornament" to the rank of a written
performance directive. And that would, in Friedlaender's sense, truly be a
"falsification."[31]

Some Ancillary Considerations

It is probably useful to bear in mind that pitch in Schubert's Vienna appears
to have been somewhat lower than the standard international A = 440 to
which we are accustomed today. "On the basis of tuning forks used in various opera houses and orchestras, pitch at the outset of the 19th century
would seem to have been generally in the region of A = 425."[32] The tuning
fork of the piano builder J. A. Stein, whose instruments were popular in
Vienna—Mozart is reputed to have purchased one—was A = 421.6.[33] It
should be noted, however, that while the lower pitch would be helpful in
the high register for songs of *Schwanengesang,* it would be the reverse for the
lowest notes, for example the tenor's low *A* at the beginning of "Kriegers
Ahnung" and the many low *B*'s of "Aufenthalt."

Of more relevance may be the fact that during Schubert's lifetime a vast
majority of the performances of his songs took place in private homes. According to Otto Erich Deutsch in the *Schubert Reader,* the first public performances of Schubert's songs were consistently in small or moderately sized
halls.[34] The first song heard in a public concert, "Schäfers Klaglied," for example, was at a hall in a small hotel, the Roman Emperor Inn, on 28 February 1819. Two years later the songs "Der Wanderer" and "Der Jüngling auf
dem Hügel" were first performed publicly at the same location. "Erlkönig,"
"Sehnsucht," and "Gruppe aus dem Tartarus" received their first public performances at the Gundelhof, a hall in a building where Leopold von
Sonnleithner had his residence.[35] Sonnleithner, a close friend of Schubert's,
was a major figure in the establishment of the Gesellschaft der Musikfreunde (Vienna Philharmonic Society), and Deutsch reports that "from
1815 to 1824 he held domestic concerts [at the Gundelhof]. Each Friday
evening, and later every other Friday, more than 120 music lovers gathered
there during the winter months."[36] Another inn, the Red Hedgehog, was the
location for the first performances of some twenty additional songs by
Schubert, as well as some of his chamber music.[37]

Theaters and large concert halls were primarily used for performances
of those few stage works by Schubert that were publicly presented, or for
occasional performances of such larger vocal works as "Gesang der Geister

über den Wasser."[38] The difference in style between the music for Schubert's operas, clearly intended for presentation in a theater, and that of his songs is considerable. The intimate surroundings the composer had in mind for his Lieder undoubtedly explain a stylistic orientation toward greater flexibility and rhythmic freedom.

Finally, it has been suggested that "during the history of Western Artistic Singing the steady trend has been towards the cultivation of stronger, wider and slower vibrato . . . [and] the gradual transition to continuous vibrato took place during the 19th century [when it] was a subject of much debate."[39] Mozart's remarks about Joseph Meissner's "bad habit of intentionally vibrating his voice"—that it was "contrary to nature" inasmuch as "the voice has its own natural vibrations"[40]—probably reflected Schubert's attitude as well. He was, after all, trained as a singer in the conservative Royal Court Chapel in Vienna and by vocal masters who were for the most part contemporaries of Mozart.

NOTES

1. Helm, "Johann Friedrich Reichardt," *New Grove*, vol. 15, 705. The quotation is taken from Stein, *Poem and Music*, 35.

2. Cited in Stein, *Poem and Music*, 42.

3. Cited in Schwab, *Sangbarkeit, Popularität und Kunstlied*, 68. Unless otherwise indicated, all translations in this chapter are by M. Chusid.

4. Deutsch, *Schubert: Memoirs by His Friends*, 131.

5. Ibid., 111.

6. Sonnleithner, "Bemerkungen zur Gesangskunst," in *Recensionen und Mittheilungen über Theater und Musik*, vol. 6 (1860), 217–219, 281–284, 313–316, 697–701, and vol. 7 (1861), 129–138. The section cited below is from chapter 4, "Über den Vortrag des Liedes, mit besonderer Beziehung auf Franz Schubert" (vol. 6, 697ff.). English translation is from Deutsch, *Schubert: Memoirs by His Friends*, 337f.

7. *Franz Schubert: Die Texte seiner einstimmig komponierten Lieder und ihre Dichter*.

8. Barr, "Lied, III, 1: c1750–c1800, Berlin," *New Grove*, vol. 10, 836.

9. Stein, *Poem and Music*, 28.

10. See the biographical section on Heine in Chapter 2 on which of the two Klein brothers Heine was referring to, and see especially Chapter 2 n. 37.

11. Blume, "Goethe," *Musik in Geschichte und Gegenwart*, vol. 5, col. 432.

12. Schwab, *Sangbarkeit*, 19–20.

13. Letters dated 29 March 1784 and 30 July 1787. Ibid., 21.

14. Letter dated 19 March 1802. Ibid.

15. Stein, *Poem and Music*, 16. Original German in Schwab, *Sangbarkeit*, 69.

16. Schwab, *Sangbarkeit*, 68.

17. Analyses of these songs may be found in Part II (Chapters 3 and 4) of this volume.

18. Schilling, *Musikalische Dynamik*, 254.

19. In this regard see Dürr, "Schubert and Johann Michael Vogl," 126–140.

20. See Friedlaender, "Fälschungen," 166–185.

21. Compare *Neue-Schubert Ausgabe,* series IV, vols. 1a and 1b, 35ff., 208 ff.

22. Deutsch, *Schubert Reader,* 458.

23. The varied version from the Witteczek-Spaun collection is printed in *Neue-Schubert Ausgabe,* series IV, vol. 14b, 290ff.

24. In this regard see, for example, Krones and Schollum, *Vokale,* 177–203.

25. See the prefaces to the Lieder volumes (series IV) of the *Neue-Schubert Ausgabe* (e.g., vol. 14a, xiiif.) as well as Dürr, "'Manier' und 'Veränderung,'" 124–139.

26. In this regard compare mm. 4–5 and 11–13 in the third Finale of the opera *Alfonso und Estrella.*

27. Rochlitz, "Beytrag zur Lehre," 130f.

28. Schilling, *Musikalische Dynamik,* 264.

29. Printed in *Neue-Schubert Ausgabe,* series IV, vol. 1, 279ff.

30. Schilling, *Musikalische Dynamik,* 255.

31. See Friedlaender, "Fälschungen."

32. Carp, "Pitch," 164.

33. Ibid.

34. See appendix 4, "First Performances of Works by Schubert in his Lifetime."

35. Deutsch, *Schubert Reader,* 934f.

36. Ibid., 112.

37. Ibid., 935–937.

38. Ibid., 935.

39. Crutchfield, "Voices," 296.

40. Ibid.

CHAPTER 7

The Three Styles of *Schwanengesang*
A Pianist's Perspective

STEVEN LUBIN

From the pianist's point of view *Schwanengesang* is heterogeneous. So must it be to the singer and listener. The Müller cycles, after all, are what Schubert has in mind in constructing a cycle, and the stupendous unificatory accomplishment they represent is no more likely to leap out from an unintended assemblage than a royal flush from a shuffled deck. (*Winterreise* is like some vast preplanned ritual system, with its consistency of tone and purpose infusing all that variety of meticulous detail.) How, then, can *Schwanengesang* be so eminently performable as a collection? It is strange that its inner stylistic diversity should be both so marked and so capable of creating an impression of blending. The strange miscible heterogeneity of *Schwanengesang* extends to Schubert's late style as a whole.

Taking the *Schwanengesang* accompaniments as exemplary, there are three contributants to this heterogeneous late style that come to the fore. One is the perennial, overtly innocent and cheerful song-like phrase-process that is inclined to appear anywhere in Schubert: it has a diatonic, unstylized melody in the major, and a closed (though often charmingly de-symmetrized) phrase structure. The harmonic underpinning typically is graced by Schubert's supremely economical and convincing voice-leading, whose very air of normalcy can sometimes distract one from the shock of uncommon harmonic moves. When these harmonic underpinnings are the piano parts of songs, they display a certain "song-accompaniment" conventionality, wherein Schubert's stunning variety of chordal and arpeggiated patterns remains within the bounds of an accessible quasi-popular manner. We might call this Schubert's "pleasing" style. Of the fourteen *Schwanengesang* songs, five are in the pleasing style: "Liebesbotschaft," "Frühlingssehnsucht," "Abschied," "Das Fischermädchen," and "Die Taubenpost." All three poets are represented.

A second late-Schubert voice is learned (though without ever becoming academic) rather than quasi-popular, and surprising and eclectic (though without exceeding the bounds of a reasonable stylistic decorum) rather than conventional. This second voice sounds often in the minor, and obsessively intermingles major and minor in an unprecedented way. The intermingling is not of the (deliberately) naïve sort wherein the minor might be taken as the emotional obverse of the pleasing style, in the manner of Papageno contemplating suicide, who arouses pathos by varying a pleasing-style strain in the minor. Schubert's usage is far more complex. Its *locus classicus*, if not its *fons et origo*, is *Winterreise*. Sometimes the minor is interspersed with flashing admixtures of the major that seem grimmer than the minor-mode passages they gloss, as though their potential for sweetness had been corrupted. The major-mode setting of "und seine Zweige rauschten" in "Der Lindenbaum" from *Winterreise* is one haunting example among many; something quite similar appears in *Schwanengesang*'s "Ihr Bild" at "und ach, ich kann es nicht glauben."

This second voice of the late Schubert is represented in *Schwanengesang* by much of Rellstab's "Kriegers Ahnung," "Aufenthalt," and "In die Ferne," and by Heine's "Ihr Bild" and "Am Meer." Even in "Ständchen," with its plucking accompaniment and Mediterranean-boat-song air, the emotionally complex intercourse between major and minor, full of a world-weary bitterness and obvious irony, is far removed from the overt ingenuousness of the pleasing style, and so I classify it here. For want of a more convenient name we might call this second late-Schubert voice his "serious" style. Near the end of his life, as syphilis advanced, this manner became Schubert's stylistic mainstream.

The late minor-mode writing shades into a third stylistic tendency, one branching off from the mainstream in the opposite direction from that of the pleasing style. We can call it "avant-garde." Here, rather than clinging to convention, Schubert flouts it. The assault on stylistic decorum becomes disturbing, and this alienation becomes the expressive point. The style moves from lyricism to expressionism. It is easy to find this tendency in the three *Schwanengesang* songs in the avant-garde style, "Der Atlas," "Die Stadt," and "Der Doppelgänger."

In "Der Atlas," the first of the Heine songs in the published sequence, a new stylistic iconoclasm seems to leap out. There is a blurring of harmonic function at the very beginning brought about by a violent abbreviating of decorum: the rising appoggiatura (leading tone to tonic note) in the accompaniment's second bar serves as a savagely foreshortened dominant grafted onto the tonic. The commission of an outrageous foreshortening suggests an unnaturally vast outrage.

"Die Stadt" also evokes an unnatural state. That weird diminished harmony in the piano engulfing the tonic note is really the raised supertonic seventh chord (even though Schubert spells it, in C minor, with an *E flat* rather than a *D sharp*), a harmony that even in the best of times, when it embellishes a major-mode tonic and so has two leading tones, only weakly apes the dominant ninth's powers as an embellishing diminished harmony. As Schubert uses the raised supertonic here, it is downright non-functional. Its harmonic meaning is deliberately unreadable; it collapses, and our alienation from harmonic normalcy arouses an expressionistic nausea.

"Der Doppelgänger" is the most celebrated example of Schubert's avant-garde style. At "Du Doppelgänger! / du bleicher Geselle! / was äffst du nach mein Liebesleid," perhaps the song's most harrowing passage, the accompaniment bears much of the expressionistic burden, with its uncanny modulation from (minor) tonic to mediant minor (Ex. 7.1). The rising line, wreaking havoc with voice-leading norms like a tsunami flattening a landscape, seems to represent the poem's surging wavefront of nightmarish pain.

It is sometimes suggested that it took Heine's poetry to release in Schubert this expressionism, this liberating freedom to rise above convention, this alleged new engagement with larger issues in his final year. More generally, there is a tendency among some commentators to assume that the avant-garde style is the most original, powerful, large-scaled and forward-looking of Schubert's late stances, and that the pleasing style in particular is a throwback to a less highly developed stage. There is this implication, for instance, in Robert Schumann's charge that the B-flat Trio exemplifies the "feminine" Schubert, as opposed to the more iconoclastic E-flat Trio; and something of his attitude has probably survived into our age. With Beethoven as a paradigm for greatness, it is hard to think of music as being imposing unless it sweeps away conventions rather than clings to them. And yet these attitudes do no justice to the extreme expressive power of Schubert's late style, a power that depends on the participation, and sometimes the intermixing, of all three stylistic voices.

As regards Heine, first of all, no doubt he did stimulate Schubert to explore new kinds of settings. Heine, whose immense intellect and magical verbal skills made him a poet capable of comprehending in a sweeping perspective his own sense of Romantic alienation, was indeed exceptional. Heine was not, perhaps, a great poet of the sort who invents his own poetical scenario, but rather of the sort who works with the accepted one of his

Ex. 7.1. "Der Doppelgänger," mm. 43–47

era in an extraordinary way. Along with Rellstab, Seidl, Müller, and many other poets Schubert set, Heine often stays within a fashionable Werther-esque scenario that might be summarized thus: I (the poet's persona) have great, wide, rich affective and imaginative gifts; but Woman rejects me and Nature's promised solace proves insufficient; I am hopelessly alienated; I wither; this is tragic, and therefore I am ennobled; also, my tragedy is witnessed by the kindred reader, and so I make an artistic connection with my fellow humans, the only kind of connection worthy of me. Good poets, like Rellstab, try to find unmannered images and language to make the most of this, the prevailing convention; Heine, even when he seems to deal in conventional images, sees beyond and questions them, and can be self-critical about them. It is the subversiveness implicit in this questioning that perhaps affects Schubert, whose "liberated" avant-garde settings of Heine are powerful, imposing, and disturbing.

And yet, his settings in the serious and pleasing styles, including settings of narrowly conventional poems like "Die Taubenpost," are often no less great. There is surely no simple calculus for evaluating the contribution of poetic quality to that of a composite song. Purely formal elements in a poem, those not contributing to its poetic quality, can serve as a substrate for a musical construction of surpassing greatness, as I shall suggest in connection with Die Taubenpost. But in any case, the late Schubert employs all three stylistic voices with equal conviction and power. He can step in and out among conventions, can use irony in complex and varied ways, and can employ musical convention or iconoclasm to complement, comment upon, or even undercut poetic convention or iconoclasm. And in his last year he seems to have worked at devising some frameworks to encompass all three. The A-major Piano Sonata from 1828, for instance, opens in the serious style. Midway through the second movement we suffer the onset of a frightful avant-garde episode, surely one of the nineteenth century's most terrifying musical portrayals of a psyche becoming unhinged, one that haunts the memory no less terribly than Modest Mussorgsky's analogous passage

from Boris's Monologue (written half a century later). There is then a gradual transition back to the serious style of the movement's "A" section, like an
awakening from a nightmare; and before long we hear a theme in the purest
pleasing style, opening the final movement. The E-flat Trio is a similar mixture. It is no doubt this breadth of stylistic tolerance for heterogeneity in
Schubert's late style generally that conditions us to accept *Schwanengesang* as
making a coherent impression in performance, even at that most jarring of
all moments when the lilting diatonic piano introduction to "Die Taubenpost" breaks in upon the hypercharged atmosphere of "Der Doppelgänger."
In this very juxtaposition, in fact, "Die Taubenpost" demonstrates that the
pleasing style, far from being small-scaled or regressive, remains to the end
one of Schubert's most powerful expressive resources. The notion to the
contrary is probably a distortion due to Beethoven's paradigm.

   The young Beethoven had in his repertoire a "pleasing" style of his own,
exemplified by such movements as the Andante favori and the variation
movement of Op. 47. I have elsewhere called this Beethoven's "Biedermeyer" style,[1] to suggest that it makes a certain cloyingly artificial or merely
decorative impression, and that it seems not to issue directly from an inner
conviction, unlike many other early stylistic traits that Beethoven continued
to practice throughout his career (his foreground use of eighteenth-century
"connective tissue," for instance, or his patented short-breathed, unstylized
way with melodic declamation, or his motoric adaptation of "murkybass"
pianistic figures). Beethoven's replacement of the Andante favori in the
Waldstein Sonata by the Adagio cantabile we now think of as integral to it
was probably an event of great symbolic importance. With it, Beethoven
shed his Biedermeyer style like a snakeskin. The exigencies of the heroic
style now take over. Beethoven invents the vast phrase-structure landscapes
that become his private world. And once in this private world, he finds himself no longer beholden to many inherited conventions. He needn't "please"
any more. He suffers in his isolation but exults in his triumphs as a god
would; for the terms of success are of his own making.

   Schubert is far different. He inhabits this world and is capable of de-
lighting in it, and suffering loss in it, with a directness unknown to Beethoven. He holds fast to conventions and concrete musical elements that
Beethoven, in his mature abstractness, relinquishes.[2] Here, for example, is
Schubert rejoicing in a newly confirmed tonic, playing with its triad like a
child with a just-discovered toy wagon (Ex. 7.2).

   This way of playing with materials without first transforming them is
foreign to Beethoven. Beethoven plays too, in certain moods, but when he
does, it is with abstract things like tonalities and textures. Schubert's pleas-

Ex. 7.2. *Trout* Quintet, last movement, piano part, mm. 84ff.

ing style is a prime example of his concreteness—his engagement with what is immediately given in everyday experience, in this case represented by song conventions. Once this surface representation of the "immediately given" is in place, however, there is nothing to prevent its taking on other accompanying layers of meaning. In Schubert's late pleasing style these complex layered meanings are subtle and varied—"irony" is no more than a catch-all term for them. *Die schöne Müllerin,* for instance, owes much of its pathos to the partial persistence of the pleasing style it starts out with, before the loss of innocence; whereas in *Winterreise,* the pleasing style is reserved for bitter counterfactual episodes of contrast to the prevailing reality, as in "Frühlingstraum" and "Täuschung." The pleasing-style songs in *Schwanengesang* resemble the usage in *Die schöne Müllerin,* as do many other instances in Schubert's late music.

Coming at the very end of Schubert's life, "Die Taubenpost," with its flat refusal at the surface level to acknowledge anguish, is somewhat akin to the strange geniality of late Beethoven as we find it, for instance, in the themes of Opp. 109/III and 111/II. Neither Beethoven nor Schubert, at least openly, seems to rage against the dying of the light. But the late styles of the two—their styles "conditioned by death," in Thomas Mann's phrase—are really very different. Beethoven's heartfelt, "simple" diatonic themes are no more a return to the attempt to write in a conventional song-like style than the Fifth Symphony is. The song conventions are transformed, and the abstractness of the themes gives them a grandiosity. "Die Taubenpost," by contrast, is breathtakingly ingenuous, or at least it so appears on the surface. And yet, no less than Beethoven's, it lives up to its obligations as a great composer's parting utterance. Not uncharacteristically, it does so without the cooperation of a great poem. The extended metaphor of the pigeon is charming, but it has trouble supporting its own weight, particularly at the point where the pigeon is asked to deliver the poet's tears!

What Seidl's poem does offer, just by virtue of its patterning, is a great opportunity for a master of tonal form. By drawing out the metaphor for six quatrains and interpreting it for us in the seventh, Seidl follows the strategy of the old sonnet writers—he first carries out a long process of spinning and baiting a web of connections, pulling us in, and then springs the trap in a final drawing together of connections, unforeseen but already overdetermined, that completes the web. In music, this strategy recalls, more than anything else, the many textless tonal plans of J. S. Bach in which that completing of the web, near the end, becomes the telling moment of the piece, the moment we anticipate with galvanized attention and experience with delight, the moment when implicit interconnectedness, hitherto only unconsciously grasped, is suddenly made explicit in a kind of aphoristically concentrated summation. This disciplined self-limitation to an interconnected system of discourse is the heart of closed form, and Schubert, at least in his "pleasing" mode, turns out paradoxically to be one of its greatest masters. With Bach as a model, one would think that masters of closed form should write in an exaltedly abstract voice, with all that is topical or picturesque stripped away; but Schubert here unabashedly exercises his exquisitely rarefied formal gift in an unassuming, quasi-popular manner.

Very often in Bach, as in "Die Taubenpost," a few main motifs, a piece's dramatis personae, align themselves in recurring arrays, like the elements in the periodic table, whereby their functions become more and more clearly defined as the piece unfolds. Finally, the personalities of these characters become completely clear, and their interaction seems to compel the denouement. In "Die Taubenpost," Schubert generates such a purely tonal denouement and, in a staggeringly effective way, coordinates it with the one embedded in the poem.

The musical dramatis personae of "Die Taubenpost" are, first of all, a pair of unmatched ten-bar periods (each four bars + four bars + a two-bar extension). These ten-bar periods set, respectively, quatrains 1 and 2, and then, in a musical reprise, quatrains 5 and 6, all in the tonic. A condensed version of the two periods in the flat mediant major makes a tonally contrasting enclosed episode out of quatrain 4.

Quatrain 3, by contrast, is set over a dominant pedal, with a repeated four-bar rising scalewise texture above. It is the accumulated energy of this prolonged dominant that launches the move to flat III, and there is a sense of momentum being transferred in effecting the distancing that keeps the overtly cheerful flow of the song undisturbed throughout the flat III episode and into the reprise.

There are, furthermore, some salient details spun into the web. There is an inverted-bowl motif that appears in many guises: most locally it appears in the recurring rollicking dotted figure for the pianist's right hand, but also it suffuses the vocal line of the main expository periods, most noticeably concluding the second principal ten-bar period (first 3–5–3 and then, more conclusively, 3–5–1) and in the little treble keyboard scale recurrently bridging the latter two cadences. (Perhaps this motif connotes the idea of a trajectory joining two locales, with the physical image of a bird's flight entailing a less visualizable imaginative connection.) Impelling the little bird's-flight passage each time is an unobtrusively arrived-at deceptive cadence, with the bass rising from 5 to 6. Thereby hangs a tail, as Tovey might have said.

The culminating intensified interweaving of all these elements begins at bar 72 ("Drum heg") with a condensed and altered reappearance of the dominant-pedal passage that had launched the earlier episode of tonal distancing. In this recurrence the dominant is of IV rather than I, and it resolves on the fourth bar of the phrase. Apart from this mild harmonic arrival, this time the accumulated momentum of the pedal remains untransferred, and it is allowed to attenuate in an extra bar of unchanged subdominant harmony. In this extraordinary extra bar, the accompaniment becomes uncoupled from the vocal line; suddenly unpropelled harmonically, it drifts through a diminuendo to pianissimo. This moment of change from an ongoing propelled flow to a drifting is the crux of Schubert's setting of the poem: there occurs here, both poetically and musically, a breakthrough from an outward, "normal" pattern of activity (the busy harmonic flow, the poem's busy filling in of metaphoric detail) into an inner awareness. The pigeon is no more and no less than my longing! At the pianissimo, activity ceases and a new inner consciousness arises. Its newness is conveyed by the astonishing major-supertonic tonicization at "Sehnsucht." Each of the three concentrated vocal utterances at this juncture ("die Sehnsucht; kennt ihr sie?; kennt ihr sie?") renders the inverted-bowl motif in the concisest form possible. Meanwhile the drift toward the tonicization of II becomes the occasion for a broadly ascending bass line, which Schubert makes culminate in the often prefigured deceptive cadence, now given a transcendent preface. As though this were not a sufficient climax, Schubert then devises a second phrase-process that delivers the same effect of summation but via a wholly new route (flat VI, theretofore unexplored, but with the revelation of "Sehnsucht" coming this last time in the tonic).

In this song, the picturesque pleasing style is maintained with perfect consistency throughout at the surface, matching the naïveté of the poem. Underlying the setting, however, is the evidence of a formal mastery not outdone, it seems to me, by the many Bach movements that leap to mind as exemplars of hierarchical design. This way of leaving concreteness un-transformed and surface and substrate unhomogenized is not Beethoven's way, but it is perhaps not less powerful and moving than Beethoven's.

A consideration of the piano Schubert wrote for might be relevant in these considerations. The magic major-supertonic pianissimo chord at "Sehnsucht," I believe, is designed for, and most successfully rendered by, a period piano. I am not among those who argue that modern pianos are categorically inferior to early ones for early repertoire, or that effective and satisfying modern-piano accompaniments of Schubert are impossible, since the contrary is patently true. But period pianos can offer many ravishing advantages. The "Sehnsucht" bar is a good point of entry.

In Schubert's piano music, from time to time, one encounters moments suggestive of a sudden shift of focus from an outer to an inner awareness. I have argued elsewhere that a striking example of such a moment occurs in the first movement of the E-flat Trio, near the end of the exposition.[3] Here the shift is elaborately prepared by a soaring passage with a bustling, piquantly chromatic triplet accompaniment, and with ecstatically singing strains in the strings. As this passage runs its course, activity attenuates in a long, smooth diminuendo, finally leaving nothing but a single tone in the cello marked "ppp." This cello tone, I proposed, is like a barrier marking off a point where outer stimuli cease. What ensues, "on the other side of silence," as I described it somewhat dramatically (borrowing a phrase from George Eliot), is one of those unforgettable moments portraying subjectivity. The soaring melody of the earlier passage recurs, but in a simplified, diatonic form, pared down to its essence, the triplets gone, the chromaticism all concentrated in a single touching chord. The texture is homophonic, the dynamic pianissimo: it is an echo so rarefied it is barely there at all. It is a recollection "flashing upon our inner eye." Performed on modern instruments this whole sequence can be greatly moving. But upon first playing the "echo" passage on a fine replica of a Graf piano of the 1820s, I was persuaded that an intended effect of great importance was achievable thereby that a modern instrument could not duplicate. The six-and-a-half-octave Viennese piano of Schubert's era was (relative to ours) lightly strung, on account of its all-wood case; its hammers were therefore relatively small and hard, and the ictus of its tones incisive but capable of extreme softness, with the help of action-shifting and moderating pedals. The "echo" passage can therefore be played with hammerstrokes of almost infinitesimal gentleness, direct and uncushioned by layers of felt, but rarefied and intimate.

My clairvoyant moment in "Die Taubenpost" is analogous. The point of cessation of a harmonically propelled flow at m. 72 is like the membrane separating public and private in the trio. The entry into subjectivity here calls up a kind of hushed awe, a veneration of its sacredness, that is merely suggested by Schubert's poets (it is explicit in the early Wordsworth). The major supertonic harmony in pianissimo is the breakthrough, and a period piano renders it ideally (direct and unbuffered in declamation, yet ethereally fine-grained). Really masterful and reliable period pianos are rare things to encounter. They are usually replicas by unusually sensitive makers (Rodney Regier of Freeport, Maine, has built most of the early pianos I have used for recordings).[4] An exception is the Franz Brodmann piano of 1820 employed by Jörg Ewald Dähler in his excellent *Schwanengesang* recording with Ernst Häfliger (Claves CD 50-8506).

The period piano can enhance, in its own way, a great many other details in *Schwanengesang*. One feature often pointed out is that its relatively rapid die-away of sound becomes an advantage in controlling and exploiting the various weights of articulation that composers writing for these pianos specify in their notation. The framing five-bar introduction and postlude in "Die Taubenpost" is an apt example (Ex. 7.3). It displays a layering of three levels of articulation—legato, staccato, and unmarked (slightly detached).

A period piano can point up these differences and thereby heighten the picturesque, conventional sprightliness of the accompaniment. (Dähler in his recording moves through the syncopations and arrives slightly early at the middle of the bar, producing a quasi-popular, dance-like effect.) The period piano for this song heightens, then, the unique Schubertian counterpoint already described between an unassuming surface and a substrate crafted by one possessed of "the profoundest knowledge of composition." The piano postlude seems to call out, "I am no more than a genre piece!" with a modesty that is itself a contributant to pathos.

The timbre and attack characteristics of the Schubert-era piano are charming for all the pleasing-style songs. The woody timbre is particularly agreeable in the songs with woodland imagery. In "Liebesbotschaft" (an apt framing partner for the collection along with "Die Taubenpost"), the churning accompaniment gains in energy from the edge on the attack, and the bass lines emerge in a satisfyingly clear way. Much the same is true of "Frühlingssehnsucht"; here, the pianissimo cessations of motion, with tonal distancing ("Wohin?" etc.), benefit from the same ethereal effect discussed above, where there is a shift toward introspection suggested by the poem. In "Abschied," the snarl of the period piano's deep bass has a special pungency contributing to the effect of hoofbeats. The long monotextural accompaniment of this song (as of other comparable ones) benefits markedly from the

Ex. 7.3. "Die Taubenpost," mm. 1–5

Ex. 7.4. "Ständchen," mm. 9–10

color-changing pedals: the una corda modifies the timbre more than its analogue on the modern piano, and the moderator can change the sound by
cutting out the high partials.

In "Das Fischermädchen," Schubert spins out an untroubled Siciliana
while Heine compares his psyche to the complex, layered ocean. The fortepiano sweetens the (deliberate?) undercutting of the poem's darkness by
lyricism. There seem to lurk no hints of irony here. "Ständchen's" accompaniment resembles the "pleasing" accompaniments texturally. It exploits
the piano's ability to imitate both a plucked instrument and a singer. The period piano makes the contrast between the two particularly clear, as in
Ex. 7.4, where the period piano's incisiveness and quick decay allow the staccato left-hand dyads to sound plucked against the right hand's legato line
(provided that the damper pedal not be invoked to help out with the legato).

In the darker "serious" and "avant-garde" songs, the period piano makes
its contribution partly through the immediacy of its attack, which can produce a menacing effect or a sinister rattling, and partly through its complexity of timbre, which can add to the spookiness of the atmosphere. The
soft pedals, separately or ganged up, can modify the effect of both.

In "Kriegers Ahnung," the accompaniment's dotted, military, prefatory
announcement, an almost Wagnerian-sounding foreboding of death, has a
ghastly severity on period piano. At "hier fühlt die Brust sich ganz allein,"
the style becomes avant-garde, with the two uncanny modulations symbolizing the protagonist's displacement and alienation. The period piano aug-

ments the mood with rageful, pointed outbursts that immediately sink back into the prevailing texture of soft repeated chords with low-bass octaves. Pedaling these articulate chords only lightly, one can keep this depiction of the warrior's oppressed psychological state isolated in the foreground, so to speak, expressionistically, rather than blended with the general background sounds of the world, as one usually hears it on a modern piano.

In "Aufenthalt," if the period piano's bass has a particularly complex and distinguished timbre, the counterpoint with the singer can be real duet, soundwise. Once again, the climactic outburst ("starrender Fels") has a particularly penetrating impact on a Graf or other period piano. And its edgy attack has other pertinent uses. It adds venom to the strident low octaves and to the roaring tremolandi of "Der Atlas." And in "Die Stadt," in pianissimo, even bathed in the damper-pedal resonance Schubert calls for, the sharp-etched period-piano attack can produce a remarkable glassy, expressionistic effect. Dähler handles this passage memorably in his recording.

"In die Ferne," like "Kriegers Ahnung," verges on the avant-garde at times. The accompaniment's introduction is again called upon to depict a somber psychological state. The *fzp* suggests a clash between a wrath-venting impulse and a prevailing mood of subdued gloom. The Viennese fortepiano, with its light stringing and hard hammers, renders this particularly well. The modern piano is capable of a far wider dynamic range between soft and loud, but the period piano, within its narrow absolute range, creates a kind of contrast of which the modern piano is incapable: struck sharply, its hard hammers set up a shock wave that puts a burr on the attack, making a violent impression completely unlike that of the clear resonance of a normal stroke. After the snarl of the *fz*, the remainder of the phrase, with its neatly articulated bass sixteenths in piano, evokes the requisite change of demeanor. Farther along, a similar sound contrast underlines a still more violent outburst, at "Mutterhaus hassenden," where the blasphemy in the poem calls forth a brutal flouting of voice-leading norms (Ex. 7.5).[5] The effect of varied attack quality pertains also in "Ihr Bild," where the violent piano postlude vents an anguish previously suppressed, and in "Der Doppelgänger," where the changes as the isolated chords grow and ebb intensify the impression of rising and falling waves of nightmarish horror. Here, too, the relatively quick decay of the period piano leaves the intervals between chords empty and desolate. (It is striking that the accompaniment to the first two quatrains opens with the first subject of Bach's "archaic" fugue from WTC I/4. Could this be a "Doppelgänger" in its own right?)[6]

If there is an avant-garde aspect to "Am Meer," it is the unearthly softness of the piano part. Here the quietude is not indicative of a turn into sub-

Ex. 7.5. "In der Ferne," mm. 17–18

jectivity, as above, contrasting with a more outgoing and public gesture, but of an extreme and febrile steady state of despair. The rapid tremolandi in pianissimo need to sound like morbid tremors rather than sources of energy. This accompaniment, it would seem, was specifically written for the period piano, with its action-shifting and moderator pedals.

Given the heterogeneity of Schubert's late style, with its three disparate voices, and given our modern misconception that early pianos are relatively limited in expressive scope, it might seem remarkable how flexible and versatile the period piano manages to be in meeting all the varied demands Schubert makes upon it, and how apt it turns out to be for the expressive tasks at hand. But things probably happened the other way around: in all likelihood it was the possibilities suggested to Schubert by the instruments available to him that determined the particular directions his piano style took. The Canadian scholar John Glofcheskie suggests that for Schubert, the piano was perhaps his chief solace in his mature years, that he was much concerned with exploiting all its special features, that he used it as idiomatically as anyone, and that he was "a composer with a resourceful and spontaneous approach to his instrument."[7] It seems not unreasonable to think that a continuing exploration of his music on the instruments for which he wrote it might well continue to yield interpretive insights.

NOTES

1. In a panel presentation at the 1994 Beethoven conference sponsored by the Early Keyboard Society of Milwaukee.

2. Another early picturesque stylistic tendency of Beethoven's after the *Waldstein* period that becomes transformed into something far more abstract is the French Revolutionary mannerism of such pieces as the slow movements of Opp. 17 and 26.

3. In a lecture at the 1994 Schubertiade at New York's 92nd Street Y and in liner notes for

my recording of the E-flat Trio, D. 929, with the Mozartean Players, for Harmonia Mundi, HM907094.

4. Schubert recordings: Trio in E flat, cited above; Trio in B flat, D. 898, Adagio in E flat, D. 897, Allegro in B flat, D. 28, with the Mozartean Players, on Harmonia Mundi, HM907094; the *Trout* Quintet, with the Academy of Ancient Music Chamber Ensemble; and seven Lieder with John Mark Ainsley, on L'Oiseau Lyre, 433848-2. Reissued as L'Oiseau Lyre 455724-20F2.

5. Brahms cited the fifths and octaves in this passage and suggested an orthodox revision; at the same time, however, he acknowledged that they were undoubtedly deliberate, and he seemed to leave open the question as to whether the aims of tone-painting might justify them. See F. Salzer and C. Schachter, eds., *Music Forum* 5 (1980), 62–63. Schenker, glossing Brahms's comments and revision, declared Schubert's version superior but rationalized this by recourse to voice-leading considerations in the surrounding context—the thought of Schubert committing a deliberate solecism was apparently repugnant to him. See ibid., 148–149.

6. I am grateful to Christopher Gibbs for pointing out to me that Schubert also used this motive as the main subject in the *Agnus Dei* of the E-flat Mass and in the overture to *Fierrabras*.

7. Glofcheskie, "Schubert and the Gentle Fortepiano," 2.

CHAPTER 8

A *Schwanengesang* Discography

RICHARD LESUEUR

This discography is confined to recordings of the complete *Schwanengesang* and does not include recordings of individual songs. That is better left to a complete Schubert Lieder discography, as several of the individual songs have been recorded more than one hundred times outside the complete cycle. The discography is arranged in alphabetical order by vocalist with the pianist as a second factor if the vocalist recorded the cycle more than once. In the case of Dietrich Fischer-Dieskau and Gerald Moore, I have had to go one step further and have arranged their recordings in chronological order. Dates preceded by an "r" indicate recording dates; if the recording date is not known, then the date of first publication is provided, preceded by a "p." In several instances I have had to make educated guesses as to release dates. I have included all issue numbers known to me; any additions or corrections would be greatly appreciated.

The earliest complete *Schwanengesang* was recorded around 1934 by Hans Duhan. I have been unable to trace an LP or CD reissue of this pioneering effort. The first recording by Dietrich Fischer-Dieskau and Gerald Moore was not conceived as a recording of the cycle. In October 1951 they recorded the six Heine Lieder. These were originally issued in 78 rpm format but were soon added to the LP catalogue. The other songs of the cycle were recorded for various Schubert mixed-recital discs issued in the 1950s. It was not until much later that these performances were brought together and issued as a cycle. Fischer-Dieskau recorded the complete cycle with Moore in three successive decades, the 1950s, 1960s, and 1970s, whereas his earliest recording, in 1948, is with Klaus Billing, and the last, in 1982, is with Alfred Brendel. The recording with Billing is a transcription of a radio broadcast.

I am surprised at the scarcity of complete recordings by women. Unlike *Winterreise* or *Die schöne Müllerin,* this is not a narrative cycle, and each of the individual songs has been recorded by females; however, there have been only four recordings of the complete set by women. Also unlike *Winterreise* or *Die schöne Müllerin,* this cycle has never been recorded in translation. Nevertheless, with more than fifty complete recordings, listeners or researchers should be able to find an interpretation that reflects their own concept of *Schwanengesang.*

Discography

Laser Disc

Hermann Prey; Leonard Hokanson (1986)
  Philips 070237-1

Sound Recordings

Olaf Bär; Geoffrey Parsons (r. 8/89)
  CD: EMI CDC7 49997-2
L. Daine; V. Tsrule (p. 1974)
  LP: Melodyia D 035525/26
Hans Duhan; Ferdinand Foll (r. 1934?)
  78: HMV (Czech) ER 292–295, ES 460, ES 471, ES 507
Brigitte Fassbaender; Alibert Reimann (r. 11/89 and 6/91)
  CD: DG 429 766-2
Dietrich Fischer-Dieskau; Klaus Billing (r. 1/48)
  CD: Melodram MEL 18017//Verona 27064
Dietrich Fischer-Dieskau; Alfred Brendel (r. 9/82)
  LP: Philips 6514 383
  CD: Philips 411 051-2
Dietrich Fischer-Dieskau; Gerald Moore (r. 10/51, 5/55, 9/57, and 5/58)
  LP: EMI 1 C127-01764/01766
  CD: EMI CMS7 63559-2//EMI 7243 5 65670-2
Dietrich Fischer-Dieskau; Gerald Moore (r. 9/62)
  LP: Angel S-36127//EMI 60128/30//EMI SLS 840
    EMI 1C063-00222//HMV ASD 544//HMV ALP 1993

Electrola SME 91222
 CD: EMI CDC7 49081-2
Dietrich Fischer-Dieskau; Gerald Moore (r. 3/72)
 LP: DG 2720 059//DG 2531 383
 CD: DG 415 188-2
Shura Gehrman; Nina Walker (p. 1973)
 LP: Nimbus 45001
 CD: Nimbus NI 5022
Ernst Häfliger; Jörg Ewald Dähler (r. 4/85)
 LP: Claves D 8506
 CD: Claves CD 50-8506
Ernst Häfliger; Eric Werba (1964?)
 LP: DG 138905//DG 410 544-1
Håkan Hagegård; Emmanual Ax (r. 10–11/84 and 8/85)
 LP: RCA ARC1-5476//RCA RL 85476
 CD: RCA RCD1-5476
Ralph Herbert; Frederic Waldman (1950?)
 LP: Allegro 3089//Allegro 16
Andriej Hoilski; Jerzy Marschwinski (1965?)
 LP: Muza SXL 695
Robert Holl; David Lutz (r. 7/94)
 CD: Preiser 93042
Wolfgang Holzmair; Imogen Cooper (r. 1/94)
 CD: Philips 442 460-2
Hans Hotter; Gerald Moore (r. 5/54)
 LP: Angel 35219//EMI CX 1269//EMI 2C 151 01274/75
 EMI 1C147-01274/75//EMI HMV XLP 30102/03//Seraphim IC 6051
 CD: EMI Jap TOCE 8164/77
Gerhard Hüsch; Manfred Gurlitt (r. 5/52)
 78: Japanese Victor SD 3073/75, SF 715/18
 LP: Japanese Victor LS 103-4//World Records Club 65
Gerhard Hüsch; Michio Kobayashi (r. 1962)
 LP: Japanese Victor RA 2184
Georg Jelden; Vera Cech (p. 1975)
 LP: Saphir/Intercord 120 864//Intercord INT 185 756//
  Intercord 180 900
Rudolf Knoll; Paul Schilhawsky (1978)
 LP: Euphoria E-2115//Euponia E-2113
Rudolf Knoll; Hugo Steurer (1992)
 CD: Pilz CD 160 270

Ralph Kohn; Graham Johnson (5/95)
  CD: Priory PRI 571
Tom Krause; Irwin Gage (p. 1973)
  LP: London OS 26328//Decca SXL 6590
Siegfried Lorenz; Norman Shetler (r. 11/85)
  CD: Capriccio 10097
Daniel Lichti; Janina Fialkowska (p. 1994)
  CD: Doremi DHR 9302
Benjamin Luxon; David Willison (r. 9/88)
  LP: Chandos ABRD 1361
  CD: Chandos CHAN 8721
Kevin MacMillan; Lev Natochenny (r. 10/93)
  CD: Marquis ERAD 151
Inez Matthews; Lowell Farr (1955)
  LP: Period SPL 717
Petre Munteanu; Franz Holetschek (1952)
  LP: Westminster WL 5165//Westminster XWN 18695
Thomas Pfeiffer; Fritz Rieger (1988?)
  CD: Bayer 100 012
Berthold Possemeyer; Thomas Palm (1992?)
  CD: Ars Produktion ARS 368 326
Hermann Prey; Philippe Bianconi (r. 4/84 and 8/85)
  CD: Denon C33-7906
Hermann Prey; Leonard Hokanson (r. 1978)
  LP: DG 2531 325
Hermann Prey; Walter Klien (1963)
  LP: London OS 25797//Decca SXL 6069//Decca DK 115091-2
Hermann Prey; Gerald Moore (r. 11/71)
  LP: Philips 6747 059//Philips 6520 016//Philips 6767 300
  CD: Philips 422 243-2
Michael Schopper; Jos van Immerseel (r. 4/90)
  CD: Globe GLO 542
Peter Schreier; Walter Olbertz (p. 1972)
  LP: DG 2530 469//DG 2542 144
Peter Schreier; Andreas Schiff (r. 8/89)
  CD: London 425 612-2
Peter Schreier; Norman Shetler (r. 1985)
  LP: Eterna 725132

John Shirley Quirk; Stuart Bedford (1977)
  LP: Enigma VAR 1043
  CD: ASV ASQ 6171
Bo Skovhus; Helmut Deutsch (r. 9/94)
  CD: Sony SK 66835
Bernhard Sönnerstedt, Folmer Jensen (1954?)
  LP: HMV KALP 3
Gérard Souzay; Dalton Baldwin (r. 4/72 and 6/72)
  LP: EMI 2C 065-12532
Eduard Stocker; Magda Rusy (1960?)
  LP: Livre d'Or de France Culture 1002
Bryn Terfel; Malcolm Martineau (1991)
  CD: Sain SCDC 4035
Robert Titze; Walter Bohle (1958?)
  LP: Discophile Francais DF 218
José van Dam; Valéry Afanassiev (r. 5/91)
  CD: Forlane UCD 16647
Max van Egmond; Irwin Gage (1973)
  LP: Telefunken SAT 22509
Weis (sop.); Ferdinand (1972?)
  LP: Electrecord ST-ECE 1507

Bibliography

Catalogues and Music

Deutsch, Otto Erich. *Franz Schubert: Thematisches Verzeichnis seiner Werke in chronol-
ogischer Folge.* New ed. prepared by the Editorial Board of the *Neue Schubert-
Ausgabe* [Walther Dürr, Arnold Feil, Christa Landon] and Werner Aderhold (Kassel, 1978). First ed. published as *Schubert: Thematic Catalogue of All His Works in
Chronological Order,* in collaboration with Donald R. Wakeling (London, 1951).

Dürr, Walther, ed. *Franz Schubert: 'Schwanengesang,' 13 Lieder nach Gedichten von Rellstab und Heine. Faksimile nach dem Autograph* (Hildesheim, 1978).

———. "Dreizehn Lieder nach Gedichten von Rellstab und Heine" (D. 957) and
"Die Taubenpost" (D. 965A), *Neue Schubert-Ausgabe,* series IV, vols. 14a and 14b
(Kassel, 1988).

Friedlander, Max, ed. *Schwanengesang,* vol. 1: *Schubert-Album* (Leipzig, n.d.). Also
*Schubert-Album Supplement: Varianten und Revisionsbericht zum ersten Bande der
Lieder* (Leipzig, [1884]).

Kralik, Heinrich, ed. *Schuberts Liederzyklen 'Die schöne Müllerin,' 'Winterreise,' und
'Schwanengesang': In verkleinerter Nachbildung der Originalausgaben* (Vienna, n.d.).

Kreutzer, Conradin. *'Frühlingslieder' and 'Wanderlieder,'* facs. ed., trans. Luise Eitel
Peake (Stuyvesant, N.Y., 1989).

Mandyczewski, Eusebius, ed. *Schwanengesang,* series 20, "Für eine Singstimme mit
Begleitung des Pianoforte," nos. 554–567 in *Franz Schubert's Werke: Erste kritisch
durchgesehene Gesammtausgabe* (Leipzig, 1895). *Revisionsbericht* to this edition published in 1897. Reprint, New York, 1969. *Schwanengesang* in vol. 17, Critical Commentary in vol. 19.

Nottebohm, Gustav. *Thematisches Verzeichnis der in Druck erschienenen Werke von
Franz Schubert* (Vienna, 1874).

Weissmann, Wilhelm, ed. *Franz Schubert, Die Sieben Rellstab Lieder aus dem 'Schwanengesang' im Faksimile der Urschrift* (Leipzig, 1941). Not examined.

Bibliographies, Documents, Letters, and Memoirs Concerning Schubert

Brusatti, Otto. *Schubert im Wiener Vormärz: Dokumente 1829–48* (Graz, 1978).

Deutsch, Otto Erich. *Schubert: A Documentary Biography*, trans. Eric Blom (London, 1946). Published in the United States as *The Schubert Reader: A Life of Franz Schubert in Letters and Documents* (New York, 1947). Translated into German and revised as *Schubert: Die Dokumente seines Leben* (Kassel, 1964), *Neue Schubert-Ausgabe*, series VIII, supplementary vol. 5.

————. *Schubert: Memoirs by His Friends*, trans. R. Ley and J. Nowell (New York, 1958). Second (German) ed. published as *Schubert: Die Erinnerungen seiner Freunde* (Leipzig, 1966).

Fink, Gottfried Wilhelm. [Review of *Winterreise* and *Schwanengesang*], *Allgemeinen musikalische Zeitung* (29 October 1829). Reprinted in *Franz Schubert: Dokumente*, ed. Till G. Waidelich ([Tutzing], 1993).

Kahl, Willi. *Verzeichnis des Schriftum über Franz Schubert, 1828–1928* (Regensburg, 1938).

King, A. Hyatt. "Bibliography." In *The Music of Schubert*, ed. Gerald Abraham (New York, 1948).

Litschauer, Walburga. *Dokumente zum Leben der Anna Revertera*, vol. 2 of *Neue Dokumente zum Schubert-Kreis: Aus Briefe und Tagebücher* (Vienna, 1993).

Norwood, Eugene L., and David Bonnell Green. "A New Schubert Letter," *Music and Letters* 37 (1956).

Seaton, Douglass. "Schubert" and "Heine." In *The Art Song: A Research and Information Guide* (New York, London, 1987).

Snyder, Lawrence D. *German Poetry in Song: An Index of Lieder* (Berkeley, 1995).

Waidelich, Till G., ed. *Franz Schubert: Dokumente, 1817–1830*. Vol. 1: *Texts: Programs, Reviews, Announcements, Necrology, Musical Supplements and Other Printed Sources* ([Tutzing], 1993). Publication of the Internationalen Franz Schubert Instituts, vol. 10, part 1.

Books, Dissertations, Theses, and Articles

Abraham, Gerald, ed. *The Music of Schubert* (New York, 1947). Published in England as *Schubert: A Symposium* (London, 1952).

Auhagen, Wolfgang. *Studien zur Tonartencharakteristik in theoretischen Schriften und Kompositionen von späten 17. bis zum Beginn des 20. Jahrhundert* (Frankfurt, 1983).

Badura-Skoda, Eva, and Peter Branscombe, eds. *Schubert Studies: Problems in Style and Chronology* (Cambridge, England, 1982).

Barr, Raymond A. "Lied, III." In *New Grove*, vol. 10.

Bendiner, M. "Rellstab, Heinrich Friedrich Ludwig." In *Allgemeinen Deutsche Biographie*, vol. 28 (Leipzig, 1889).

Berlioz, Hector. *Memoirs of Hector Berlioz Including his Travels in Italy, Germany, Russia, and England, 1803–1865*, trans. and ed. David Cairns (London, 1969).

Bingham, Ruth Otto. *The Song Cycle in German-Speaking Countries, 1790–1840: Approaches to a Changing Genre*. Ph.D. diss., Cornell University, 1993 (Ann Arbor, Mich.: UMI).

Bird, George, and Richard Stokes. *The Fischer-Dieskau Book of Lieder* (New York, 1977).

Blume, Friedrich. "Goethe." In *Musik in Geschichte und Gegenwart*, vol. 5 (1956).

Branscombe, Peter. "Adolf Müller [Schmid]." In *New Grove*, vol. 12.

———. "Heinrich Heine." In *New Grove*, vol. 8.

Brauner, Charles S. "Irony in the Heine Lieder of Schubert and Schumann." *Musical Quarterly* 67 (1981).

Brendel, Alfred. *Musical Thoughts and Afterthoughts* (London, 1976).

Brown, Maurice J. E. *Schubert: A Critical Biography* (London, 1958).

———. *Schubert's Songs* (Seattle, 1969). BBC Music Guide, originally published in 1967.

Brusatti, Otto, ed. *Schubert-Kongress Wien 1978: Bericht* (Graz, 1979).

Capell, Richard. *Schubert's Songs*, 3rd ed. (London, 1973; reprint, New York, 1977).

Carleton, Stephen E. *Schubert's Working Methods: An Autograph Study with Particular Reference to the Piano Sonatas*. Ph.D. diss., University of Pittsburgh, 1981 (Ann Arbor, Mich.: UMI).

Chochlow, Jurij N. "Zur Frage vom Verhältnis der Musik und des poetischen Textes in Schuberts Liedern." In *Schubert Kongress Wien, 1978: Bericht*, ed. Otto Brusatti (Graz, 1979).

Chusid, Martin. "The Chamber Music of Schubert." Ph.D. diss., University of California, Berkeley, 1961.

———. "Schubert's Chamber Music: Before and after Beethoven." In *The Schubert Companion*, ed. Christopher Gibbs (Cambridge, England, 1997).

Clive, Peter. *Schubert and His World: A Biographical Dictionary* (Oxford, 1997).

Cone, Edward T. "Beethoven's Experiments in Composition: The Late Bagatelles." In *Beethoven Studies 2*, ed. Alan Tyson (London, 1977).

———. *The Composer's Voice* (Berkeley, 1974).

———. "Poet's Love or Composer's Love?" In *Music and Text: Critical Inquiries*. Ed. Steven P. Scher (Cambridge, 1992).

———. "'Am Meer' Reconsidered: Strophic, Binary, or Ternary?" In *Schubert Studies*, ed. Brian Newbould (Aldershot, 1997).

———. "Words into Music: The Composer's Approach to the Text." In *Sound and Poetry*, ed. Northrop Frye (New York, 1957).

Crutchfield, Will. "Voices." In *Performance Practice: Music after 1600*, ed. Howard Meyer Brown and Stanley Sadie (New York, 1989).

Daverio, John. "The Song Cycle: Journeys Through a Romantic Landscape." In *German Lieder in the Nineteenth Century*, ed. Rufus Hallmark (New York, 1996).

Davis, Shelley. "Rellstab, Ludwig." In *New Grove*, vol. 15.

Dittrich, Marie-Agnes. "Die Lieder." In *Schubert Handbuch*, ed. Walther Dürr and Andreas Krause ([Kassel], 1997).

Dürr, Walther. "Ausweichungen ohne Sinn, Ordnung und Zweck—Zu Tonalität bei Schubert." In *Franz Schubert—Der Fortschrittliche*, ed. Wolfgang Partsch (Tutzing, 1989).

———. *Das deutsche Sololied im 19. Jahrhundert: Untersuchungen zu Sprache und Musik* (Wilhelmshaven, 1984).

———. "'Manier' und 'Veränderung' in Kompositionen Franz Schuberts." In *Zur Aufführungspraxis der Werke Franz Schuberts*, ed. Vera Schwarz (Munich, 1981).

———. "Schubert and Johann Michael Vogl: A Reappraisal," *Nineteenth-Century Music* 3 (1979).

———. "Schubert's Songs and Their Poetry: Reflections on Poetic Aspects of Song Composition." In *Schubert Studies*, ed. Eva Badura-Skoda and Peter Branscombe (Cambridge, 1982).

———. "Vorwort." In *Neue Schubert-Ausgabe*, series IV, vol. 14a (Kassel, 1988).

Dürr, Walther, and Arnold Feil. *Franz Schubert* (Stuttgart, 1991).

Dürr, Walther, and Andreas Krause. *Schubert Handbuch* ([Kassel, 1997]).

Earle, Don L. "The Solo Song Cycle in Germany (1800–1850)." Ph.D. diss., Indiana University, 1952.

Eggebrecht, Heinrich. "Prinzipien der Schubert-Liedes," *Archiv für Musikwissenschaft* 27 (1970).

Einstein, Alfred. *Schubert: A Musical Portrait* (New York, 1951). Published in England as *Schubert: The Man and His Music* (London, 1951).

Fairley, Barker. *Heinrich Heine: An Interpretation* (Oxford, 1954).

Fischer, Kurt von. "Some Thoughts on Key Order in Schubert's Song Cycles." In *Kurt von Fischer: Essays in Musicology*, ed. Tamara S. Evans (New York, 1989).

———. "Zur semantischen Bedeutung von Text Repetitionen in Schuberts Liederzyklen." In *Schubert-Kongress Wien, 1978: Bericht*, ed. Otto Brusatti (Graz, 1979).

Fischer-Dieskau, Dietrich. *Schubert: A Biographical Study of His Songs*, transl. and ed. K. S. Whitton (London, 1976). Original German ed. published as *Auf den Spuren der Schubert-Lieder* (Wiesbaden, 1971).

Flothuis, Marius. "Schubert Revises Schubert." In *Schubert Studies*, ed. Eva Badura-Skoda and Peter Branscombe (Cambridge, England, 1982).

Friedlander, Max. "Fälschungen in Schubert's Liedern," *Vierteljahrschrift für Musikwissenschaft* 9 (1893).

Frisch, Walter, ed. *Schubert: Critical and Analytical Studies* (Lincoln, Neb., 1986).

Georgiades, Thrasybulos. "The German Language and Music." In *Music and Language*, trans. M. L. Goellner (Cambridge, England, 1982). Originally published in German as *Musik und Sprache*, 2nd ed. (Heidelberg, 1974).

———. *Schubert: Musik und Lyrik* (Göttingen, 1967), 2 vols.

Gerstenberg, Walter. "Schubertiade: Anmerkungen zu einigen Liedern." In *Festschrift Otto Erich Deutsch*, ed. W. Gerstenberg (Kassel, 1963).

Gibbs, Christopher H. *The Presence of 'Erlkönig': Reception and Reworkings of a Schubert Lied*. Ph.D. diss., Columbia University, 1992 (Ann Arbor, Mich.: UMI).

Gibbs, Christopher H., ed. *The Schubert Companion* (Cambridge, England, 1997).

Glofcheskie, John. "Schubert and the Gentle Fortepiano," *Musick* (Early Music Vancouver) 2 (1990).

Goedeke, Karl. *Grundrisse zur Geschichte der deutschen Dichtung,* 2nd ed., ed. Edmund Goetze (Dresden, 1910).

Goldschmidt, Harry. *Franz Schubert: Ein Lebensbild* (Leipzig, 1962).

———. "Welches war die ursprüngliche Reihenfolge in Schuberts Heine-Liedern." In *Deutsche Jahrbuch der Musikwissenschaft für 1972* (Leipzig, 1974). Reprinted in Goldschmidt, *Um die Sache der Musik* (Leipzig, 1976).

———. "Zu einer Neubewertung von Schuberts letzter Schaffenzeit (1828)." In *Bericht über den siebenten internationalen musikwissenschaftlichen Kongress, Köln, 1958* (Kassel, 1959). Reprinted in Goldschmidt, *Um die Sache der Musik* (Leipzig, 1976).

Gramit, David E. *The Intellectual and Aesthetic Tenets of Franz Schubert's Circle.* Ph.D. diss., Duke University, 1987 (Ann Arbor, Mich.: UMI).

———. "Schubert and the Biedermeier: The Aesthetics of Johann Mayrhofer's Heliopolis," *Music and Letters* 74 (1993).

Gruber, Gernot. "Romantische Ironie in den Heine-Liedern." In *Schubert-Kongress Wien, 1978: Bericht,* ed. Otto Brusatti (Graz, 1979).

Hallmark, Rufus. "Schubert's *Auf dem Strom.*" In *Schubert Studies,* ed. Eva Badura-Skoda and Peter Branscombe (Cambridge, England, 1982).

Hallmark, Rufus, ed. *German Lieder in the Nineteenth Century* (New York, 1996).

Hanson, Alice M. *Musical Life in Biedermeier Vienna* (Cambridge, 1985). Based, with some omissions, on her dissertation, "The Social and Economic Context of Music in Vienna from 1815 to 1830." Ph.D. diss., University of Illinois at Urbana-Champaign, 1980.

Heine, Heinrich. *The Complete Poems of Heinrich Heine: A Modern English Version,* trans. Hal Draper (Boston, 1982).

———. *Memoirs: From His Works, Letters, and Conversations,* ed. Gustav Karpales, trans. G. Cannan (London, 1910).

———. *Poems and Ballads,* trans. Emma Lazarus (New York, 1947).

Helm, Eugene. "Reichardt, J. F." In *New Grove,* vol. 15.

Heuben, Heinrich H. "Einleitung: Ludwig Rellstab." In the novel 1812 by Rellstab (Leipzig, 1923).

Heussner, Horst. "Rellstab, Heinrich Friedrich Ludwig." In *Musik in Geschichte und Gegenwart,* vol. 11 (1963).

Hilmar, Ernst. "Kritische Betrachtungen zu Liszts Transkriptionen von Liedern von Franz Schubert: Allgemeines und Spezialles zur Niederschrift des *Schwanengesangs.*" In *Liszt Studien Band 1 (Kongress-Bericht Eisenstadt 1975),* ed. Wolfgang Suppan (Graz, 1977).

———. *Verzeichnis der Schubert-Handschriften in der Musiksammlung der Wiener Stadt- und Landesbibliothek* (Kassel, 1978).

Hilmar, Ernst, and Otto Brusatti. *Franz Schubert: Ausstellung der Wiener Stadt- und Landesbibliothek: Katalog* (Vienna, 1978).

Holloway, Robin. "Schubert: *Schwanengesang.*" In *Song on Record,* ed. Alan Blyth (Cambridge, England, 1986).

Jonas, Oswald, ed. "The Relation of Word and Tone." Appendix A of *Introduction to the Theory of Heinrich Schenker* (New York, 1982). Original German ed. 1934, revised 1972.

Kerman, Joseph. "An die ferne Geliebte." In *Beethoven Studies,* ed. Alan Tyson (New York, 1973).

———. "A Romantic Detail in Schubert's *Schwanengesang.*" In *Schubert: Critical and Analytical Studies,* ed. Walter Frisch (Lincoln, Neb., 1986). A slightly revised version of his article in *Musical Quarterly* 48 (1962).

Kinderman, William. "Schubert's Tragic Perspective." In *Schubert: Critical and Analytical Studies,* ed. Walter Frisch (Lincoln, Neb., 1986).

Kolb, Jocelyn. "Die Puppenspiel meines Humors: Heine and Romantic Irony," *Studies in Romanticism* 26 (1987).

Komar, Arthur. "Der Doppelgänger." In *Workbook in Tonal Analysis* ([Dedham, Mass.,] 1995).

König, Else. *Ludwig Rellstab: Ein Beitrag zur Geschichte der Unterhaltungsliteratur in der ersten Hälfte der 19. Jahrhundert.* Ph.D. diss., Breslau, 1938 (Würzberg-Anmühle, 1938).

Kortländer, Bernd. "Nachwort: zu Heines Ästhetik; Heine's Lebensweg bis 1827; Quellen; Zur Interpretation der Geschichte; Rezeption." In *Heinrich Heine: 'Buch der Lieder,'* ed. B. Kortländer (Stuttgart, 1990).

Kramer, Lawrence. "The Schubert Lied: Romantic Form and Romantic Consciousness." In *Schubert: Critical and Analytical Studies,* ed. Walter Frisch (Lincoln, Neb., 1986).

Kramer, Richard. "Against Recycling," *Nineteenth-Century Music* 20 (1996).

———. *Distant Cycles: Schubert and the Conceiving of Song* (Chicago, 1994).

———. "Schubert's Heine," *Nineteenth-Century Music* 8 (1985); reprinted in his *Distant Cycles.*

Kraus, Felicitas von. *Beiträge zur Erforschung des Malenden und poetisierenden Wesens in der Begleitung von Franz Schubert.* Ph.D. diss., Munich, 1926 (Mainz, 1927).

Krautwurst, Franz. "Zu Schuberts Harmonik." In *Franz Schubert 'Der Fortschrittliche,'* ed. Wolfgang Partsch (Tutzing, 1989).

Kravitt, Edward F., "The Lied in Nineteenth Century Concert Life," *Journal of the American Musicological Society* 18 (1965).

Kreissle von Hellborn, Heinrich. *Franz Schubert* (London, 1869; reprint, New York, 1972), 2 vols. Originally published in German (Vienna, 1865; reprint, Hildesheim, 1968).

Krones, Hartmut, and Robert Schollum. *Vokale und allgemeine Aufführungspraxis* (Vienna, 1983).

Kühner, Hans. "Heine, Heinrich." In *Musik in Geschichte und Gegenwart,* vol. 6 (1957).

Kurth, Richard. "Music and Poetry, a Wilderness of Doubles: Heine-Nietsche-Schubert-Derrida," *Nineteenth-Century Music* 21, no. 1 (Summer 1997): 3–37.

Lehmann, Lotte. *Eighteen Song Cycles: Studies in their Interpretation* (London, 1971).

———. *More than Singing: The Interpretation of Song,* trans. F. Holden (New York, 1945).

Liszt, Franz. *The Letters of Franz Liszt to Marie zu Sayn-Wittgenstein,* trans. and ed. H. E. Hugo (Cambridge, Mass., 1953).

Litschauer, Walburga. "Vorwort." In *Neue Schubert-Ausgabe,* series VII, Klaviermusik, part 2, vol. 3: Klaviersonaten III (Kassel, 1996).

Litterick, Louise. "Recycling Schubert: On Reading Richard Kramer's *Distant Cycles: Schubert and the Conceiving of Song*," *Nineteenth-Century Music* 20 (1996).

Lowen, Marshall H. "Symbolism in Schubert's *Winterreise*," *Studies in Romanticism* 12 (1973).

Lubin, Steven. Liner notes for a recording of Schubert's E-flat Piano Trio performed by Steven Lubin with the Mozarteum Players (Harmonia Mundi, HM 907094).

Mann, Michael. *Heinrich Heines Musikkritiken* ([Hamburg,] 1971).

Massin, Brigitte. *Franz Schubert* (Paris, 1977).

Max, Hans. "Johann Gabriel Seidl: Eine biographische Skizze." In *Johann Gabriel Seidl's Gesammelte Schriften*, vol. 6 (Vienna, 1881).

Mendelssohn, Felix. *Letters*, ed. G. Selden-Gotha (London, 1946).

Metzner, Georg. *Heine in der Musik: Bibliographie der Heine-Vertonungen*, vol. 1 (Tutzing, 1989).

Mies, Paul. "Die Bedeutung des Unisono im Schubertschen Liede," *Zeitschrift für Musikwissenschaft* 11 (1928–29).

———. *Schubert der Meister des Liedes: Die Entwicklung von Form und Inhalt im Schubertschen Lied* (Berlin, 1928).

Miller, Philip L. *Ring of Words* (Garden City, N.Y., 1966).

Moore, Gerald. *The Performance of Fifty Songs* (London, 1953).

———. *Schubert's Song Cycles* (London, 1975).

Morgan, Robert P. "Dissonant Prolongation: Theoretical and Compositional Precedents," *Journal of Music Theory* 20 (1976).

Moser, Hans J. *Das deutsche Lied seit Mozart* (Berlin, 1937; reprint, Tutzing, 1966).

Mühlhäuser, Siegfried. "' . . . Kaum wage ich das Bekenntnis—ich verstehe keine Note . . . ' Ein bisher ungedruckter Brief Heinrich Heines an Eduard Marxsen. Ein Beitrag zur Frage der Vertonung Heinescher Gedichte," *Musikforschung* 26 (1973).

Die Musik in Geschichte und Gegenwart. Ed. Friedrich Blume (Kassel, 1949–1986), 17 vols.

Mustard, Helen M. *The Lyric Cycle in German Literature* (New York, 1946).

Muxfeldt, Kristina. *Schubert Song Studies*. Ph.D. diss., State University of New York, Stony Brook, 1991 (Ann Arbor, Mich.: UMI).

Newbould, Brian. *Schubert: The Music and the Man* (Berkeley, 1997).

———. *Schubert Studies* (Aldershot, 1998).

Newcomb, Anthony. "Structure and Expression in a Schubert Song: Noch einmal 'Auf dem Flusse' zu hören." In *Schubert: Critical and Analytical Studies*, ed. Walter Frisch (Lincoln, Neb., 1986).

The New Grove Dictionary of Music and Musicians. Ed. Stanley Sadie (London, 1980; paperback ed. 1995), 20 vols.

Nollen, John S. "Heine and Wilhelm Müller," *Modern Language Notes* 17 (1902).

Obermaier, Walter. "Schubert und die Zensur." In *Schubert-Kongress Wien, 1978: Bericht*, ed. Otto Brusatti (Graz, 1979).

Orel, Alfred. "Die Skizze zu Franz Schuberts letzen Lied," *Die Musik* 29 (1937).

Osborne, Robert. "Reordering Schubert's *Schwanengesang*." In *Program, The American Schubert Institute* (Boston, 19 February 1992).

Pawel, Ernst. *The Poet Dying: Heinrich Heine's Last Years in Paris* (New York, 1995).

Peake, Luise Eitel. "The Antecedents of Beethoven's Liederkreis," *Music and Letters* 63 (1982).

―――. "Kreutzer's *Wanderlieder:* The Other *Winterreise,*" *Musical Quarterly* 65 (1979).

―――. *The Song Cycle: A Preliminary Inquiry into the Beginnings of the Romantic Song Cycle and the Nature of an Art Form.* Ph.D. diss., Columbia University, 1968 (Ann Arbor, Mich.: UMI).

Perraudin, Michael. *Heinrich Heine, Poetry in Context: A Study of "Buch der Lieder"* (Oxford, 1989).

Piston, Walter. *Harmony* (New York, 1941).

Porter, Ernest G. "Der Doppelgänger," *Music Review* 21 (1960).

―――. *Schubert's Song Technique* (London, 1961).

―――. *The Songs of Schubert* (London, 1937).

Prawer, Siegbert S. *Heine: 'Buch der Lieder'* (London, 1960).

―――. *Heine, the Tragic Satirist: A Study of the Later Poetry, 1827–1856* (Cambridge, 1961).

―――. *The Penguin Book of Lieder* ([Hammondsworth, Middlesex,] 1964).

Prod'homme, Jacques G. "Schubert's Works in France," *Musical Quarterly* 14 (1928).

Reed, John. *Schubert: The Final Years* (New York, 1972).

―――. *The Schubert Song Companion* (Manchester, 1985).

Reeves, Nigel. *Heinrich Heine: Poetry and Politics* ([London,] 1974).

Rehm, Jürgen. *Zur Musikrezeption im vormärzlichen Berlin* (Hildesheim, 1983).

Reininghaus, Friedrich. *Schubert und das Wirtshaus: Musik unter Metternich,* 2nd ed. ([Berlin,] 1980).

Reintjes, Mikki. "Aspects of Cyclical Structure in Schubert's 'Schwanengesang.'" M.A. thesis, University of Victoria, 1990.

Rellstab, Ludwig. *Aus meinem Leben* (Berlin, 1861).

―――. *Ludwig Berger: Ein Denkmal* (Berlin, 1846).

Riemann, Hugo. *Ludwig van Beethovens sämtliche Klaviersonaten, ästhetische und formal-technische Analyse mit historischer Notizen,* 3rd ed. (Berlin, 1919), 3 vols.

Robertson, Alec. "The Songs." In *Music of Schubert,* ed. Gerald Abraham (New York, 1947).

Rochlitz, Friedrich. "Beytrag zur Lehre von den Verzierungen," *Allgemeine musikalische Zeitung* 16 (1814).

Sammons, Jeffrey. *Heinrich Heine: A Modern Biography* (Princeton, 1979).

―――. *Heinrich Heine: The Elusive Poet* (New Haven, 1969).

Scheibler, Ludwig. "Schuberts einstimmige Lieder nach "österreichischen Dichtern," *Musikbuch für Österreich* 5 (1908).

Schenker, Heinrich. "Schubert: Ihr Bild," *Der Tonwille* 1 (1921).

Schilling, Gustav. *Musikalische Dynamik oder die Lehre von Vortrage in der Musik* (Kassel, 1843).

Schindler, Anton. "Erinnerungen an Franz Schubert," *Niederrheinische Musk-Zeitung für Kunstfreunde und Künstler* 5 (1857).

Schlosser, Anton. "Johann Gabriel Seidl." In *Allgemeinen Deutsche Biographie,* ed. Hermann Schulze and G. Semper (Leipzig, 1891), vol. 23.

Schnebel, Dieter. "Klangräume-Zeiträume: Zweiter Versuch über Schubert." In *Aspekte der musikalischen Interpretationen: Sava Savoff zum 70. Geburtstag*, ed. Hermann Danuser and Christoff Keller (Hamburg, 1980).

Schneider, Frank. "Franz Schuberts Heinelieder," *Sinn und Form* 31 (1979).

Schochow, Maximilian, and Lilly Schochow. *Franz Schubert: Die Texte seiner einstimmig komponierten Lieder und ihre Dichter* (Hildesheim, 1974), 2 vols.

Schubert, Franz. *'Schwanengesang': Facsimiles of the Autograph Score and Sketches, and Reprint of the First Edition*, ed. Martin Chusid (New Haven, 2000).

Schwab, Heinrich. *Sangbarkeit, Popularität und Kunstlied: Studien zu Lied und Liedästhetik der mittleren Goethezeit, 1770–1814* (Regensburg, 1968).

Seaton, Douglass. "Interpreting Schubert's Heine Songs," *Music Review* 53 (1992).

Seelig, Harry. "The Literary Context: Goethe as Source and Catalyst." In *German Lieder in the Nineteenth Century*, ed. Rufus Hallmark (New York, 1996).

Seidl, Johann Gabriel. *Dichtungen* (Vienna, 1826), 2 vols.

"Seidl, Johann Gabriel." In *Österreichischen Parnass bestiegen von einen herunterkommenden Antiquar* (Frey-sing [Freising, Bavaria], n.d. [c. 1836–1840]).

Seidlitz, Julius. "Johann Gabriel Seidl." In *Die Poesie und Poeten in Österreich* (Grimma [Saxony], 1837), vol. 2.

Seiffert, Wolf-Dieter. "Franz Schuberts Heinelied *Ihr Bild*," *Musikforschung* 43 (1990).

Seitz, Reinhold. "Johann Vesque von Püttlingen." In *Musik in Geschichte und Gegenwart*, vol. 13 (1966).

———. "Johann Vesque von Püttlingen." In *New Grove*, vol. 19.

Siegmund-Schultze, Walther. "Betrachtungen zu den Heine-Liedern von Franz Schubert," *Wissenschaftliche Zeitschrift Universität Halle* 31 (1982).

Simpson, Eugene T. "A Study, Analysis and Performance of the 'Schwanengesang' of F. Schubert, D. 957." Ph.D. diss., Teacher's College, Columbia University, 1968.

Sonnleithner, Leopold von. "Bemerkungen zur Gesangkunst" and "Über den Vortrag des Liedes, mit besonderer Beziehung an Franz Schubert." Both in *Recensionen und Mittheilungen über Theater und Musik* (Vienna, 1860–1861), vols. 6 and 7.

Spillman, Robert. "Performing Lieder: The Mysterious Mix." In *German Lieder in the Nineteenth Century*, ed. Rufus Hallmark (New York, 1996).

Steblin, Rita. *A History of Key Characteristics in the Eighteenth and Early Nineteenth Centuries* (1981; reprint, [Rochester, N.Y.,] 1996).

Stein, Jack. *Poem and Music in the German Lied from Gluck to Hugo Wolf* (Cambridge, Mass., 1971).

Steinbeck, Wolfram. "Das Prinzip der Liedbegleitung bei Schubert," *Musik Forschung* 42 (1989).

Thayer, Alexander W. *Thayer's Life of Beethoven*, rev. and ed. Elliot Forbes (Princeton, 1967). First English ed. by H. E. Krehbiel (New York, 1921).

Thomas, J. H. "Schubert's Modified Strophic Songs with Particular Reference to *Schwanengesang*," *Music Review* 24 (1973).

Thomas, Werner. "*Der Doppelgänger* von Franz Schubert," *Archiv für Musikwissenschaft* 11 (1954). Reprinted in Thomas, *Zur musikalischen Analyse* (Darmstadt, 1974).

Thym, Jürgen. "Crosscurrents in Song: Five Distinctive Voices." In *German Lieder in the Nineteenth Century*, ed. Rufus Hallmark (New York, 1996).

Tovey, Sir Donald. "Franz Schubert." In *The Mainstream of Music and Other Essays* (New York, 1959), originally published as *Essays and Lectures in Music* (London, 1949).

Turchin, Barbara P. "The Nineteenth-Century *Wanderlieder* Cycle," *Journal of Musicology* 5 (1987).

———. *Robert Schumann's Song Cycles in the Context of the Early Nineteenth-Century 'Liederkreis.'* Ph.D. diss., Columbia University, 1981 (Ann Arbor, Mich.: UMI).

Utz, Helga. *Untersuchungen zur Syntax der Lieder Franz Schuberts* (Munich, 1989).

Vetter, Walther. *Der Klassiker Schubert* (Leipzig, 1953), 2 vols.

West, Ewan. "The Musenalmanach and Viennese Song, 1770–1830," *Music and Letters* 67 (1986).

Westrup, Jack. "Some Settings of Heine." In *Festival Essays for Pauline Alderman,* ed. Burton L. Karson, Eleanor Russell, and Halsey Stevens (Provo, Utah, 1976).

Whitall, Arnold. *Romantic Music: A Concise History from Schubert to Sibelius* (London, 1987).

Wigmore, Richard. *Schubert: The Complete Song Texts* (New York, 1988).

Winter, Robert. "Paper Studies and the Future of Schubert Research." In *Schubert Studies,* ed. Eva Badura-Skoda and Peter Branscombe (Cambridge, England, 1982).

Wiora, Walter. *Das Deutsche Lied: Zur Geschichte und Aesthetik einer musikalischen Gattung* (Wolfenbüttel, 1971).

Wurzbach, Wolfgang von. "Johannes Gabriel Seidl," *Grillparzer Gesellschaft Jahrbuch* 15 (1905).

———. "Johann Gabriel Seidls Leben und Werke." In *Johann Gabriel Seidls ausgewählte Werke* (Leipzig, [c. 1905]), vol. 1.

Youens, Susan. "Behind the Scenes: *Die schöne Müllerin* before Schubert," *Nineteenth-Century Music* 15 (1991).

———. "Poetic Rhythm and Musical Meter in Schubert's *Winterreise*," *Music and Letters* 65 (1989).

———. *Schubert's Poets and the Making of Lieder* (Cambridge, 1996).

Zagari, Luciano. "Permanence in Change: Heine's Reception in Italian Culture Through Two Centuries." In *Heinrich Heine and the Occident,* ed. Peter U. Hohendahl and Sander L. Gilman (Lincoln, Neb., 1991).

Zeman, Herbert. "Franz Schuberts Teilhabe an den österreichischen literarischen Zeit." In *Schubert-Kongress Wien, 1978: Bericht,* ed. Otto Brusatti (Graz, 1979).

Contributors

MARTIN CHUSID is Professor of Music and Director of the American Institute for Verdi Studies at New York University. He has written extensively about, and edited, the music of Schubert (*Unfinished* Symphony and two volumes of chamber music) and Verdi (*Rigoletto*). He has also written on the operas of Mozart and Dvořák and the late masses of Haydn.

EDWARD T. CONE is Professor Emeritus, Princeton University. He is a composer, pianist, and author of *Musical Form and Musical Performance, The Composer's Voice,* and articles on Schubert, Beethoven, Berlioz, Stravinsky, Verdi, and others.

WALTHER DÜRR is Professor Emeritus at the University of Tübingen and chief editor of the *Neue Schubert-Ausgabe,* for which he has edited all the solo songs. He has written a history of the German Lied and has written extensively on Schubert.

RICHARD LESUEUR is Music Specialist at the Ann Arbor (Michigan) District Library. He has written extensively on vocal music and acts as repertoire consultant for singers around the world.

WALBURGA LITSCHAUER directs the Viennese office of the *Neue Schubert-Ausgabe,* for which she has edited several volumes of piano music. She has compiled a number of volumes of letters and documents relating to members of the Schubert circle and written a book on Schubert's dances.

STEVEN LUBIN is Professor at the Conservatory of Music, State University of New York at Purchase. He has concertized widely as pianist and fortepianist and has recorded extensively, especially the music of Mozart, Beethoven, and Schubert.

Index

"Frühlingssehnsucht" and, 109; Liszt piano transcriptions of, 10; major-minor dichotomy in, 107–109; ornamentation notation of, 182–183; performance review of, 11; on period piano, 201; popularity of, 10; serious-style piano accompaniment to, 192; singing of, 186–187; text of, 106–107
Steblin, Rita, 149nn3, 6
Stein, J. A., 188
Stein, Jack, 152n65
Stoepel, Franz, 169
Strauss, Richard, 38
stretching. See phrase expansion
String Quintet in C Major (Schubert), 163
strophic elements, 122; correspondence in stanzas for, 54; in "Frühlingssehnsucht," 55–58; modified, 88n2; in songs of Berlin school, 180–181; in "Ständchen," 60
Structural Hearing (Salzer), 98
Sturm oder die Geisterinsel, Der (Seidl and Riotte), 44

Talbert, W., 16
Tannhauser (Wagner and Heine), 31
Taschenbuch Aurora (periodical), 40
Taschenbuch zum geselligen Vergnügen (periodical), 42
"Taubenpost, Die" (No. 14), 85–88; commentary on, 145–149; as concluding song, 170–171; continuity draft of, 146–148, 155n121, 179; double ornaments in, 185; Fink on, 9; Hartmann on, 10; Haslinger buys, 7; on period piano, 199–200, 201; piano accompaniment to, 192, 194, 196–199; repetition in, 86–88; singing of, 186; text of, 144–145. See also Seidl, Johann Gabriel
Tedesco, Ignaz Amadeus, 11
Teltscher, Josef, 42
tempo markings, 183, 185
text, 149n1; of "Abschied," 116–119; of "Am Meer," 138; of "Der Atlas," 123–124; of "Aufenthalt," 110; of "Der Doppelgänger," 140; of "Das Fischermädchen," 131–132; of "Frühlingssehnsucht," 102–103, 151n38; of "Ihr Bild," 128; of "In der Ferne," 113–114; of "Kriegers Ahnung," 99; of "Liebesbotschaft," 94–95; reading for meaning, 176–179; Schubert's reuse of portions of, 93; of "Die Stadt," 135; of "Ständchen," 106–107; of "Die Taubenpost," 144–145
Theaterzeitung (periodical), 11
Theodor (Rellstab), 17
Theresa (Seidl), 40
Thomas, J. H., 98, 127

Thomas, Werner, 140–142, 143, 154nn114, 115 through-composed elements, 65; correspondence in text structure for, 54
Tieck, Ludwig, 16, 161
Tietze, Ludwig, 10, 11
Tovey, Donald, 99
Tragödien, nebst einem lyrischen Intermezzo (Heine), 25
"Tränenregen" (Die schöne Müllerin No. 10), 165
Travels from Munich to Genoa (Heine), 28
"Trockne Blumen" (Die schöne Müllerin No. 18), 151n30
Type A correspondence, 54–55
Type B correspondence, 55

Über mein Verhältnis als Kritiker zu Herrn Spontini als erste Komponisten und Generalmusikdirektor zu Berlin nebst einem vergnüglichen Anhange (Rellstab), 20
Uhland, Ludwig, 161
"Unterscheidung, Die" (Seidl and Schubert), 172n19. See also Four Refrain-Lieder
Utz, Helga, 127–128, 133

variation-form, correspondence types and, 55
Veilchen (periodical), 40
Verdi, Giuseppe, 19, 36, 46n21, 129, 172n18
Verein für Cultur und Wissenschaft der Juden, Heine and, 25
Verschworenen, Die (Castelli and Schubert), 18
Vetter, Walther, 23, 101, 152n65
vibrato, 189
Vienna Conservatory of the Society of the Friends of Music, 12; Prize List of, 13n31
vier Menschenälter, Die (Seidl and Lachner), 44
Vogel, Wilhelm, 38
Vogl, Johann Michael, 10, 175; ornaments in Schubert songbooks of, 182, 186, 187–188
Vogler, G. J., 149n6
Volkston (folk-like songs), 133, 154n95
Von der musikalischen Poesie (Krause), 179
Voss, Johann Heinrich, 180
Vossische Zeitung (periodical), 14, 15, 19–20, 21, 45n2

Wagner, Richard, 31, 47nn51, 52
Wanderlieder (Uhland), 161
Wanderungen durch Tirol und Steiermark (Seidl), 37
Weber, Carl Maria von, 16, 17, 18, 20–21
Weigl, Thaddäus, 41
Westrup, Jack, 123, 132, 133, 152n69, 154n100

DATE